TEXTBOOK OF FORENSIC CHEMISTRY

TEXTBOOK OF FORENSIC CHEMISTRY

By

Dr. Syed Aftab Iqbal

M.Sc. , Ph.D., FICS

FICC, FIAEM, MNASc.

Professor

Department of Chemistry

Saifia Science College

Barkatullah University

Bhopal (India)

&

Dr. Mitu Liviu

Lecturer

Department of Chemistry

Pitesti University

Arges, Romania

DPH

DISCOVERY PUBLISHING HOUSE PVT. LTD.

INDIA

Published by:
Tilak Wasan
DISCOVERY PUBLISHING HOUSE PVT. LTD.
4383/4B, Ansari Road, Darya Ganj
New Delhi-110 002 (India)
Phone : +91-11-23279245; 23253475; 43596065
E-mail : discoverybooksindia@gmail.com
discoverypublishinghouse@gmail.com
namitwasan9@gmail.com
web : www.discoverypublishinggroup.com

First Edition: **2011**

ISBN: 978-81-8356-838-8

Textbook of Forensic Chemistry

Preface

Forensic chemistry is the application of chemistry to law enforcement or the failure of products or processes. Many different analytical methods may be used to reveal what chemical changes occurred during an incident, and so help reconstruct the sequence of events. "Forensic chemistry is unique among chemical sciences in that its research, practice, and presentation must meet the needs of both the scientific and the legal communities. As such, forensic chemistry research is applied and derivative by nature and design, and it emphasizes metrology and validation."

Forensic science (often shortened to forensics) is the application of a broad spectrum of sciences to answer questions of interest to the legal system.This may be in relation to a crime or to a civil action. But besides its relevance to the underlying legal system, more generally forensics encompasses the accepted scholarly or scientific methodology and norms under which the facts regarding an event, or an artifact, or some other physical item (such as a corpse, or cadaver, for example) are to the broader notion of authentication whereby an interest outside of a legal form exists in determining whether an object is in fact what it purports to be, or is alleged as being.

The word *"forensic"* comes from the Latin adjective *"forensis"* meaning of or before the forum. During the time of the Romans, a criminal charge meant presenting the case before a group of public individuals in the forum. Both the person accused of the crime and the accuser would give speeches based on their side of the story. The individual with the best argument and delivery would determine the outcome of the case. Basically, the person with the sharpest forensic skills would win. This origin is the source of the two modern usages of the word *"forensic"* - as a form of legal evidence and as a category of public presentation.

In modern use, the term "forensics" in place of "forensic science" can be considered incorrect as the term "forensic" is effectively a synonym for "legal" or "related to courts". However, the term is now so closely associated with the scientific field that many dictionaries include the meaning that equates the word "forensics" with "forensic science".

Author

Contents

1

Introduction

Forensic chemistry is the application of chemistry to law enforcement or the failure of products or processes. Many different analytical methods may be used to reveal what chemical changes occurred during an incident, and so help reconstruct the sequence of events. "Forensic chemistry is unique among chemical sciences in that its research, practice, and presentation must meet the needs of both the scientific and the legal communities. As such, forensic chemistry research is applied and derivative by nature and design, and it emphasizes metrology and validation."

Methods

One useful method is the gas chromatograph-mass spectrometer (GCMS), which is actually two instruments that are attached. The gas chromatograph is essentially a very hot oven holding a hollow coiled column. A drug sample is diluted in a solvent (e.g.: chloroform, methanol) and is injected into this column, the solvent will evaporate very quickly leaving the drug to travel through the column. Different substances are retained in the column for different amounts of time. The retention time, as compared to a known standard sample using the same method (same column length/polarity, same flow rate, same temperature program), can help to provide a positive identification for the presence of a compound of interest. The column eluent is then fed into a mass spectrometer. A mass spectrometer bombards the eluant with electrons, causing it to fragment into ions. These ions are separated by their mass, commonly with the use of a quadrupole mass analyzer or quadrupole ion trap, and detected by an electron multiplier. This provides a fragmentation pattern, which functions as a sort of fingerprint for each compound, and is compared to a reference sample.

Spectroscopy

Another instrument used to aide in identification of compounds is the Fourier Transform infrared spectrophotometer (FTIR). The sample is bombarded with infrared radiation. Polar bonds found in organic compounds have a natural frequency of vibration similar to the frequency of infrared radiation. When the frequency of the infrared radiation matches the natural frequency of the bond, the amplitude of the vibration increases, and the infrared is absorbed. The output of an infrared spectrophotometer charts the amount of light absorbed vs. the wavelength, typically with units of percent transmission and wavenumbers(cm-1). Because both the frequency and the intensity of absorption are dependent on the type of bond, a skilled chemist can determine the functional groups present by examining the infrared spectrum.

As with the GCMS the FTIR spectrum can be compared to that of a known sample, thus providing evidence for the identification of a compound. Spectroscopy can also help to identify materials used in failed products, especially polymers, additives and fillers. Samples can be taken by dissolution, or by cutting a thin slice using a microtome from the specimen under examination. Surfaces can be examined using Attenuated total reflectance spectroscopy, and the method has also been adapted to the optical microscope with infra-red microspectroscopy.

Thermoplastics can be analysed using infra-red spectroscopy, UV spectroscopy, as NMR and ESEM. Failed samples can either be dissolved in a suitable solvent and examined directly (UV, IR and NMR spectroscopy) or as a thin film cast from solvent or cut using microtomy from the solid product. Infra-red spectroscopy is especially useful for assessing oxidation of polymers, such as the polymer degradation caused by faulty injection moulding. The spectrum shows the characteristic carbonyl group produced by oxidation of polypropylene, which made the product brittle. It was a critical part of a crutch, and when it failed, the user fell and injured herself very seriously. The spectrum was obtained from a thin film cast from a solution of a sample of the plastic taken from the failed forearm crutch.

Sample Integrity

Forensic chemists usually perform their analytical work in a sterile laboratory decreasing the risk of sample contamination. In order to prevent tampering, forensic chemists must keep track of a chain of custody for each sample. A chain of custody is a document which stays with the evidence at all times. Among other information, contains signatures and identification of all the people involved in transport, storage and analysis of the evidence.

This makes it much more difficult for intentional tampering to occur, it also acts as a detailed record of the location of the evidence at all times for record keeping purposes. It increases the reliability of a forensic chemist's work and increases the strength of the evidence in court.

A distinction is made between destructive and non-destructive analytical methods. Destructive methods involve taking a sample from the object of interest, and so injures the object. Most spectroscopic techniques fall into this category. By contrast, a non-destructive method conserves the integrity of the object, and is generally preferred by forensic examiners. Optical microscopy cannot injure the sample, so fall into this class.

Examples

Polymers for example, can be attacked by aggressive chemicals, and if under load, then cracks will grow by the mechanism of stress corrosion cracking. Perhaps the oldest known example is the ozone cracking of rubbers, where traces of ozone in the atmosphere attack double bonds in the chains of the materials. Elastomers with double bonds in their chains include natural rubber, nitrile rubber and styrene-butadiene rubber. They are all highly susceptible to ozone attack, and can cause problems like car fires (from rubber fuel lines) and tire blow-outs. Nowadays, anti-ozonants are widely added to these polymers, so the incidence of cracking has dropped. However, not all safety-critical rubber products are protected, and since only ppb of ozone will start attack, failures are still occurring.

Another highly reactive gas is chlorine, which will attack susceptible polymers such as acetal resin and polybutylene pipework. There have been many examples of such pipes and acetal fittings failing in properties in the USA as a result of chlorine-induced cracking. Essentially the gas attacks sensitive parts of the chain molecules (especially secondary, tertiary or allylic carbon atoms), oxidising the chains and ultimately causing chain cleavage. The root cause is traces of chlorine in the water supply, added for its anti-bacterial action, attack occurring even at parts per million traces of the dissolved gas.

Most step-growth polymers can suffer hydrolysis in the presence of water, often a reaction catalysed by acid or alkali. Nylon for example, will degrade and crack rapidly if exposed to strong acids, a phenomenon well known to those who accidentally spill acid onto their shirts or tights. Polycarbonate is susceptible to alkali hydrolysis, the reaction simply depolymerising the material. Polyesters are prone to degrade when treated with strong acids, and in all these cases, care must be taken to dry the raw materials for processing at high temperatures to prevent the problem occurring.

Many polymers are also attacked by UV radiation at vulnerable points in their chain structures. Thus polypropylene suffers severe cracking in sunlight unless anti-oxidants are added. The point of attack occurs at the tertiary carbon atom present in every repeat unit, causing oxidation and finally chain breakage.

Forensic science (often shortened to forensics) is the application of a broad spectrum of sciences to answer questions of interest to the legal system.This may be in relation to a crime or to a civil action. But besides its relevance to the underlying legal system, more generally *forensics* encompasses the accepted scholarly or scientific methodology and norms under which the facts regarding an event, or an artifact, or some other physical item (such as a corpse, or cadaver, for example) are to the broader notion of authentication whereby an interest outside of a legal form exists in determining whether an object is in fact what it purports to be, or is alleged as being.

The word *"forensic"* comes from the Latin adjective *"forensis"* meaning *of or before the forum*. During the time of the Romans, a criminal charge meant presenting the case before a group of public individuals in the forum. Both the person accused of the crime and the accuser would give speeches based on their side of the story. The individual with the best argument and delivery would determine the outcome of the case. Basically, the person with the sharpest forensic skills would win. This origin is the source of the two modern usages of the word *"forensic"* - as a form of legal evidence and as a category of public presentation.

In modern use, the term *"forensics"* in place of "forensic science" can be considered incorrect as the term "forensic" is effectively a synonym for "legal" or "related to courts". However, the term is now so closely associated with the scientific field that many dictionaries include the meaning that equates the word "forensics" with "forensic science".

History

The "Eureka" legend of Archimedes (287-212 BC) can be considered an early use of forensic anthropology. He determined that a crown was not completely made up of gold (as it was fraudulently claimed). This conclusion was reached by evaluating the density of the object using measurements of its displacement and its weight, as he was not allowed to damage the crown. The earliest account of fingerprint use to establish identity was during the 7th century. According to an Arabic merchant, Soleiman, a debtor's fingerprints were affixed to a bill, which would then be given to the lender. This bill was legally recognized as proof of the validity of the debt.

The first written account of using medicine and entomology to solve (separate) criminal cases is attributed to the book *Xi Yuan Ji Lu* , translated as "Collected Cases of Injustice Rectified"), written in Song Dynasty China by Song Ci 1186-1249) in 1248. In one of the accounts, the case of a person murdered with a sickle was solved by a death investigator who instructed everyone to bring his sickle to one location. Flies, attracted by the smell of blood, eventually gathered on a single sickle. In light of this, the murderer confessed. The book also offered advice on how to distinguish between a drowning (water in the lungs) and strangulation (broken neck cartilage), along with other evidence from examining corpses on determining if a death was caused by murder, suicide, or an accident.

In sixteenth century Europe, medical practitioners in army and university settings began to gather information on cause and manner of death. Ambroise Paré, a French army surgeon, systematically studied the effects of violent death on internal organs. Two Italian surgeons, Fortunato Fidelis and Paolo Zacchia, laid the foundation of modern pathology by studying changes which occurred in the structure of the body as the result of disease. In the late 1700s, writings on these topics began to appear. These included: *"A Treatise on Forensic Medicine and Public Health"* by the French physician Fodéré, and *"The Complete System of Police Medicine"* by the German medical expert Johann Peter Franck.

In 1776, Swedish chemist Carl Wilhelm Scheele devised a way of detecting arsenous oxide, simple arsenic, in corpses, although only in large quantities. This investigation was expanded, in 1806, by German chemist Valentin Ross, who learned to detect the poison in the walls of a victim's stomach, and by English chemist James Marsh, who used chemical processes to confirm arsenic as the cause of death in an 1836 murder trial.

Two early examples of English forensic science in individual legal proceedings demonstrate the increasing use of logic and procedure in criminal investigations. In 1784, in Lancaster, England, John Toms was tried and convicted for murdering Edward Culshaw with a pistol. When the dead body of Culshaw was examined, a pistol wad (crushed paper used to secure powder and balls in the muzzle) found in his head wound matched perfectly with a torn newspaper found in Toms' pocket. In Warwick, England, in 1816, a farm labourer was tried and convicted of the murder of a young maidservant. She had been drowned in a shallow pool and bore the marks of violent assault. The police found footprints and an impression from corduroy cloth with a sewn patch in the damp earth near the pool. There were also scattered grains of wheat and chaff. The breeches of a farm labourer who had been threshing wheat nearby were examined and corresponded exactly to the impression in the earth near the pool Later in the 20th century, several British pathologists, Bernard Spilsbury, Francis Camps, Sydney Smith and Keith Simpson would pioneer new forensic methods in Britain.

Subdivisions

- *Computational forensics* concerns the development of algorithms and software to assist forensic examination.
- *Criminalistics* is the application of various sciences to answer questions relating to examination and comparison of biological evidence, trace evidence, impression evidence (such as fingerprints, footwear

impressions, and tire tracks), controlled substances, ballistics, firearm and toolmark examination, and other evidence in criminal investigations. Typically, evidence is processed in a crime lab.

- *Digital forensics* is the application of proven scientific methods and techniques in order to recover data from electronic/digital media. Digital Forensic specialists work in the field as well as in the lab.
- *Forensic accounting* is the study and interpretation of accounting evidence.
- *Forensic anthropology* is the application of physical anthropology in a legal setting, usually for the recovery and identification of skeletonized human remains.
- *Forensic archaeology* is the application of a combination of archaeological techniques and forensic science, typically in law enforcement.
- *Forensic astronomy* uses methods from *astronomy* to determine past celestial constellations for forensic purposes.
- *Forensic botany* is the study of plant life in order to gain information regarding possible crimes.
- *Forensic chemistry* is the study of detection and identification of illicit drugs, accelerants used in arson cases, explosive and *gunshot residue*.
- *Forensic dactyloscopy* is the study of fingerprints.
- *Forensic DNA analysis* takes advantage of the uniqueness of an individual's DNA to answer forensic questions such as determining paternity/maternity or placing a suspect at a crime scene.
- Forensic documents examination or *questioned document examination* answers questions about a disputed document using a variety of scientific processes and methods. Many examinations involve a comparison of the questioned document, or components of the

document, to a set of known standards. The most common type of examination involves handwriting wherein the examiner tries to address concerns about potential authorship.

- *Forensic engineering* is a scientific examination and analysis of structures and products relating to their failure or cause of damage.
- *Forensic entomology* deals with the examination of insects in, on, and around human remains to assist in determination of time or location of death. It is also possible to determine if the body was moved after death.
- *Forensic geology* deals with trace evidence in the form of soils, minerals and petroleums.
- *Forensic interviewing* is a method of communicating designed to elicit information and evidence.
- *Forensic limnology* is the analysis of evidence collected from crime scenes in or around fresh water sources. Examination of biological organisms, in particular, *diatoms*, can be useful in connecting suspects with victims.
- *Forensic linguistics* deals with issues in the legal system that requires linguistic expertise.
- *Forensic meteorology* is a site specific analysis of past weather conditions for a point of loss.
- *Forensic odontology* is the study of the uniqueness of dentition better known as the study of teeth.
- *Forensic pathology* is a field in which the principles of medicine and pathology are applied to determine a cause of death or injury in the context of a legal inquiry.
- *Forensic psychology* is the study of the mind of an individual, using forensic methods. Usually it determines the circumstances behind a criminal's behaviour.

- *Forensic seismology* is the study of techniques to distinguish the seismic signals generated by underground nuclear explosions from those generated by earthquakes.
- *Forensic serology* is the study of the body fluids.
- *Forensic toxicology* is the study of the effect of drugs and poisons on/in the human body.
- *Forensic video analysis* is the scientific examination, comparison and evaluation of video in legal matters.
- *Trace evidence* analysis is the analysis and comparison of trace evidence including glass, paint, fibres, hair etc.
- *Veterinary Forensics* is forensics applied to crimes involving animals.

Questionable Techniques

Some forensic techniques, believed to be scientifically sound at the time they were used, have turned out later to have much less scientific merit, or none. Some such techniques include:

- *Comparative bullet-lead analysis* was used by the FBI for over four decades, starting with the John F. Kennedy assassination in 1963. The theory was that each batch of ammunition possessed a chemical makeup so distinct that a bullet could be traced back to a particular batch, or even a specific box. However, internal studies and an outside study by the National Academy of Sciences found that the technique was unreliable, and the FBI abandoned the test in 2005.
- *Forensic dentistry* has come under fire; in at least two cases, bite mark evidence has been used to convict people of murder who were later freed by DNA evidence. A 1999 study by a member of the American Board of Forensic Odontology found a 63 percent rate of false identifications and is commonly referenced

within online news stories and conspiracy websites. However, the study was based on an informal workshop during an ABFO meeting which many members did not consider a valid scientific setting.

Litigation Science

Litigation science describes analysis or data developed or produced *expressly* for use in a trial, versus those produced in the course of independent research. This distinction was made by the U.S. 9th Circuit Court of Appeals when evaluating the admissibility of experts.

This uses demonstrative evidence, which is evidence created in preparation of trial by attorneys or paralegals.

Examples in Fiction

Sherlock Holmes, the fictional character created by Sir Arthur Conan Doyle in works produced from 1887 to 1915, used forensic science as one of his investigating methods. Conan Doyle credited the inspiration for Holmes on his teacher at the medical school of the University of Edinburgh, the gifted surgeon and forensic detective Joseph Bell.

Decades later, the comic strip *Dick Tracy* also featured a detective using a considerable number of forensic methods, although sometimes the methods were more fanciful than actually possible.

Defense attorney Perry Mason occasionally used forensic techniques, both in the novels and television series.

Popular television series focusing on crime detection, including *CSI*, *Cold Case*, *Bones*, *Law & Order*, *NCIS*, *Criminal Minds*, *Silent Witness*, *Dexter*, and *Waking the Dead*, depict glamorized versions of the activities of 21st century forensic scientists. These related TV shows have changed individuals' expectations of forensic science, an influence termed the "CSI effect".

Controversies

Questions about forensic science, fingerprint evidence and the assumption behind these disciplines have been brought to light in some publications the latest being an article in the *New York Post* The article stated that "No one has proved even the basic assumption: That everyone's fingerprint is unique." The article also stated that "Now such assumptions are being questioned—and with it may come a radical change in how forensic science is used by police departments and prosecutors."

2

Computer Forensics

Computer forensics is a branch of forensic science pertaining to legal evidence found in computers and digital storage mediums. Computer forensics is also known as *digital forensics*.

The goal of computer forensics is to explain the current state of a digital artifact. The term digital artifact can include a computer system, a storage medium (such as a hard disk or CD-ROM), an electronic document (e.g. an email message or JPEG image) or even a sequence of packets moving over a computer network. The explanation can be as straightforward as "what information is here?" and as detailed as "what is the sequence of events responsible for the present situation?"

The field of Computer Forensics also has sub branches within it such as Firewall Forensics, Database Forensics and Mobile Device Forensics.

There are many reasons to employ the techniques of computer forensics:

- In legal cases, computer forensic techniques are frequently used to analyze computer systems belonging to defendants (in criminal cases) or litigants (in civil cases).
- To recover data in the event of a hardware or software failure.
- To analyze a computer system after a break-in, for example, to determine how the attacker gained access and what the attacker did.
- To gather evidence against an employee that an organization wishes to terminate.
- To gain information about how computer systems work for the purpose of debugging, performance optimization, or reverse-engineering.

Special measures should be taken when conducting a forensic investigation if it is desired for the results to be used in a court of law. One of the most important measures is to assure that the evidence has been accurately collected and that there is a clear chain of custody from the scene of the crime to the investigator—and ultimately to the court. In order to comply with the need to maintain the integrity of digital evidence, British examiners comply with the Association of Chief Police Officers (A.C.P.O.) guidelines . These are made up of four principles as follows:

1. No action taken by law enforcement agencies or their agents should change data held on a computer or storage media which may subsequently be relied upon in court.
2. In exceptional circumstances, where a person finds it necessary to access original data held on a computer or on storage media, that person must be competent to do so and be able to give evidence explaining the relevance and the implications of their actions.

3. An audit trail or other record of all processes applied to computer based electronic evidence should be created and preserved. An independent third party should be able to examine those processes and achieve the same result.

4. The person in charge of the investigation (the case officer) has overall responsibility for ensuring that the law and these principles are adhered to.

The Forensic Process

There are five basic steps to the computer forensics.

1. Preparation (of the investigator, not the data).
2. Collection (the data).
3. Examination.
4. Analysis.
5. Reporting.

The investigator must be properly trained to perform the specific kind of investigation that is at hand.

Tools that are used to generate reports for court should be validated. There are many tools to be used in the process. One should determine the proper tool to be used based on the case.

Collecting Digital Evidence

Digital evidence can be collected from many sources. Obvious sources include computers, cell phones, digital cameras, hard drives, CD-ROM, USB memory devices, and so on. Non-obvious sources include settings of digital thermometers, black boxes inside automobiles, RFID tags, and web pages (which must be preserved as they are subject to change).

Special care must be taken when handling computer evidence: most digital information is easily changed, and once changed it is usually impossible to detect that a change has taken place (or to revert the data back to its original state) unless other measures have been taken. For this reason it is common practice to calculate a cryptographic hash of an evidence file and to record that hash elsewhere, usually in an investigator's notebook, so that one can establish at a later point in time that the evidence has not been modified since the hash was calculated.

Other specific practices that have been adopted in the handling of digital evidence include:

- Imaging computer media using a writeblocking tool to ensure that no data is added to the suspect device.
- Establish and maintain the chain of custody.
- Documenting everything that has been done.
- Only use tools and methods that have been tested and evaluated to validate their accuracy and reliability.

Some of the most valuable information obtained in the course of a forensic examination will come from the computer user. An interview with the user can yield valuable information about the system configuration, applications, encryption keys and methodology. Forensic analysis is much easier when analysts have the user's passphrases to access encrypted files, containers, and network servers.

In an investigation in which the owner of the digital evidence has not given consent to have his or her media examined (as in some criminal cases) special care must be taken to ensure that the forensic specialist has the legal authority to seize, copy, and examine the data. Sometimes authority stems from a search warrant. As a general rule, one should not examine digital information unless one has the legal authority to do so. Amateur forensic examiners should keep this in mind before starting any unauthorized investigation.

Live vs. Dead Analysis

Traditionally computer forensic investigations were performed on data at rest—for example, the content of hard drives. This can be thought of as a dead analysis. Investigators were told to shut down computer systems when they were impounded for fear that digital time-bombs might cause data to be erased.

In recent years there has increasingly been an emphasis on performing analysis on live systems. One reason is that many current attacks against computer systems leave no trace on the computer's hard drive—the attacker only exploits information in the computer's memory. Another reason is the growing use of cryptographic storage: it may be that the only copy of the keys to decrypt the storage are in the computer's memory, turning off the computer will cause that information to be lost.

Imaging Electronic Media (Evidence)

The process of creating an exact duplicate of the original evidentiary media is often called Imaging. Using a standalone hard-drive duplicator or software imaging tools such as DCFLdd or IXimager, the *entire* hard drive is completely duplicated. This is usually done at the sector level, making a bit-stream copy of every part of the user-accessible areas of the hard drive which can physically store data, rather than duplicating the filesystem. The original drive is then moved to secure storage to prevent tampering. During imaging, a write protection device or application is normally used to ensure that no information is introduced onto the evidentiary media during the forensic process.

The imaging process is verified by using the SHA-1 message digest algorithm (with a program such as sha1sum) or other still viable algorithms such as MD5. At critical points throughout the analysis, the media is verified again, known as "hashing", to ensure that the evidence is still in its original state. In corporate environments seeking civil or internal charges, such steps are generally overlooked due to the time required to perform them. They are essential for evidence that is to be presented in a court room, however.

Collecting Volatile Data

If the machine is still active, any intelligence which can be gained by examining the applications currently open is recorded. If the machine is suspected of being used for illegal communications, such as terrorist traffic, not all of this information may be stored on the hard drive. If information stored solely in RAM is not recovered before powering down it may be lost. This results in the need to collect volatile data from the computer at the onset of the response.

Several Open Source tools are available to conduct an analysis of open ports, mapped drives (including through an active VPN connection), and open or mounted encrypted files (containers) on the live computer system. Utilizing open source tools and commercially available products, it is possible to obtain an image of these mapped drives and the open encrypted containers in an unencrypted format. Open Source tools for PCs include Knoppix and Helix. Commercial imaging tools include Access Data's Forensic Toolkit and Guidance Software's EnCase application.

The aforementioned Open Source tools can also scan RAM and Registry information to show recently accessed web-based email sites and the login/password combination used. Additionally these tools can also yield login/password for recently accessed local email applications including MS Outlook.

In the event that partitions with EFS are suspected to exist, the encryption keys to access the data can also be gathered during the collection process. With Microsoft's most recent addition, Vista, and Vista's use of BitLocker and the Trusted Platform Module (TPM), it has become necessary in some instances to image the logical hard drive volumes before the computer is shut down.

RAM can be analyzed for prior content after power loss. Although as production methods become cleaner the impurities used to indicate a particular cell's charge prior to power loss are becoming less common. However, data held statically in an area of RAM for long periods of time are more likely to be detectable using these methods. The likelihood of such recovery increases as the originally applied voltages, operating temperatures and duration of data storage increases. Holding unpowered RAM below - 60 °C will help preserve the residual data by an order of magnitude, thus improving the chances of successful recovery. However, it can be impractical to do this during a field examination.

Analysis

All digital evidence must be analyzed to determine the type of information that is stored upon it. For this purpose, specialty tools are used that can display information in a format useful to investigators. Such forensic tools include: AccessData's FTK, Guidance Software's EnCase, and Brian Carrier's Sleuth Kit. In many investigations, numerous other tools are used to analyze specific portions of information.

Typical forensic analysis includes a manual review of material on the media, reviewing the Windows registry for suspect information, discovering and cracking passwords, keyword searches for topics related to the crime, and extracting e-mail and images for review.

Reporting

Once the analysis is complete, a report is generated. This report may be a written report, oral testimony, or some combination of the two.

Comparison to Physical Forensics

There are many core differences between computer forensics and "physical forensics." At the highest level, the physical forensic sciences focus on identification and individualization. Both of these processes compare an item from a crime scene with other substances to identify the class of the item (i.e. is the red liquid fruit juice or blood?) or the source of the item (i.e. did this blood come from person X?). Computer forensics on the other hand focuses on finding the evidence and analyzing it. Therefore, it is more analogous to a physical crime scene investigation than the physical forensic processes.

Examples of Computer Forensics

Computer forensics has played a pivotal role in many cases:

Chandra Levy

Chandra Levy was a Washington, D.C. intern who disappeared on April 30, 2001. She had used the web and e-mail to make travel arrangements and communicate with her parents. Information found on her computer led police to search most of Rock Creek Park, where her body was eventually found one year later by a man walking his dog.

BTK Killer

Dennis Rader was convicted of a string of serial killings that occurred over a period of sixteen years. Towards the end of this period, Rader sent letters to the police on a floppy disk. Metadata within the documents implicated an author named "Dennis" at "Christ Lutheran Church"; this evidence helped lead to Rader's arrest.

Aside from uncovering evidence to assist the prosecution in high-profile murder cases, an in-depth knowledge of computer forensics is integral when presenting digital evidence for legal proceedings.

ANTI-COMPUTER FORENSICS

Anti-computer forensics is a general term for a set of techniques used as countermeasures to forensic analysis.

Definition

Anti-forensics has only recently been recognized as a legitimate field of study. Within this field of study, numerous definitions of anti-forensics abound. One of the more widely known and accepted definitions comes from Dr. Marc Rogers of Purdue University. Dr. Rogers uses a more traditional "crime scene" approach when defining anti-forensics. "Attempts to negatively affect the existence, amount and/ or quality of evidence from a crime scene, or make the analysis and examination of evidence difficult or impossible to conduct"

A more abbreviated definition is given by Scott Berinato in his article entitled, The Rise of Anti-Forensics. "Anti-forensics is more than technology. It is an approach to criminal hacking that can be summed up like this: Make it hard for them to find you and impossible for them to prove they found you." Interestingly, neither author takes into account using anti-forensics methods to ensure the privacy of one's personal data.

Sub-categories

Anti-forensics methods are often broken down into several sub categories to make classification of the various tools and techniques simpler. One of the more widely accepted subcategory breakdowns was developed by Dr. Marcus Rogers. He has proposed the following sub-categories, data hiding, artifact wiping, trail obfuscation and attacks against the CF (computer forensics) process/tools.

Purpose and Goals

Within the field of digital forensics there is much debate over the purpose and goals of anti-forensic methods. The common conception is that anti-forensic tools are purely malicious in intent and design. Others believe that these tools should be used to illustrate deficiencies in digital forensic procedures, digital forensic tools, and forensic examiner education. This sentiment was echoed at the 2005 Blackhat Conference by anti-forensic tool authors, James Foster and Vinnie Liu. They stated that by exposing these issues, forensic investigators will have to work harder to prove that collected evidence is both accurate and dependable. They believe that this will result in better tools and education for the forensic examiner.

Data Hiding

Data hiding is the process of making data difficult to find while also keeping it accessible for future use. "Obfuscation and encryption of data give an adversary the ability to limit identification and collection of evidence by investigators while allowing access and use to themselves." Some of the more common forms of data hiding include encryption, steganography, and other various forms of hardware/software based data concealment. Each of the different data hiding methods makes digital forensic examinations difficult. When the different data hiding methods are combined, they can make a successful forensic investigation nearly impossible.

Encryption

One of the more commonly used techniques to defeat computer forensics is data encryption. In a presentation he gave on encryption and anti-forensic methodologies the Vice President of Secure Computing, Paul Henry, referred to encryption as a "forensic analysis's nightmare".

The majority of publicly available encryption programs allow the user to create virtual encrypted disks which can only be opened with a designated key. Through the use of modern encryption algorithms and various encryption techniques these programs make the data virtually impossible to read without the designated key.

File level encryption encrypts only the file contents. This leaves important information such as file name, size and timestamps unencrypted. Parts of the content of the file can be reconstructed from other locations, such as temporary files, swap file and deleted, unencrypted copies.

Most encryption programs have the ability to perform a number of additional functions that make digital forensic efforts increasingly difficult. Some of these functions include the use of a keyfile, full-volume encryption, and plausible deniability. The widespread availability of software containing these functions has put the field of digital forensics at a great disadvantage.

Steganography

Steganography is a technique where information or files are hidden within another file in an attempt to hide data by leaving it in plain sight. "Steganography produces dark data that is typically buried within light data (e.g., a non-perceptible digital watermark buried within a digital photograph)." Some experts have argued that the use of steganography techniques are not very widespread and therefore shouldn't be given a lot of thought. Most experts will agree that steganography has the capability of disrupting the forensic process when used correctly.

According to Jeffrey Carr, a 2007 edition of *Technical Mujahid* (a bi-monthly terrorist publication) outlined the importance of using a steganography programme called Secrets of the Mujahedeen. According to Carr, the program was touted as giving the user the capability to avoid detection by current steganalysis programs. It did this through the use of steganography in conjunction with file compression.

Other Forms of Data Hiding

Other forms of data hiding involve the use of tools and techniques to hide data throughout various different locations in a computer system. Some of these places can include "memory, slack space, hidden directories, bad blocks, alternate data streams, hidden partitions." One of the more well known tools that is often used for data hiding is called Slacker (part of the Metasploit framework). Slacker breaks up a file and places each piece of that file into the slack space of other files, thereby hiding it from the forensic examination software. Another data hiding technique involves the use of bad sectors. To perform this technique, the user changes a particular sector from good to bad and then data is placed onto that particular cluster. The belief is that forensic examination tools will see these clusters as bad and continue on without any examination of their contents.

Artifact Wiping

The methods used in artifact wiping are tasked with permanently eliminating particular files or entire file systems. This can be accomplished through the use of a variety of methods that include disk cleaning utilities, file wiping utilities and disk degaussing/destruction techniques.

Disk Cleaning Utilities

Disk cleaning utilities use a variety of methods to overwrite the existing data on disks (see data remanence). The effectiveness of disk cleaning utilities as anti-forensic tools is often challenged as some believe they are not completely effective. Experts who don't believe that disk cleaning utilities are acceptable for disk sanitization base their opinions off current DOD policy, which states that the only acceptable form of sanitization is degaussing. (See National Industrial Security Program) Disk cleaning utilities are also criticized because they leave signatures that the file system was wiped, which in some cases is unacceptable. Some of the widely used disk cleaning utilities include DBAN, srm, KillDisk, PC Inspector and CyberScrubs cyberCide. Another option which is approved by the NIST and the NSA is CMRR Secure Erase, which uses the Secure Erase command built into the ATA specification.

File Wiping Utilities

File wiping utilities are used to delete individual files from an operating system. The advantage of file wiping utilities is that they can accomplish their task in a relatively short amount of time as opposed to disk cleaning utilities which take much longer. Another advantage of file wiping utilities is that they generally leave a much smaller signature than disk cleaning utilities. There are two primary disadvantages of file wiping utilities, first they require user involvement in the process and second some experts believe that file wiping programs don't always correctly and completely wipe file information. Some of the widely used file wiping utilities include R-Wipe & Clean, Eraser, Aevita Wipe & Delete and CyberScrubs PrivacySuite.

Trail Obfuscation

The purpose of trail obfuscation is to confuse, disorientate and diver s. By using programs such as Timestomp, a user can render any number of files useless in a legal setting by directly calling in to question the files credibility.

Another well known trail obfuscation program is Transmogrify (also part of the Metasploit framework). In most file types the header of the file contains identifying information. A (.jpg) would have nduct a search for images on a machine, it would simply see a (.doc) file and skip over it.

Attacks Against Computer Forensics

In the past anti-forensic tools have focused on attacking the foren ge information. Anti-forensics has recently moved into a new realm where tools and techniques are focused on attacking forensic tools that perform the examinations. These new anti-forensic methods have benefited from a number of factors to include well documented forensic examination procedures, widely known forensic tool vulnerabilities and digital forensic examiners heavy reliance on their tools.

During a typical forensic examination, the examiner would create an image of the computers disks. This keeps the original computer (evidence) from being tainted by forensic tools. Hashes are created by the forensic ex mination software to verify the integrity of the image. One of the recent anti-tool techniques targets the integrity of the hash that is created to verify the image. By affecting the integrity of the hash, any evidence that is collected during the subsequent investigation can be challenged.

FORENSIC DISK CONTROLLER

A forensic disk controller or hardware write-block device is a specialized type of computer hard disk controller made for the purpose of gaining read-only access to computer hard drives without the risk of damaging the drive's contents. The device is named forensic because its most common application is for use in investigations where a computer hard drive may contain evidence. Such a controller historically has been made in the form of a dongle that fits between a computer and an IDE or SCSI hard drive, but with the advent of USB and SATA, forensic disk controllers supporting these newer technologies have become widespread.

Using hardware to protect the hard drive from writes is very important for several reasons. First, many operating systems, including Windows, may write to any hard disk that is connected to the system. At the very least, Windows will update the access time for any file accessed, and may write things to the disk unexpectedly - such as creating hidden folders for the recycle bin or saved hardware configuration. Virus infections or malware on the system used for analysis may attempt to infect the disk being inspected. Additionally, the NTFS file system may attempt to commit or rollback unfinished transactions, and/or change flags on the volume to mark it as "in use". At the worst, undesired files may allocate and overwrite deleted space on the hard disk which may potentially destroy evidence in the form of previously deleted files.

Protecting an evidence drive from writes during investigation is also important to counter potential allegations that the contents of the drive were altered during the investigation. Of course, this can be alleged anyway, but in the absence of technology to protect a drive from writes, there is no way for such an allegation to be refuted.

Hardware write blocking was invented by Mark Menz and Steve Bress (US patent 6,813,682 and EU patent EP1, 342, 145)

The United States National Institute of Justice operates a Computer Forensics Tool Testing (CFTT) program which formally identifies the following top-level tool requirements:

- *A hardware write block* (HWB) device shall not transmit a command to a protected storage device that modifies the data on the storage device.
- An HWB device shall return the data requested by a read operation.
- An HWB device shall return without modification any access-significant information requested from the drive.
- Any error condition reported by the storage device to the HWB device shall be reported to the host.

How it Works

All forensic disk controllers work by capturing commands from the host operating system that request the drive to overwrite sectors, and preventing them from reaching the drive. Whenever the host bus architecture supports it, the forensic disk controller reports to the host operating system that the drive is read-only.

- A forensic disk controller works in one of two ways. The disk controller can either deny all writes to the disk and report them as failures, or use on-board memory to cache the writes for the duration of the session.

- A disk controller that denies all writes will likely not be tolerated by an operating system that assumes that all hard disks can be written to. Although the controller could report the writes as successful, subsequent reads will return the original data, which will be unexpected by the operating system and which will cause it to malfunction due to the internal inconsistency between the operating system and the drive's actual state.
- A disk controller that caches writes in memory presents the appearance to the operating system that the drive is writable, and uses the memory to ensure that the operating system sees changes to the individual disk sectors it attempted to overwrite. It does this by retrieving sectors from the disk if the operating system hasn't attempted to change them, and retrieving the changed version from memory for sectors that have been changed. This method is transparent to and compatible with all operating systems, and ensures that when the device is powered off, the disk remains unchanged and in its original state. Because the operating system's internal state persists only as long as the drive is mounted or powered on, assuming none of the writes were desired there is no adverse consequence to losing the data in the change buffer.

3
Data Recovery

Data recovery is the process of salvaging data from damaged, failed, corrupted, or inaccessible secondary storage media when it cannot be accessed normally. Often the data are being salvaged from storage media formats such as hard disk drives, storage tapes, CDs, DVDs, RAID, and other electronics. Recovery may be required due to physical damage to the storage device or logical damage to the file system that prevents it from being mounted by the host operating system.

The most common "data recovery" issue involves an operating system (OS) failure (typically on a single-disk, single-partition, single-OS system), where the goal is to simply copy all wanted files to another disk. This can be easily accomplished with a Live CD, most of which provide a means to:

1. mount the system drive;
2. mount and backup disk or media drives; and
3. move the files from the system to the backup with a file manager or optical disc authoring software.

Further, such cases can be mitigated by disk partitioning and consistently moving valuable data files to a different partition from the replaceable OS system files.

The second type involves a disk-level failure such as a compromised file system, disk partition, or a hard disk failure —in each of which the data cannot be easily read. Depending on the case, solutions involve repairing the file system, partition table or MBR, or hard disk recovery techniques ranging from software-based recovery of corrupted data to hardware replacement on a physically damaged disk. These last two typically indicate the permanent failure of the disk, thus "recovery" means sufficient repair for a one-time recovery of files.

A third type involves the process of retrieving files that have been deleted from a storage media. Although there is some confusion as to the term, the term "data recovery" may be used to refer to such cases in the context of forensic purposes or spying.

Recovering Data After Physical Damage

A wide variety of failures can cause physical damage to storage media. CD-ROMs can have their metallic substrate or dye layer scratched off; hard disks can suffer any of several mechanical failures, such as head crashes and failed motors; tapes can simply break. Physical damage always causes at least some data loss, and in many cases the logical structures of the file system are damaged as well. This causes logical damage that must be dealt with before any files can be salvaged from the failed media.

Most physical damage cannot be repaired by end users. For example, opening a hard disk in a normal environment can allow airborne dust to settle on the platter and become caught between the platter and the read/write head, causing new head crashes that further damage the platter and thus compromise the recovery process. Furthermore, end users generally do not have the hardware or technical expertise required to make these repairs. Consequently, costly data recovery companies are often employed to salvage important data. These firms often use "Class 100"/ISO-5 cleanroom facilities to protect the media while repairs are being made. (Any data recovery firm without a pass certificate of ISO-5 or better will not be accepted by hard drive manufacturers for warranty purposes.)

Recovery Techniques

Recovering data from physically-damaged hardware can involve multiple techniques. Some damage can be repaired by replacing parts in the hard disk. This alone may make the disk usable, but there may still be logical damage. A specialized disk-imaging procedure is used to recover every readable bit from the surface. Once this image is acquired and saved on a reliable medium, the image can be safely analysed for logical damage and will possibly allow for much of the original file system to be reconstructed.

Hardware Repair

Examples of physical recovery procedures are: removing a damaged PCB (printed circuit board) and replacing it with a matching PCB from a healthy drive, performing a live PCB swap (in which the System Area of the HDD is damaged on the target drive which is then instead read from the donor drive, the PCB then disconnected while still under power and transferred to the target drive), read/write head assembly with matching parts from a healthy drive, removing the hard disk platters from the original damaged drive and installing them into a healthy drive, and often a combination of all of these procedures. Some data recovery companies have procedures that are highly technical in nature and are not recommended for an untrained individual. Any of them will almost certainly void the manufacturer's warranty.

DISK IMAGING

The extracted raw image can be used to reconstruct usable data after any logical damage has been repaired. Once that is complete, the files may be in usable form although recovery is often incomplete.

Open source tools such as DCFLdd v1.3.4-1 or DOS tools such as HDClone can usually recover data from all but the physically-damaged sectors. A 2007 Defense Cyber Crime Institute study shows that the DCFLdd v1.3.4-1 installed on a Linux 2.4 Kernel system produces extra "bad sectors", resulting in the loss of information that is actually available. The study states that when installed on a FreeBSD Kernel system, only the bad sectors are lost. Another tool that can correctly image damaged media is ILook IXImager, a tool available only to government and Law Enforcement.

Typically, Hard Disk Drive data recovery imaging has the following abilities:

1. Communicating with the hard drive by bypassing the BIOS and operating system which are very limited in their abilities to deal with drives that have "bad sectors" or take a long time to read.
2. Reading data from "bad sectors" rather than skipping them (by using various read commands and ECC to recreate damaged data).
3. Handling issues caused by unstable drives, such as resetting/repowering the drive when it stops responding or skipping sectors that take too long to read (read instability can be caused by minute mechanical wear and other issues).
4. Pre-configuring drives by disabling certain features, such a SMART and G-List re-mapping, to minimize imaging time and the possibility of further drive degradation.

Recovering data after logical damage Logical damage is primarily caused by power outages that prevent file system structures from being completely written to the storage medium, but problems with hardware (especially RAID controllers) and drivers, as well as system crashes, can have the same effect. The result is that the file system is left in an inconsistent state. This can cause a variety of problems, such as strange behavior (e.g., infinitely recursing directories, drives reporting negative amounts of free space), system crashes, or an actual loss of data. Various programs exist to correct these inconsistencies, and most operating systems come with at least a rudimentary repair tool for their native file systems. Linux, for instance, comes with the fsck utility, Mac OS X has Disk Utility and Microsoft Windows provides chkdsk. Third-party utilities such as The Coroners Toolkit and The Sleuth Kit are also available, and some can produce superior results by recovering data even when the disk cannot be recognized by the operating system's repair utility. Utilities such as TestDisk can be useful for reconstructing corrupted partition tables.

Some kinds of logical damage can be mistakenly attributed to physical damage. For instance, when a hard drive's read/write head begins to click, most end-users will associate this with internal physical damage. This is not always the case, however. Another possibility is that the firmware of the drive or its controller needs to be rebuilt in order to make the data accessible again.

PREVENTING LOGICAL DAMAGE

The increased use of journaling file systems, such as NTFS 5.0, ext3, and XFS, is likely to reduce the incidence of logical damage. These file systems can always be "rolled back" to a consistent state, which means that the only data likely to be lost is what was in the drive's cache at the time of the system failure. However, regular system maintenance should still include the use of a consistency checker. This can protect both against bugs in the file system software and latent incompatibilities in the design of the storage hardware. One such incompatibility is the result of the disk controller reporting that file system structures have been saved to the disk when it has not actually occurred. This can often occur if the drive stores data in its write cache, then claims it has been written to the disk. If power is lost, and this data contains file system structures, the file system may be left in an inconsistent state such that the journal itself is damaged or incomplete. One solution to this problem is to use hardware that does not report data as written until it actually is written. Another is using disk controllers equipped with a battery backup so that the waiting data can be written when power is restored. Finally, the entire system can be equipped with a battery backup that may make it possible to keep the system on in such situations, or at least to give enough time to shut down properly.

RECOVERY TECHNIQUES

Two common techniques used to recover data from logical damage are consistency checking and data carving. While most logical damage can be either repaired or worked around using these two techniques, data recovery software can never guarantee that no data loss will occur. For instance, in the FAT file system, when two files claim to share the same allocation unit ("cross-linked"), data loss for one of the files is essentially guaranteed.

CONSISTENCY CHECKING

The first, consistency checking, involves scanning the logical structure of the disk and checking to make sure that it is consistent with its specification. For instance, in most file systems, a directory must have at least two entries: a dot (.) entry that points to itself, and a dot-dot (..) entry that points to its parent. A file system repair program can read each directory and make sure that these entries exist and point to the correct directories. If they do not, an error message can be printed and the problem corrected. Both chkdsk and fsck work in this fashion. This strategy suffers from two major problems. First, if the file system is sufficiently damaged, the consistency check can fail completely. In this case, the repair program may crash trying to deal with the mangled input, or it may not recognize the drive as having a valid file system at all. The second issue that arises is the disregard for data files. If chkdsk finds a data file to be out of place or unexplainable, it may delete the file without asking. This is done so that the operating system may run smoother, but the files deleted are often important user files which cannot be replaced. Similar issues arise when using system restore disks (often provided with proprietary systems like Dell and Compaq), which restore the operating system by removing the previous installation. This problem can often be avoided by installing the operating system on a separate partition from your user data.

DATA CARVING

Data Carving is a data recovery technique that allows for data with no file system allocation information to be extracted by identifying sectors and clusters belonging to the file. Data Carving usually searches through raw sectors looking for specific desired file signatures. The fact that there is no allocation information means that the investigator must specify a block size of data to carve out upon finding a matching file signature. This presents the challenge that the beginning of the file is still present and that there is (depending on how common the file signature is) a risk of many false hits. Also, data carving requires that the files recovered be located in sequential sectors (rather than fragmented) as there is no allocation information to point to fragmented file portions. This method can be time and resource intensive.

RECOVERING OVERWRITTEN DATA

When data have been physically overwritten on a hard disk it is generally assumed that the previous data are no longer possible to recover. In 1996, Peter Gutmann, a respected computer scientist, presented a paper that suggested overwritten data could be recovered through the use of Scanning transmission electron microscopy In 2001, he presented another paper on a similar topic Substantial criticism has followed, primarily dealing with the lack of any concrete examples of significant amounts of overwritten data being recovered. To guard against this type of data recovery, he and Colin Plumb designed the Gutmann method, which is used by several disk scrubbing software packages.

Although Gutmann's theory may be correct, there's no practical evidence that overwritten data can be recovered. Moreover, there are good reasons to think that it cannot.

Recovery Software

Bootable

Data recovery cannot always be done on a running system. As a result boot disk, Live CD, Live USB, or any other type of Live Distro containing a minimal operating system and a set of repair tools.

- **Knoppix:** The original Linux Live CD. It contains many useful utilities for data recovery.
- **Ubuntu Rescue Remix:** A GNU/Linux live system that runs from CD or USB pen drive that includes free-libre, open source data recovery and forensics tools.
- **System Rescue CD:** A Gentoo based Live CD, useful for repairing unbootable computer systems and retrieving data after a system crash.
- **Nero Back It Up Image Tool:** A user friendly bootable environment, through which you can restore your image created by Nero Back It Up and/or Nero Back It Up Image Tool to make your machine back to consistent state.
- **Selkie Rescue Data Recovery:** A bootable cd that runs before Windows with a user friendly interface. Allows you to retrieve files to a second computer via crossover cable or a network.
- **Spin Rite:** Bootable CD running Free DOS. Drive recovery software written by Steve Gibson of Gibson Research Corporation. Will run on most PC (x86, non-Apple) hardware regardless of installed operating system.

Consistency Checkers

- **CHKDSK:** A consistency checker for DOS and Windows systems.

- **Disk First Aid:** A consistency checker for Mac OS 9.
- **Disk Utility:** A consistency checker for Mac OS X.
- **fsck:** A consistency checker for UNIX file systems.

File Recovery

- **Photo Rec:** Multi-platform console program used to recover files.
- **San Disk Rescue PRO:** Software introduced by SanDisk and distributed through LC Technology International Inc.

Forensics

- **The Coroner's Toolkit:** A suite of utilities aimed at assisting in forensic analysis of a UNIX system after a break-in.
- **The Sleuth Kit:** Also known as TSK, The Sleuth Kit is a suite of forensic analysis tools developed by Brian Carrier for UNIX, Linux and Windows systems. TSK includes the Autopsy forensic browser.
- **En Case:** A suite of forensic tools developed by Guidance Software that is used for imaging and forensic analysis for UNIX, Linux, and Windows systems.
- FTK by Access Data (Forensic Tool Kit) Used by law enforcement.

Imaging Tools

Data Loss

In the field of information technology, data loss refers to the unforeseen loss of data or information. An occurrence of data loss can be called a *Data Loss Event* and there are several possible root causes. *Data loss* must be distinguished from *data unavailability*, such as may arise from a network outage. Although the two have substantially similar effects, *data unavailability* is temporary while *data loss* is permanent. Backup and recovery schemes are developed to restore lost data.

Types of Data Loss Events

- Intentional Action
  - Intentional deletion of a file or programme
- Unintentional Action
  - Accidental deletion of a file or programme
  - Misplacement of CDs or floppies
  - Administration errors
  - Inability to read unknown file format
- Failure
  - Power failure, resulting in data in volatile memory not being saved to permanent memory.
  - Hardware failure, such as a head crash in a hard disk.
  - A software crash or freeze, resulting in data not being saved.
  - Software bugs or poor usability, such as not confirming a file delete command.
  - Data corruption, such as filesystem corruption or database corruption.
- Disaster
  - Natural disaster, earthquake, flood, tornado, etc.
  - Fire
- Crime
  - Theft, hacking, sabotage, etc.
  - A malicious act, such as a worm, virus, hacker or theft of physical media.

Studies have consistently shown hardware failure and human error to be two most common causes of data loss, accounting for roughly three quarters of all incidents. A commonly overlooked cause is a natural disaster. Although the probability is small, the only way to recover from data loss due to a natural disaster is to store backup data in a physically separate location.

Cost of Data Loss

The cost of a Data Loss event is directly related to the value of the data and the length of time that it is needed, but unavailable. Consider:

- The cost of continuing without the data.
- The cost of recreating the data
- The cost of notifying users in the event of a compromise.

Organizational Responsibility

Recent statistics show the number of publicized data loss events involving sensitive data is on the rise, in part due to recent legislation, including the landmark California SB 1386, requiring the notification of data loss. This and other legislation has forced organizations to notify victims that their identity has potentially been compromised.

Preventing Data Loss

There is no guaranteed way to prevent data loss. However, the frequency of data loss events and their impact can be greatly mitigated by taking proper precautions. The different types of data loss events demand different types of precautions. For example, multiple power circuits with battery backup and a generator will only protect against power failures. Similarly, using a journaling filesystem and RAID storage will only protect against certain types of software and hardware failure. Regular data backups are an important asset to have when trying to recover after a data loss event, but they don't do much to prevent user errors or system failures.

A well rounded approach to data protection has the best chance of avoiding data loss events. Such an approach will also include such mundane tasks as maintaining antivirus protection and network firewalls, as well as staying up to date with all published security fixes and system patches. User education is probably the most important, and most difficult, aspect of preventing data loss. Nothing else will prevent users from making mistakes that jeopardize data security.

Recovery from Data Loss

Successful recovery from a Data Loss Event generally requires an effective backup strategy. Without a backup strategy, recovery requires reinstallation of programs and regeneration of data. Even with an effective backup strategy, restoring a system to the precise state it was in prior to the Data Loss Event is extremely difficult. Some level of compromise between granularity of recoverability and cost is necessary. Furthermore, a Data Loss Event may not be immediately apparent. An effective backup strategy must also consider the cost of maintaining the ability to recover lost data for long periods of time.

The most convenient backup system would have duplicate copies of every file and program that were immediately accessible whenever a Data Loss Event was noticed. However, in most situations, there is an inverse correlation between the value of a unit of data and the length of time it takes to notice the loss of that data. Taking this into consideration, many backup strategies decrease the granularity of restorability as the time increases since the potential Data Loss Event. By this logic, recovery from recent Data Loss Events is easier and more complete than recovery from Data Loss Events that happened further in the past.

Recovery is also related to the type of *Data Loss Event.* Recovering a single lost file is going to be substantially different than recovering a whole system that was destroyed in a flood. An effective backup regimen will have some proportionality between the magnitude of *Data Loss* and the magnitude of effort required to recover. For example, it should be far easier to restore the single lost file than to recover the whole system destroyed in a flood.

ERROR DETECTION AND CORRECTION

In mathematics, computer science, telecommunication, and information theory, error detection and correction has great practical importance in maintaining data (information) integrity across noisy channels and less-than-reliable storage media.

General Definitions of Terms

Definitions of error detection and error correction:

- *Error detection* is the ability to detect the presence of errors caused by noise or other impairments during transmission from the transmitter to the receiver.
- *Error correction* is the additional ability to reconstruct the original, error-free data.

There are two basic ways to design the channel code and protocol for an error correcting system:

- **Automatic repeat-request (ARQ):** The transmitter sends the data and also an error detection code, which the receiver uses to check for errors, and requests retransmission of erroneous data. In many cases, the request is implicit; the receiver sends an acknowledgement (ACK) of correctly received data, and the transmitter re-sends anything not acknowledged within a reasonable period of time.
- **Forward error correction (FEC):** The transmitter encodes the data with an error-correcting code (ECC) and sends the coded message. The receiver never sends any messages back to the transmitter. The receiver decodes what it receives into the "most likely" data. The codes are designed so that

it would take an "unreasonable" amount of noise to trick the receiver into misinterpreting the data.

It is possible to combine the two, so that minor errors are corrected without retransmission, and major errors are detected and a retransmission requested. The combination is called hybrid automatic repeat-request.

Error Detection Schemes

Several schemes exist to achieve error detection, and generally they are quite simple. All error detection codes (which include all error-detection-and-correction codes) transmit more bits than were in the original data. Most codes are "systematic": the transmitter sends a fixed number of original data bits, followed by fixed number of *check bits* (usually referred to as redundancy in the literature) which are derived from the data bits by some deterministic algorithm. The receiver applies the same algorithm to the received data bits and compares its output to the received check bits; if the values do not match, an error has occurred at some point during the transmission. In a system that uses a "non-systematic" code, such as some raptor codes, data bits are transformed into at least as many code bits, and the transmitter sends only the code bits.

Repetition Schemes

Variations on this theme exist. Given a stream of data that is to be sent, the data is broken up into blocks of bits, and in sending, each block is sent some predetermined number of times. For example, if we want to send "1011", we may repeat this block three times each.

Suppose we send "1011 1011 1011", and this is received as "1010 1011 1011". As one group is not the same as the other two, we can determine that an error has occurred. This scheme is not very efficient, and can be susceptible to problems if the error occurs in exactly the same place for each group (e.g. "1010 1010 1010" in the example above will be detected as correct in this scheme).

The scheme however is extremely simple, and is in fact used in some transmissions of numbers stations.

Parity Schemes

A parity bit is an error detection mechanism that can only detect an odd number of errors.

The stream of data is broken up into blocks of bits, and the number of 1 bits is counted. Then, a "parity bit" is set (or cleared) if the number of one bits is odd (or even). (This scheme is called even parity; odd parity can also be used.) If the tested blocks overlap, then the parity bits can be used to isolate the error, and even correct it if the error affects a single bit. This is the principle behind the Hamming code.

There is a limitation to parity schemes. A parity bit is only guaranteed to detect an odd number of bit errors (one, three, five, and so on). If an even number of bits (two, four, six and so on) are flipped, the parity bit appears to be correct, even though the data is corrupt.

Checksum

A checksum of a message is an arithmetic sum of message code words of a certain word length, for example byte values, and their carry value. The sum is negated by means of ones-complement, and stored or transferred as an extra code word extending the message.

On the receiver side, a new checksum may be calculated from the extended message. If the new checksum is not 0, an error has been detected.

Checksum schemes include parity bits, check digits, and longitudinal redundancy check.

Cyclic Redundancy Checks

More complex error detection (and correction) methods make use of the properties of finite fields and polynomials over such fields.

The cyclic redundancy check considers a block of data as the coefficients to a polynomial and then divides by a fixed, predetermined polynomial. The coefficients of the result of the division is taken as the redundant data bits, the CRC.

On reception, one can recompute the CRC from the payload bits and compare this with the CRC that was received. A mismatch indicates that an error occurred.

Hamming Distance Based Checks

If we want to detect d bit errors in an n bit word we can map every n bit word into a bigger $n+d+1$ bit word so that the minimum Hamming distance between each valid mapping is $d+1$. This way, if one receives a $n+d+1$ word that doesn't match any word in the mapping (with a Hamming distance $x <= d+1$ from any word in the mapping) it can successfully detect it as an erroneous word. Even more, d or fewer errors will never transform a valid word into another, because the Hamming distance between each valid word is at least $d+1$, and such errors only lead to invalid words that are detected correctly. Given a stream of $m*n$ bits, we can detect $x <= d$ bit errors successfully using the above method on every n bit word. In fact, we can detect a maximum of $m*d$ errors if every n word is transmitted with maximum d errors.

Horizontal and Vertical Redundancy Check

Other types of redundancy check include horizontal redundancy check, vertical redundancy check and "double", "dual" or "diagonal" parity (used in RAID-DP).

Polarity Schemes

One less commonly used form of error correction and detection is transmitting a polarity reversed bitstream simultaneously with the bitstream it is meant to correct. This scheme is very weak at detecting bit errors, and marginally useful for byte or word error detection and correction.

However, at the physical layer in the OSI model, this scheme can aid in error correction and detection.

Polarity symbol reversal is (probably) the simplest form of Turbo code, but technically not a Turbo code at all.

- Turbo codes do not work at the bit level.
- Turbo codes typically work at the character or symbol level depending on their placement in the OSI model.
- Character here refers to Baudot, ASCII-7, the 8-bit byte or the 16-bit word.

Original transmitted symbol 1011

- transmit 1011 on carrier wave 1 (CW1)
- transmit 0100 on carrier wave 2 (CW2)

Receiver end

- do bits polarities of (CW1) <> (CW2)?
- if CW1 == CW2, signal *bit error* (triggers more complex ECC)

This polarity reversal scheme works fairly well at low data rates (below 300 baud) with very redundant data like telemetry data.

Error Correction

Automatic Repeat Request

Automatic Repeat-re Quest (ARQ) is an error control method for data transmission which makes use of error detection codes, acknowledgment and/or negative acknowledgement messages and timeouts to achieve reliable data transmission. An acknowledgment is a message sent by the receiver to the transmitter to indicate that it has correctly received a data frame.

Usually, when the transmitter does not receive the acknowledgment before the timeout occurs (i.e. within a reasonable amount of time after sending the data frame), it retransmits the frame until it is either correctly received or the error persists beyond a predetermined number of retransmissions.

A few types of ARQ protocols are Stop-and-wait ARQ, Go-Back-N ARQ and Selective Repeat ARQ.

Hybrid Schemes

Hybrid ARQ is a combination of ARQ and forward error correction.

Error-correcting Code

An error-correcting code (ECC) or forward error correction (FEC) code is a code in which each data signal conforms to specific rules of construction such that departures from that construction in the received signal can be automatically detected and corrected. Error-correcting codes are used in computer data storage, for example in dynamic RAM, and in data transmission.

Shannon's theorem is an important theorem in error correction which describes the maximum attainable efficiency of an error-correcting scheme versus the expected levels of noise interference. In general, these methods put redundant information into the data stream following certain algebraic or geometric relations so that the decoded stream can be corrected if damaged in transmission. The effectiveness of the coding scheme is measured in terms of code rate, which is the code length divided by the useful information, and the coding gain, which is the difference of the signal-to-noise ratio levels of the uncoded and coded systems required to reach the same bit error rate levels.

Error-correcting Memory

Because soft errors are extremely common in the DRAM of computers used in satellites and space probes, such memory is structured as ECC memory (also called "EDAC protected memory"). Such memory controllers traditionally use a Hamming code, although some use triple modular redundancy. Even though a single cosmic ray can upset many physically neighboring bits in a DRAM, such memory systems are designed so that neighboring bits belong to different words, so that a single event upset (SEU) causes only a single error in any particular word, and so can be corrected by a single-bit error correcting code. As long as no more than a single bit in any particular word is affected by an error between accesses, such a memory system presents the illusion of an error-free memory.

Applications

Applications that require low latency (such as telephone conversations) cannot use Automatic Repeat reQuest (ARQ); they must use Forward Error Correction (FEC). By the time an ARQ system discovers an error and re-transmits it, the re-sent data will arrive too late to be any good.

Applications where the transmitter immediately forgets the information as soon as it is sent (such as most television cameras) cannot use ARQ; they must use FEC because when an error occurs, the original data is no longer available. (This is also why FEC is used in data storage systems such as RAID and distributed data store).

Applications that use ARQ must have a return channel. Applications that have no return channel cannot use ARQ.

Applications that require extremely low error rates (such as digital money transfers) must use ARQ.

The Internet

In a typical TCP/IP stack, error detection is performed at multiple levels:

- Each Ethernet frame carries a CRC-32 checksum. The receiver discards frames if their checksums do not match.

- The IPv4 header contains a header checksum of the contents of the header (excluding the checksum field). Packets with checksums that don't match are discarded.
- The checksum was omitted from the IPv6 header, because most current link layer protocols have error detection.
- UDP has an optional checksum. Packets with wrong checksums are discarded.
- TCP has a checksum of the payload, TCP header (excluding the checksum field) and source- and destination addresses of the IP header. Packets found to have incorrect checksums are discarded and eventually get retransmitted when the sender receives a triple-ack or a timeout occurs.

Deep-space Telecommunications

NASA has used many different error correcting codes. For missions between 1969 and 1977 the Mariner spacecraft used a Reed-Muller code. The noise these spacecraft were subject to was well approximated by a "bell-curve" (normal distribution), so the Reed-Muller codes were well suited to the situation.

The Voyager 1 & Voyager 2 spacecraft transmitted colour pictures of Jupiter and Saturn in 1979 and 1980.

- Colour image transmission required 3 times the amount of data, so the Golay (24, 12, 8) code was used.
- This Golay code is only 3-error correcting, but it could be transmitted at a much higher data rate.
- Voyager 2 went on to Uranus and Neptune and the code was switched to a concatenated Reed-Solomon code-Convolutional code for its substantially more powerful error correcting capabilities.
- Current DSN error correction is done with dedicated hardware.

- For some NASA deep space craft such as those in the Voyager program, Cassini-Huygens (Saturn), New Horizons (Pluto) and Deep Space 1—the use of hardware ECC may not be feasible for the full duration of the mission.

The different kinds of deep space and orbital missions that are conducted suggest that trying to find a "one size fits all" error correction system will be an ongoing problem for some time to come.

- For missions close to the earth the nature of the "noise" is different from that on a spacecraft headed towards the outer planets.
- In particular, if a transmitter on a spacecraft far from earth is operating at a low power, the problem of correcting for noise gets larger with distance from the ear.

Satellite Broadcasting (DVB)

The demand for satellite transponder bandwidth continues to grow, fueled by the desire to deliver television (including new channels and High Definition TV) and IP data. Transponder availability and bandwidth constraints have limited this growth, because transponder capacity is determined by the selected modulation scheme and Forward error correction (FEC) rate.

Overview

- QPSK coupled with traditional Reed Solomon and Viterbi codes have been used for nearly 20 years for the delivery of digital satellite TV.
- Higher order modulation schemes such as 8PSK, 16QAM and 32QAM have enabled the satellite industry to increase transponder efficiency by several orders of magnitude.

- This increase in the information rate in a transponder comes at the expense of an increase in the carrier power to meet the threshold requirement for existing antennas.
- Tests conducted using the latest chipsets demonstrate that the performance achieved by using Turbo Codes may be even lower than the 0.8 dB figure assumed in early designs.

Data Storage

Error detection and correction codes are often used to improve the reliability of data storage media.

A "parity track" was present on the first magnetic tape data storage in 1951. The "Optimal Rectangular Code" used in group code recording tapes not only detects but also corrects single-bit errors.

Some file formats, particularly archive formats, include a checksum (most often CRC32) to detect corruption and truncation and can employ redundancy and/or parity files to recover portions of corrupted data.

Reed Solomon codes are used in compact discs to correct errors caused by scratches.

Modern hard drives use CRC codes to detect and Reed-Solomon codes to correct minor errors in sector reads, and to recover data from sectors that have "gone bad" and store that data in the spare sectors.

RAID systems use a variety of error correction techniques, to correct errors when a hard drive completely fails.

The Vandermonde matrix is used in some RAID techniques.

INFORMATION THEORY AND ERROR DETECTION AND CORRECTION

Information theory tells us that whatever the probability of error in transmission or storage, it is possible to construct error-correcting codes in which the likelihood of failure is arbitrarily low, although this requires adding increasing amounts of redundant data to the original, which might not be practical when the error probability is very high. Shannon's theorem sets an upper bound to the error correction rate that can be achieved (and thus the level of noise that can be tolerated) using a fixed amount of redundancy, but does not tell us how to construct such an optimal encoder.

Error-correcting codes can be divided into block codes and convolutional codes. Other block error-correcting codes, such as Reed-Solomon codes, transform a chunk of bits into a (longer) chunk of bits in such a way that errors up to some threshold in each block can be detected and corrected.

However, in practice errors often occur in bursts rather than at random. This is often compensated for by shuffling (interleaving) the bits in the message after coding. Then any burst of bit-errors is broken up into a set of scattered single-bit errors when the bits of the message are unshuffled (de-interleaved) before being decoded.

List of Error-correction, Error-detection Methods

This list contains methods of error correction (Reed-Solomon, for example is a method) and practical techniques for error correction (like the Check digit, a practical method).

- Berger code
- Chipkill, an application of ECC techniques to volatile system memory.
- Constant-weight code.
- Convolutional codes are usually decoded with iterative Viterbi decoding techniques.
- Differential space–time codes, related to space–time block codes.
- Dual modular redundancy, subset of N-modular redundancy, related to triple modular redundancy.

- Erasure codes are a superset of Fountain codes.
- Forward error correction.
- Group code.
- Golay code, the Binary Golay codes are the most commonly used Golay codes.
- Goppa code that is used to create the McEliece crypto system.
- Hadamard code.
- Hagelbarger code.
- Hamming code.
- Lexicographic code.
- Longitudinal redundancy check.
- Low-density parity-check code.
- LT codes are near optimal rateless erasure correcting codes.
- m of n codes.
- Online codes are an example of rateless erasure codes.
- Parity bit.
- Raptor codes are high speed (near real time) fountain codes.
- Reed-Solomon error correction.
- Reed-Muller code.
- Repeat-accumulate code.
- Sparse graph code.
- Space–time code.
- Space–time trellis code.
- Tornado codes are optimal fountain codes
- Triple modular redundancy
- Turbo code.

- Viterbi algorithm
- Walsh code used in cellular telephony for its high noise immunity, not just its ECC capabilities.

Practical uses of Error Correction Methods

- Concatenated error correction codes, the Compact Disc and Voyager Program spacecraft use concatenated error correction technologies.
- Check digit, commonly used on UPC barcodes.
- Luhn algorithm, the most commonly used base 10 checksum that can perform limited error detection but not error correction.
- Luhn mod N algorithm, the above algorithm but implementable in a non base 10 form.
- Verhoeff algorithm, a modular based form not related to the Luhn algorithms that can detect most forms of transposition errors in financial cryptographic applications

Undeletion

Undeletion is a feature for restoring computer files which have been removed from a file system by file deletion. Deleted data can be recovered on many file systems, but not all file systems provide an undeletion feature. Recovering data without an undeletion facility is usually called data recovery, rather than undeletion. Although undeletion can help prevent users from accidentally losing data, it can also pose a computer security risk, since users may not be aware that deleted files remain accessible.

Support

Not all file systems or operating systems support undeletion. Undeletion is supported by DOS, but is not supported by most modern UNIX file systems, though AdvFS is a notable exception. The ext2 file system has an addon program called e2unde which allows file undeletion. The similar ext3 file system does not officially support undeletion, but ext3grep was written to automate the undeletion of ext3 volumes Undelete was proposed in ext4, but was yet to be implemented However, trash bin feature was posted as a patch back in 2006-12-04 The Trash bin feature use.

Graphical user environments often take a different approach to undeletion by introducing a "holding area" for files to be deleted. Undesired files are moved to this holding area, and all of the files in the holding area are periodically deleted. This approach is used by the *Trash can* in Macintosh operating systems and by the recycle bin in Microsoft Windows. This is a natural continuation of the approach taken by earlier systems, such as the limbo group used by CP/M This approach is not subject to the risk that other files being written to the filesystem will disrupt a deleted file very quickly; permanent deletion will happen on a predictable schedule or with manual intervention only.

Another approach is offered by programs such as *Norton GoBack* (formerly *Roxio GoBack*): a portion of the hard disk space is set aside for file modification operations to be recorded in such a way that they may later be undone. This process is usually much safer in aiding recovery of deleted files than the undeletion operation as described below.

Limitations

Undeletion is not fail-safe. In general, the sooner undeletion is attempted, the more likely it will be successful. Fragmentation of the deleted file may also reduce the probability of recovery, depending on the type of file system. A fragmented file is scattered across different parts of the disk, instead of being in a contiguous area.

Mechanics

The workings of undeletion depend on the file system on which the deleted file was stored. Some file systems, such as HFS, can not provide an undeletion feature because no information about the deleted file is retained (except by additional software, which is not usually present). Some file systems, however, do not erase all traces of a deleted file, including the *FAT* file system:

FAT File System

When a file is deleted on a FAT file system, its directory entry remains stored on the disk, slightly renamed in a way that marks the entry in FAT table as available for use by newly created files thereafter. Most of its name, and its time stamp, file length and—most importantly—location on the disk, remain unchanged in the directory entry. The list of disk clusters occupied by the file will be erased from the File Allocation Table, however, marking those sectors available for use by other files created or modified thereafter.

When undeletion operation is attempted, the following conditions must be met for a successful recovery of the file:

- The entry of the deleted file must still exist in the directory, meaning that it must not yet be overwritten by a new file (or folder) that has been created in the same directory. Whether this is the case can fairly easily be detected by checking whether the remaining name of the file to be undeleted is still present in the directory.
- The sectors formerly used by the deleted file must not be overwritten yet by other files. This can fairly well be verified by checking that the sectors are not marked as used in the *File Allocation Table*. However, if, in the meantime, a new file had been written to, using those sectors, and then deleted again, freeing those sectors again, this cannot be detected automatically by the undeletion program. In this case an undeletion operation, even if appearing successful, might fail because the recovered file contains different data.
- The file must not have been fragmented, meaning that the sectors its data occupied on the disk must have all

been in one uninterrupted sequence. Whether this was the case may or may not be detectable by the undeletion program, depending on the arrangement of other files on the disk.

Chances of recovering deleted files is higher in FAT16 as compared to FAT32 drives; fragmentation of files is usually less in FAT16 due to large cluster size support (1024 Bytes, 2KB, 4KB, 8KB, 16KB, 32KB and 64KB which is supported only in Windows NT) as compared to FAT32 (4KB, 8KB, 16KB only).

If the undeletion program can not detect clear signs of the above requirements not being met, it will restore the directory entry as being in use and mark all consecutive sectors (clusters), beginning with the one as recorded in the old directory entry, as used in the *File Allocation Table*. It is then up to the user to open the recovered file and to verify that it contains the complete data of the formerly deleted file.

If the data of the recovered file is not correct, parts of the file may still be stored in other sectors of the disk. Recovery of those is not possible by automatic processes but only by manual examination of each (unused) block of the disk. This usually must be done by specialists that have very good knowledge of both the disk structure and the data being sought.

Norton UNERASE was an important component in Norton Utilities version 1.0 in 1981. Microsoft included a similar UNDELETE program in the final version of MS-DOS, but applied the Recycle Bin approach instead in later operating systems using FAT.

Prevention

There are several ways to prevent file undeletion. In UNIX environments with the GNU Core Utilities, the shred command will delete a file and then repeatedly overwrite the sectors to make recovery difficult for even very expensive hardware probing techniques. In Windows, defragmenting (on FAT file systems, at least) after deletion may overwrite the original position of the file, making recovery more difficult, but is not recommended for secure data deletion. "SDelete", "Eraser" add to the difficulty by overwriting files many times before deletion.

Data Erasure

Data erasure is a method of software-based overwriting that completely destroys all electronic data residing on a hard drive or other digital media. Permanent data erasure goes beyond basic file deletion commands, which only remove direct pointers to data disk sectors and make data recovery possible with common software tools. Unlike degaussing and physical destruction, which render the disk unusable, data erasure removes all information while leaving the disk operable, preserving assets and the environment.

Software-based overwriting uses a software application to write patterns of meaningless data onto each of a hard drive's sectors. There are key differentiators between data erasure and other overwriting methods, which can leave data intact and raise the risk of data breach or spill, identity theft and failure to achieve regulatory compliance. Data erasure also provides multiple overwrites so that it supports recognized government and industry standards. It provides verification of data removal, which is necessary for meeting certain standards.

To protect data on lost or stolen media, some data erasure applications remotely destroy data if the password is incorrectly entered. Data erasure tools can also target specific data on a disk for routine erasure, providing a hacking protection method that is a less time-consuming than encryption.

Importance

Information technology (IT) assets commonly hold large volumes of confidential data. Social security numbers, credit card numbers, bank details, medical history and classified information are often stored on computer hard drives or servers and can inadvertently or intentionally make their way onto other media such as printer, USB, flash, Zip, Jaz, and REV drives.

Data Breach

Increased storage of sensitive data, combined with rapid technological change and the shorter lifespan of IT assets, has driven the need for permanent data erasure of electronic devices as they are retired or refurbished. Also, compromised networks and laptop theft and loss, as well as that of other portable media, are increasingly common sources of data breaches.

If data erasure does not occur when a disk is retired or lost, an organization or user faces that possibility that data will be stolen and compromised, leading to identity theft, loss of corporate reputation, threats to regulatory compliance and financial impacts. Companies have spent nearly $5 million on average to recover when corporate data was lost or stolen. High profile incidents of data theft include:

- *Oklahoma Corporation Commission* (*2008-05-21*): Server sold at auction compromises more than 5,000 Social Security numbers.
- *University of Florida College of Medicine, Jacksonville* (*2008-05-20*): Photographs and identifying information of 1,900 on improperly disposed computer.
- *Compass Bank* (*2008-03-21*): Stolen hard drive hard drive contains 1,000,000 customer records.
- *Lifeblood* (*2008-02-13*): Missing laptops contain personal information including dates of birth and some Social Security numbers of 321,000.

- *Hannaford* (*2008-03-17*): Breach exposes 4.2 million credit, debit cards.
- *CardSystems Solutions* (*2005-06-19*): Credit card breach exposes 40 million accounts.

Regulatory Compliance

Strict industry standards and government regulations are in place that force organizations to mitigate the risk of unauthorized exposure of confidential corporate and government data. These regulations include HIPAA (Health Insurance Portability and Accountability Act); FACTA (The Fair and Accurate Credit Transactions Act of 2003); GLB (Gramm-Leach Bliley); Sarbanes-Oxley Act (SOx); and Payment Card Industry Data Security Standards (PCI DSS). Failure to comply can result in fines and damage to company reputation, as well as civil and criminal liability.

Preserving Assets and the Environment

Data erasure offers an alternative to physical destruction and degaussing for secure removal of all disk data. Physical destruction and degaussing destroy the digital media, requiring its disposal and contributing to electronic waste while negatively impacting the carbon footprint of individuals and companies. Data erasure allows secure disposal of obsolete equipment and preserves the potential to refurbish a computer for future use, protecting viable IT assets.

Differentiators

Software-based data erasure uses a special application to write a combination of 1's and 0's onto each hard drive sector. The level of security depends on the number of times the entire hard drive is written over.

Full Disk Overwriting

There are many overwriting programs, but data erasure offers complete security by destroying data on all areas of a hard drive. Disk overwriting programs that cannot access the entire hard drive, including hidden/locked areas like the host protected area (HPA), device configuration overlay (DCO), and remapped sectors, perform an incomplete erasure, leaving some of the data intact. By accessing the entire hard drive, data erasure eliminates the risk of data remanence.

Data erasure also bypasses the BIOS and OS. Overwriting programs that operate through the BIOS and OS will not always perfo and may report back a complete and successful erasure even if they do not access the entire hard disk, leaving data accessible.

Hardware Support

Data erasure can be deployed over a network to target multiple PCs rather than having to erase each one sequentially. In cont s directly with sector sizes such as 520, 524, and 528, removing the need to first reformat back to 512 sector size.

Standards

Many government and industry standards exist for software-based overriting that removes data. A key factor in meeting these standards is the number of times the data is overwritten. Also, some standards require a method to verify that all data has been removed from the entire hard drive and to view the overwrite pattern. Complete data erasure should account for hidden areas, typically DCO, HPA and remapped sectors.

The 1995 edition of the National Industrial Security Program Operating Manual (DoD 5220.22-M) permitted the use of overwriting techniques to sanitize some types of media by writing all addressable locations with a character, its complement, and then a random character. This provision was removed in a 2001 change to the manual and was never permitted for Top Secret media, but it is still listed as a technique by many offerors of data erasure software.

Data erasure software should provide the user with a validation certificate indicating that the overwriting procedure was completed properly. Data erasure software should also comply with requirements to erase hidden areas, provide a defects log list, and list bad sectors that could not be overwritten.

Number of Overwrites Needed

Data on floppy disks can sometimes be recovered by forensic analysis even after the disks have been overwritten once with zeros (or random zeros and ones). This is not the case with modern hard drives. The bits on modern drives are so small that deviation of tracks between writes cannot be discerned by any means.

According to the 2006 NIST Special Publication 800-88 (p. 7): "Studies have shown that most of today's media can be effectively cleared by one overwrite" and "for ATA disk drives manufactured after 2001 (over 15 GB) the terms clearing and purging have converged.

According to the Centre for Magnetic Recording Research, "Secure erase does a single on-track erasure of the data on the disk drive. The U.S. National Security Agency published an Information Assurance Approval of single pass overwrite, after technical testing at CMRR showed that multiple on-track overwrite passes gave no additional erasure." "Secure erase" is a utility built into modern ATA hard drives that overwrites all data on a disk, including remapped (error) sectors.

Further analysis by Wright et al. seems to also indicate that one overwrite is all that is generally required

Sanitization (Classified Information)

Sanitization (also 'redaction') is the process of removing sensitive information from a document or other medium, so that it may be distributed to a broader audience. When dealing with classified information, sanitization attempts to reduce the document's classification level, possibly yielding an unclassified document. Originally, the term sanitization was applied to printed documents; it has since been extended to apply to computer media and the problem of data remanence as well.

Redaction generally refers to the editing or blacking out of text in a document, or to the result of such an effort. It is intended to allow the selective disclosure of information in a document while keeping other parts of the document secret. Typically the result is a document that is suitable for publication, or for dissemination to others than the intended audience of the original document. For example, when a document is subpoenaed in a court case, information not specifically relevant to the case at hand is often redacted.

Government Secrecy

In the context of government documents, redaction (also called sanitization) generally refers more specifically to the process of removing sensitive or classified information from a document prior to its publication, during declassification.

Secure Document Redaction Techniques

The traditional technique of redacting confidential material from a paper document before its public release involves crossing out portions of text with a wide black pen, followed by photocopying the result. This is a relatively easy to understand process and has only minor risks associated with it. For example, if the black pen is not wide enough, careful examination of the resulting photocopy may still reveal partial information about the text, such as the difference between short and tall letters. The exact length of the removed text also remains recognizable, which may help to guess plausible wordings for shorter redacted sections. Where computer-generated proportional fonts were used, even more information can leak out of the redacted section in the form of the exact position of nearby visible characters.

The National Archives (UK) published a document, Redaction Toolkit, Guidelines for the Editing of Exempt Information from Documents Prior to Release (2004), "to provide guidance on the editing of exempt material from information held by public bodies."

Secure redacting is a far more complicated problem with word processing file formats. These may also save a revision history of the edited text that still contains the redacted text. In some file formats, unused portions of memory are saved that may still contain fragments of previous versions of the text. Where text is redacted by overlaying graphical elements (usually black rectangles) on top of text, the original text remains in the file and can be uncovered by simply deleting the overlaying graphics. Effective redaction of electronic documents requires the actual removal of the text or image data from the document file. This either requires a very detailed understanding of the internal operation of the document processing software and file formats used, which most computer users lack, or software tools designed for sanitizing electronic documents.

Redaction usually requires a marking of the redacted area with the reason why the content is being restricted. Government documents being released under the Freedom Act are marked with exemption codes that denote the reason why the content has been sanitized.

The National Security Agency published a document, Redacting with Confidence: How to Safely Publish Sanitized Reports Converted from Word to PDF, which provides instructions for redacting Microsoft Word generated PDF files.

Printed Matter

A printed document which contains classified or sensitive information will frequently contain a great deal of information which is less sensitive. There may be a need to release the less sensitive portions to uncleared personnel. The printed document will thus be sanitized to obscure or remove the sensitive information. The term redaction is also used to describe this process, though that term is more often used in literary contexts.

In some cases, sanitizing a classified document removes enough information to reduce the classification from a higher level to a lower one. For example, raw intelligence reports may contain highly classified information, like the identities of spies, that is removed before the reports are distributed outside the intelligence agency: the initial report may be classified as Top Secret while the sanitized report may be classified as Secret.

In other cases, like the U.S. National Security Agency's report on the USS Liberty incident (right), the report may be sanitized to remove all sensitive data, so that the report may be released to the general public.

As is seen in the USS Liberty report, paper documents are generally sanitized by covering the classified and sensitive portions and then photocopying the document, resulting in a sanitized document suitable for distribution.

Computer Media and Files

Computer (electronic or digital) documents are more difficult to sanitize. In many cases, when information in an information system is modified or erased, some or all of the data remains in storage. This may be an accident of design, where the underlying storage mechanism (disk, RAM, etc.) still allows information to be read, despite its nominal erasure. The general term for this problem is data remanence. In some contexts (notably the US NSA, DoD, and related organizations), sanitization typically refers to countering the data remanence problem; redaction is used.

However, the retention may be a deliberate feature, in the form of an undo buffer, revision history, "trash can", backups, or the like. For example, word processing programs like Microsoft Word will sometimes be used to edit out the sensitive information. Unfortunately, these products do not always show the user all of the information stored in a file, so it is possible that a file may still contain sensitive information. In other cases, inexperienced users will use ineffective methods which fail to sanitize the document.

In May, 2005, the US military published a report on the death of Nicola Calipari, an Italian secret agent, at a US military checkpoint in Iraq. The report was published in Adobe PDF format and had apparently been sanitized using commercial word processing tools. Shortly thereafter, readers discovered that the blocked-out portions could be retrieved using simple cut and paste operations on the posted document.

Similarly, on May 24, 2006, lawyers for the communications service provider AT&T filed a legal brief regarding their cooperation with domestic wiretapping by the NSA. Text on pages 12 through 14 of the Adobe PDF document were blacked out in an attempt to sanitize the document, but the hidden text could be retrieved using cut and paste.

At the end of 2005, the NSA released a report giving recommendations on how to safely sanitize a Word document.

Issues such as these make it difficult to reliably implement multilevel security systems, in which computer users of differing security clearances may share documents. The Challenge of Multilevel Security gives an example of a sanitization failure caused by unexpected behavior in Microsoft Word's change tracking feature.

Censorship

Censorship is the suppression of speech or deletion of communicative material which may be considered objectionable, harmful, sensitive, or inconvenient to the government or media organisations as determined by a censor.

Rationale

The rationale for censorship is different for various types of information censored:

- Moral censorship, is the removal of materials that are obscene or otherwise morally questionable. Pornography, for example, is often censored under this rationale, especially child pornography, which is censored in most jurisdictions in the world.
- Military censorship is the process of keeping military intelligence and tactics confidential and away from the enemy. This is used to counter espionage, which is the process of gleaning military information. Very often, militaries will also attempt to suppress politically inconvenient information even if that information has no actual intelligence value.
- Political censorship occurs when governments hold back information from their citizens. The logic is to exert control over the populace and prevent free expression that might foment rebellion.
- Religious censorship is the means by which any material objectionable to a certain faith is removed. This often involves a dominant religion forcing limitations on less prevalent ones. Alternatively, one religion may shun the works of another when they believe the content is not appropriate for their faith.
- Corporate censorship is the process by which editors in corporate media outlets intervene to halt the publishing of information that portrays their business or business partners in a negative light.

Political Censorship

Strict censorship existed in the Eastern Bloc Throughout the bloc, the various ministries of culture held a tight reign on their writer arly years. In the Stalinist period, even the weather forecasts were changed if they had the temerity to sugest that the sun might not shine on May Day. Under Nicolae Ceausescu in Romania, weather reports were doctored so that the temperatures were not seen to rise above or fall below the levels which dictated that work must stop.

Independent journalism did not exist in the Soviet Union until Mikhail Gorbachev became its leader; all reporting was directed by the Communist Party or related organizations. Pravda, the predominant newspaper in the Soviet Union, had a monopoly. Foreign newspapers were available only if they were published by Communist Parties sympathetic to the Soviet Union.

Possession and use of copying machines was tightly controlled in order to hinder production and distribution of samizdat, illegal self-published books and magazines. Possession of even a single samizdat manuscript such as a book by Andrei Sinyavsky was a serious crime which might involve a visit from the KGB. Another outlet for works which did not find favor with the authorities was publishing abroad.

The People's Republic of China, which continues Communist rule in politics, if not in the controlled economy, employs some 30,000 'Internet police' to monitor the internet and popular search engines such as Google and Yahoo.

Iraq under Arab socialist Saddam Hussein had much the same techniques of press censorship as did Romania under Nicolae Ceausescu but with greater potential violence.

Cuban media is operated under the supervision of the Communist Party's Department of Revolutionary Orientation, which "develops and coordinates propaganda strategies". Connecting to Internet is illegal. Computer ownership is banned.

Censorship of State Secrets and Prevention of Attention

In wartime, explicit censorship is carried out with the intent of preventing the release of information that might be useful to an enemy. Typically it involves keeping times or locations secret, or delaying the release of information (e.g., an operational objective) until it is of no possible use to enemy forces. The moral issues here are often seen as somewhat different, as release of tactical information usually presents a greater risk of casualties among one's own forces and could possibly lead to loss of the overall conflict. During World War I letters written by British soldiers would have to go through censorship. This consisted of officers going through letters with a black marker and crossing out anything which might compromise operational secrecy before the letter was sent. The World War II catchphrase "Loose lips sink ships" was used as a common justification to exercise official wartime censorship and encourage individual restraint when sharing potentially sensitive information.

An example of "sanitization" policies comes from the USSR under Joseph Stalin, where publicly used photographs were often altered to remove people whom Stalin had condemned to execution. Though past photographs may have been remembered or kept, this deliberate and systematic alteration to all of history in the public mind is seen as one of the central themes of Stalinism and totalitarianism.

Censorship of Educational Sources

The content of school textbooks is often the issue of debate, since their target audience is young people, and the term "whitewashing" is the one commonly used to refer to selective removal of critical or damaging evidence or comment. The reporting of military atrocities in history is extremely controversial, as in the case of the Bombing of Dresden, the Nanking Massacre, the Armenian Genocide, The Holocaust (or Holocaust denial), and the Winter Soldier Investigation of the Vietnam War.

In the context of secondary-school education, the way facts and history are presented greatly influences the interpretation of contemporary thought, opinion and socialization. One argument for censoring the type of information disseminated is based on the inappropriate quality of such material for the young. The use of the "inappropriate" distinction is in itself controversial, as it changed heavily. A Ballantine Books version of the book Fahrenheit 451 which is the version used by most school classes contained approximately 75 separate edits, omissions, and changes from the original Bradbury manuscript.

Censorship in Music and Popular Culture

After Fidel Castro established his communist dictatorship, Che Guevara suggested ban on jazz and rock&roll, which he saw as "imperialist music".

The original cover of nude Yoko Ono and John Lennon's Unfinished Music No. 1: Two Virgins provoked an outrage, prompting distributors to sell the album in a plain brown wrapper.

Music censorship has been implemented by states, religions, educational systems, families, retailers and lobbying groups – and in most cases they violate international conventions of human rights.

Aside from the usual justifications of pornography, language and violence, some movies are censored due to changing racial attitudes or political correctness in order to avoid ethnic stereotyping and/or ethnic offense despite its historical or artistic value. One example is the still withdrawn "Censored Eleven" series of animated cartoons, which may be innocent then but "incorrect" now.

Copy, Picture, and Writer Approval

Copy approval is the right to read and amend an article, usually an interview, before publication. Many publications refuse to give copy approval but it is increasingly becoming common practice when dealing with publicity anxious celebrities. Picture approval is the right given to an individual to choose which photos will be published and which will not. Robert Redford is well known for insisting upon picture approval. Writer approval is when writers are chosen based on whether they will write flattering articles or not. Hollywood publicist Pat Kingsley is known for banning certain writers who wrote undesirably about one of her clients from interviewing any of her other clients.

Censorship of Maps

Censorship of maps was also used in former East Germany, especially for the areas near the border to West Germany in order to make attempts of defection more difficult. Censorship of maps is also applied by Google maps, where certain areas are greyed out or areas are purposely left out-dated with old imagery.

Meta Censorship

In this form of censorship, any information about existence of censorship and the legal basis of the censorship is censored. Rules of censoring were classified. Removed texts or phrases were not marked.

Creative Censorship

In this form of censorship, censors rewrite texts, giving these texts secret co-authors.

Censorship Implementation

The former Soviet Union maintained a particularly extensive program of state-imposed censorship. The main organ for official censorship in the Soviet Union was the *Chief Agency for Protection of Military and State Secrets* generally known as the *Glavlit*, its Russian acronym. The *Glavlit* handled censorship matters arising from domestic writings of just about any kind — even beer and vodka labels. *Glavlit* censorship personnel were present in every large Soviet publishing house or newspaper; the agency employed some 70,000 censors to review information before it was disseminated by publishing houses, editorial offices, and broadcasting studios. No mass medium escaped *Glavlit*'s control. All press agencies and radio and television stations had *Glavlit* representatives on their editorial staffs.

Sometimes, a specific and unique information whose very existence is barely known to the public, is kept in a subtle, near-censorship situation, being regarded as "subversive" or "inconvenient". Michel Foucault's 1978 text "Sexual Morality and the Law" (later republished as "The Danger of Child Sexuality"), for instance - originally published as *La loi de la pudeur,* literally, "the law of decency", defends the decriminalization of statutory rape and the abolition of age of consent laws.

4

Cryptanalysis

Cryptanalysis (from the Greek *kryptós*, "hidden", and *analýein*, "to loosen" or "to untie") is the study of methods for obtaining the meaning of encrypted information, without access to the secret information which is normally required to do so. Typically, this involves finding a secret key. In non-technical language, this is the practice of codebreaking or cracking the code, although these phrases also have a specialised technical meaning.

"Cryptanalysis" is also used to refer to any attempt to circumvent the security of other types of cryptographic algorithms and protocols in general, and not just encryption. However, cryptanalysis usually excludes methods of attack that do not primarily target weaknesses in the actual cryptography, such as bribery, physical coercion, burglary, keystroke logging, and social engineering, although these types of attack are an important concern and are often more effective than traditional cryptanalysis.

Even though the goal has been the same, the methods and techniques of cryptanalysis have changed drastically through the history of cryptography, adapting to increasing cryptographic complexity, ranging from the pen-and-paper methods of the past, through machines like Enigma in World War II, to the computer-based schemes of the present. The results of cryptanalysis have also changed — it is no longer possible to have unlimited success in codebreaking, and there is a hierarchical classification of what constitutes a rare practical attack. In the mid-1970s, a new class of cryptography was introduced: asymmetric cryptography. Methods for breaking these cryptosystems are typically radically different from before, and usually involve solving carefully-constructed problems in pure mathematics, the best-known being integer factorization.

History of Cryptanalysis

Cryptanalysis has coevolved together with cryptography, and the contest can be traced through the history of cryptography—new ciphers being designed to replace old broken designs, and new cryptanalytic techniques invented to crack the improved schemes . In practice, they are viewed as two sides of the same coin: in order to create secure cryptography, you have to design against possible cryptanalysis.

Classical Cryptanalysis

Although the actual word *"cryptanalysis"* is relatively recent (it was coined by William Friedman in 1920), methods for breaking codes and ciphers are much older. The first known recorded explanation of cryptanalysis was given by 9th-century Arabian polymath, Al-Kindi (also known as "Alkindus" in Europe), in *A Manuscript on Deciphering Cryptographic Messages*. This treatise includes a description of the method of frequency analysis (Ibrahim Al-Kadi, 1992- ref-3). Italian scholar Giambattista della Porta was author of a seminal work on cryptanalysis *"De Furtivis Literarum Notis"*.

Frequency analysis is the basic tool for breaking most classical ciphers. In natural languages, certain letters of the alphabet appear more frequently than others; in English, "E" is likely to be the most common letter in any sample of plaintext. Similarly, the digraph "TH" is the most likely pair of letters in English, and so on. Frequency analysis relies on a cipher failing to hide these statistics. For example, in a simple substitution cipher (where each letter is simply replaced with another), the most frequent letter in the ciphertext would be a likely candidate for "E".

In practice, frequency analysis relies as much on linguistic knowledge as it does on statistics, but as ciphers became more complex, mathematics became more important in cryptanalysis. This change was particularly evident during World War II, where efforts to crack Axis ciphers required new levels of mathematical sophistication. Moreover, automation was first applied to cryptanalysis in that era with the Polish Bomba device, use of punched card equipment, and in the Colossus — one of the earliest computers (arguably the first programmable electronic digital computer).

Modern Cryptanalysis

Even though computation was used to great effect in cryptanalysis in World War II, it also made possible new methods of cryptography orders of magnitude more complex than ever before. Taken as a whole, modern cryptography has become much more impervious to cryptanalysis than the pen-and-paper systems of the past, and now seems to have the upper hand against pure cryptanalysis. The historian David Kahn notes, "Many are the cryptosystems offered by the hundreds of commercial vendors today that cannot be broken by any known methods of cryptanalysis. Indeed, in such systems even a chosen plaintext attack, in which a selected plaintext is matched against its ciphertext, cannot yield the key that unlock other messages. In a sense, then, cryptanalysis is dead. But that is not the end of the story. Cryptanalysis may be dead, but there is - to mix my metaphors - more than one way to skin a cat." Kahn goes on to mention increased opportunities for interception, bugging, side channel attacks and quantum computers as replacements for the traditional means of cryptanalysis.

Kahn may have been premature in his cryptanalysis postmortem; weak ciphers are not yet extinct, and cryptanalytic methods employed by intelligence agencies remain unpublished. In academia, new designs are regularly presented, and are also frequently broken: the 1984 block cipher Madryga was found to be susceptible to ciphertext-only attacks in 1998; FEAL-4, proposed as a replacement for the DES standard encryption algorithm, was demolished by a spate of attacks from the academic community, many of which are entirely practical. In industry, too, ciphers are not free from flaws: for example, the A5/1, A5/2 and CMEA algorithms, used in mobile phone technology, can all be broken in hours, minutes or even in real-time using widely-available computing equipment. In 2001, Wired Equivalent Privacy (WEP), a protocol used to secure Wi-Fi wireless networks, was shown to be susceptible to a practical related-key attack.

The Results of Cryptanalysis

Successful cryptanalysis has undoubtedly influenced history; the ability to read the presumed-secret thoughts and plans of others can be a decisive advantage, and never more so than during wartime. For example, in World War I, the breaking of the Zimmermann Telegram was instrumental in bringing the United States into the war. In World War II, the cryptanalysis of the German ciphers — including the Enigma machine and the Lorenz cipher — has been credited with everything between shortening the end of the European war by a few months to determining the eventual result. The United States also benefited from the cryptanalysis of the Japanese PURPLE code.

Governments have long recognised the potential benefits of cryptanalysis for intelligence, both military and diplomatic, and established dedicated organisations devoted to breaking the codes and ciphers of other nations, for example, GCHQ and the NSA, organisations which are still very active today. In 2004, it was reported that the United States had broken Iranian ciphers. (It is unknown, however, whether this was pure cryptanalysis, or whether other factors were involved.

Types of Cryptanalytic Attack

Cryptanalytic attacks vary in potency and how much of a threat they pose to real-world cryptosystems. A *certificational weakness* is a theoretical attack that is unlikely to be applicable in any real-world situation; the majority of results found in modern cryptanalytic research are of this type. Essentially, the practical importance of an attack is dependent on the answers to the following three questions:

- What knowledge and capabilities are needed as a prerequisite?
- How much additional secret information is deduced?
- How much effort is required? (What is the computational complexity?

Prior Knowledge: Scenarios for Cryptanalysis

Cryptanalysis can be performed under a number of assumptions about how much can be observed or found out about the system under attack. As a basic starting point it is normally assumed that, for the purposes of analysis, the general algorithm is known; this is Kerckhoffs' principle of "the enemy knows the system". This is a reasonable assumption in practice — throughout history, there are countless examples of secret algorithms falling into wider knowledge, variously through espionage, betrayal and reverse engineering. (On occasion, ciphers have been reconstructed through pure deduction; for example, the German Lorenz cipher and the Japanese Purple code, and a variety of classical schemes).

Other assumptions include:

- *Ciphertext-only*: the cryptanalyst has access only to a collection of ciphertexts or codetexts.
- *Known-plaintext*: the attacker has a set of ciphertexts to which he knows the corresponding plaintext.
- *Chosen-plaintext (chosen-ciphertext)*: the attacker can obtain the ciphertexts (plaintexts) corresponding to an arbitrary set of plaintexts (ciphertexts) of his own choosing.
- *Adaptive chosen-plaintext*: like a chosen-plaintext attack, except the attacker can choose subsequent plaintexts based on information learned from previous encryptions. Similarly adaptive chosen ciphertext attack.
- *Related-key attack*: Like a chosen-plaintext attack, except the attacker can obtain ciphertexts encrypted under two different keys. The keys are unknown, but the relationship between them is known; for example, two keys that differ in the one bit.

These types of attack clearly differ in how plausible they would be to mount in practice. Although some are more likely than others, cryptographers will often take a conservative approach to security and assume the worst-case when designing algorithms, reasoning that if a scheme is secure even against unrealistic threats, then it should also resist real-world cryptanalysis as well.

The assumptions are often more realistic than they might seem upon first glance. For a known-plaintext attack, the cryptanalyst might well know or be able to guess at a likely part of the plaintext, such as an encrypted letter beginning with "Dear Sir", or a computer session starting with "LOGIN:". A chosen-plaintext attack is less likely, but it is sometimes plausible: for example, you could convince someone to forward a message you have given them, but in encrypted form. Related-key attacks are mostly theoretical, although they can be realistic in certain situations, for example, when constructing cryptographic hash functions using a block cipher.

Classifying Success in Cryptanalysis

The results of cryptanalysis can also vary in usefulness. For example, cryptographer Lars Knudsen classified various types of attack on block ciphers according to the amount and quality of secret information that was discovered:

- *Total break* — the attacker deduces the secret key.
- *Global deduction* — the attacker discovers a functionally equivalent algorithm for encryption and decryption, but without learning the key.
- *Instance (local) deduction* — the attacker discovers additional plaintexts (or ciphertexts) not previously known.
- *Information deduction* — the attacker gains some Shannon information about plaintexts (or ciphertexts) not previously known.
- *Distinguishing algorithm* — the attacker can distinguish the cipher from a random permutation.

Similar considerations apply to attacks on other types of cryptographic algorithm.

Complexity

Attacks can also be characterised by the amount of resources they require. This can be in the form of:

- Time — the number of "primitive operations" which must be performed. This is quite loose; primitive operations could be basic computer instructions, such as addition, XOR, shift, and so forth, or entire encryption methods.
- Memory — the amount of storage required to perform the attack.

- Data — the *quantity* of plaintexts and ciphertexts required.

In academic cryptography, a weakness or a break in a scheme is usually defined quite conservatively. Bruce Schneier sums up this approach: "Breaking a cipher simply means finding a weakness in the cipher that can be exploited with a complexity less than brute force. Never mind that brute-force might require 2128 encryptions; an attack requiring 2110 encryptions would be considered a break. . . simply put, a break can just be a certificational weakness: evidence that the cipher does not perform as advertised." (Schneier, 2000).

Cryptanalysis of Asymmetric Cryptography

Asymmetric cryptography (or public key cryptography) is cryptography that relies on using two keys; one private, and one public. Such ciphers invariably rely on "hard" mathematical problems as the basis of their security, so an obvious point of attack is to develop methods for solving the problem. The security of two-key cryptography depends on mathematical questions in a way that single-key cryptography generally does not, and conversely links cryptanalysis to wider mathematical research in a new way.

Asymmetric schemes are designed around the (conjectured) difficulty of solving various mathematical problems. If an improved algorithm can be found to solve the problem, then the system is weakened. For example, the security of the Diffie-Hellman key exchange scheme depends on the difficulty of calculating the discrete logarithm. In 1983, Don Coppersmith found a faster way to find discrete logarithms (in certain groups), and thereby requiring cryptographers to use larger groups (or different types of groups). RSA's security depends (in part) upon the difficulty of integer factorization — a breakthrough in factoring would impact the security of RSA.

In 1980, one could factor a difficult 50-digit number at an expense of 1012 elementary computer operations. By 1984 the state of the art in factoring algorithms had advanced to a point where a 75-digit number could be factored in 1012 operations. Advances in computing technology also meant that the operations could be performed much faster, too. Moore's law predicts that computer speeds will continue to increase. Factoring techniques may continue do so as well, but will most likely depend on mathematical insight and creativity, neither of which has ever been successfully predictable. 150-digit numbers of the kind once used in RSA have been factored. The effort was greater than above, but was not unreasonable on fast modern computers. By the start of the 21st century, 150-digit numbers were no longer considered a large enough key size for RSA. Numbers with several hundred digits are still considered too hard to factor in 2005, though methods will probably continue to improve over time, requiring key size to keep pace or new algorithms to be used.

Another distinguishing feature of asymmetric schemes is that, unlike attacks on symmetric cryptosystems, any cryptanalysis has the opportunity to make use of knowledge gained from the public key.

Quantum Computing Applications for Cryptanalysis

Quantum computers, which are still in the early phases of development, have potential use in cryptanalysis. For example, Shor's Algorithm could factor large numbers in polynomial time, in effect breaking some commonly used forms of public-key encryption.

By using Grover's algorithm on a quantum computer, brute-force key search can be made quadratically faster. However, this could be countered by increasing the key length.

Methods of Cryptanalysis

Classical Cryptanalysis

- Frequency analysis
- Index of coincidence
- Kasiski examination

Symmetric Algorithms

- Boomerang attack
- Brute force attack
- Davies' attack
- Differential cryptanalysis
- Impossible differential cryptanalysis
- Integral cryptanalysis
- Linear cryptanalysis
- Meet-in-the-middle attack
- Mod-n cryptanalysis
- Related-key attack
- Slide attack
- XSL attack

Hash Functions

- Birthday attack

Attack Models

- Chosen-ciphertext attack
- Chosen-plaintext attack
- Ciphertext-only attack
- Known-plaintext attack

Side channel attacks:

- Power analysis
- Timing attack

Network Attacks

- Man-in-the-middle attack
- Replay attack

External Attacks

- Black bag cryptanalysis
- Rubber-hose cryptanalysis

CRYPTANALYSIS OF THE ENIGMA

Cryptanalysis of the Enigma enabled the Allies in World War II to read substantial amounts of secret Morse-coded radio communications of the Axis powers enciphered using Enigma machines. This Allied reading yielded military intelligence which, along with that from other decrypted German radio transmissions, was given the name *Ultra*.

Enigma cryptanalysis contributed greatly to the success of Allied war efforts—in the Battle of Matapan in March 1941; in reversing the early disastrous course of the Battle of the Atlantic, beginning in the latter part of 1941; in frustrating Rommel's efforts to capture Cairo in 1942; in the invasion of Sicily (1943) and mainland Italy (1943-44); in the planning and execution of Operation Overlord (the Allied invasion of France, 1944); and in the subsequent drive to and through Germany Evidence suggests that Soviet strategy and tactics against Nazi Germany likewise benefited from Ultra intelligence, conveyed to the Soviets by a variety of conduits.

The Enigma machines were a family of portable cipher machines with rotor-based scramblers. Various German armed and secret services and civilian agencies used Enigma in somewhat different ways, and at various times made changes to their procedures for operating Enigma. The greatest differences in operating procedures were between those of the German Navy *(Reichsmarine* and *Kriegsmarine)* and those of other services and agencies.

The German plugboard-equipped Enigma that would be the Third Reich's principal crypto-system was reconstructed, with the aid of French-supplied intelligence material, by the Polish General Staff's Cipher Bureau in December 1932, on the eve of Adolf Hitler's rise to power in Germany in January 1933. From then until the outbreak of World War II, the Poles held a monopoly of decryption of this Enigma model.

As war drew near, at a Warsaw conference on 25 July 1939 the Polish Cipher Bureau initiated the French and British into its Enigma-breaking techniques and technology, thus greatly broadening the Allied (Polish, French, and particularly British and American) foundations for wartime decryption of German Enigma-enciphered communications.

General Principles

Analysis of a monoalphabetic substitution cipher is relatively easy, so long as a message is long enough to provide a reasonably representative count of the letters of the alphabet. The resultant frequency count can then be compared with the known letter frequencies of the language in which the message is written.

In the 15th and 16th centuries, in Europe, the idea of a polyalphabetic substitution cipher was developed, among others by the French diplomat Blaise de Vigenère (1523-96). For some three centuries, the Vigenère cipher was considered to be completely secure (*le chiffre indéchiffrable*—"the indecipherable cipher"). Nevertheless, Charles Babbage (1791–1871) and later, independently, Friedrich Kasiski (1805–81) succeeded in breaking this cipher.

The cryptographic key for the Vigenère cipher consists of a word or phrase that is repeated many times to cover the length of the message. The key's letters indicate which line of the

Vigenère square is used to encipher each letter of the plaintext so as to produce the ciphertext. It was this repetition that allowed Babbage and Kasiski to achieve their breaks.

During World War I, inventors in several countries realized that a purely random key sequence, containing no repetitive pattern, would make a polyalphabetic substitution, in principle, unbreakable This led to the development, in several countries, of rotor cipher machines such as Arthur Scherbius' Enigma.

Rotor cipher machines alter each character in the plaintext to produce the ciphertext, by means of a scrambler comprising a set of *rotors* (or *wheels*) that alter the electrical path from character to character, between the input device (in Enigma, a keyboard) and the output device (in Enigma, a lampboard). This constant altering of the electrical pathway produces a very long period before the pattern—the key sequence or substitution alphabet—repeats.

Although Kerckhoffs' principle states that a crypto-system should be secure even when everything about the system except the key is known to the enemy, the internal wiring of machines such as Enigma has so many possibilities that an important aspect of breaking them is deducing their logical structure.

The presence of repetition or of guessable elements in either the key or the message are the weaknesses that allow cryptanalysts to seek patterns that can enable them to break a cipher. Finding such weak points in Enigma encipherment, before and during World War II, led to sustained Allied decryption of German Enigma ciphers.

STRENGTHS OF ENIGMA

The Enigma was potentially an excellent system. It was designed to defeat cryptanalytic techniques by continually changing the substitution alphabet through the use of a scrambler comprising three—in some cases, four—rotors.

Like other rotor cipher-machines, Enigma generated a polyalphabetic substitution cipher with a long period. Given three single-notched rotors, the period was 16,900 (= 26 25 26) Such a long period prevented any detectable repetition in the enciphering sequence.

The mechanism of the Enigma consisted of a keyboard connected to an entry plate or wheel (German: *Eintrittswalze*), at the right hand end of the scrambler (usually via a plugboard in the military versions). This contained a set of 26 contacts that made electrical connection with the set of 26 spring-loaded pins on the right hand rotor. The left hand side of each rotor in turn made electrical connection with the rotor to its left, and in the case of the leftmost, with the reflector (German: *Umkehrwalze*). The reflector provided a set of thirteen paired connections to return the current back through the scrambler rotors, and eventually to the lampboard.

There are 403 trillion trillion (26 factorial) ways that the connections within each scrambler rotor—and between the entry plate and the keyboard or plugboard or lampboard—can be arranged. For the reflector plate there are a mere six billion (13 factorial) options to its possible wirings.

Whenever a key on the keyboard was pressed, the stepping motion was actuated, moving the rightmost rotor on one position. Because it advanced with each key pressed it is sometimes called the 'fast' rotor. When the notch on that rotor engaged with a pawl on the middle rotor, that too moved; and similarly with the leftmost ('slow') rotor.

Each scrambler rotor could be set to any one of its 26 starting positions (any letter of the alphabet). For the Enigma machines with only three rotors, their sequence in the scrambler could be selected from the six that are possible.

Later Enigma models added a variable *alphabet ring* like a tyre around the core of each rotor, that specified which letter was opposite the notch that caused the next wheel to advance.

Later still, the three rotors that were in use were selected from a set of five or, in the case of the German Navy, eight rotors.

Most military Enigmas also featured a plugboard (German: *Steckerbrett*) which exchanged letters reciprocally, so that if *A* was plugged to *G* then *A* would become *G* and *G* would become *A* either on input from the keyboard to the scrambler, or on output from the scrambler to the lamp panel. With six plugboard leads, the number of different ways that letters could be re-arranged was some 100 billion.

Key Setting

The machine featured the operational convenience of being symmetrical (or self-inverse). This meant that decipherment worked in the same way as encipherment—when the ciphertext was typed in, the sequence of lamps that lit yielded the plaintext. This of course required that the deciphering machine's plugboard and scrambler rotors be set identically to those of the enciphering machine.

In order to ensure that this would be the case, the complex *ground-key* setting (German: *Grundstellung*) was distributed to all users of a network by means of *setting sheets* in a *codebook* These setting sheets changed the ground key regularly (at first monthly or weekly but soon daily and even, toward war's end in some networks, several times a day). The setting sheets had columns specifying, for each date, the rotors to be used and their positions (German: *Walzenlage*), the ring positions (German: *Ringstellung*) and the plugboard connections (German: *Steckerverbindungen*). The dates were in reverse chronological order down the page. Each row was cut off when it was finished with, so that, in the event of capture, previous keys would not be revealed.

Lastly, for each message, the transmitting operator would send the *message key* (the key specific to that message) so that the receiving operator could align his rotors identically. This was called the *indicator*[14] for that message and was the initial letters that would be visible through the windows on Enigma's top plate. This key setting was itself enciphered on the machine using an *indicator setting*. At first the indicator setting was specified on the setting sheets, but later on it was selected by the operator or, in the case of the German Navy, by a more complicated and secure procedure. Because of the danger that poor radio reception might lead to the message key being garbled, it was, until May 1940, sent twice.

Security Properties

Despite the undoubted strengths of Enigma when used properly, if the settings for one day (or whatever period was represented by each row of the setting sheet) were established, the rest of the messages for that network on that day could be decrypted.

The various Enigma models provided different levels of security. The presence of a plugboard (*Steckerbrett*) substantially increased the security of the encipherment. Each pair of letters that were connected together by a plugboard lead, were referred to as *stecker partners*, and the letters that remained unconnected were said to be *self-steckered*. In general, the unsteckered Enigma was used for commercial and diplomatic traffic and could be broken relatively easily using hand methods, while attacking versions with a plugboard was much more difficult. The British read unsteckered Enigma messages sent during the Spanish Civil War, and also some Italian traffic enciphered early in World War II.

The Enigma machine did, however, have major weaknesses that proved helpful to cryptanalysts. First, a letter could never be encrypted to itself (with the exception of the early models A and B, which lacked a reflector). This property was of great help in using *cribs*—short sections of plaintext thought to be somewhere in the ciphertext—and could be used to eliminate a crib in a particular position. For a possible location, if any letter in the crib matched a letter in the ciphertext at the same position, the location could be ruled out; at Britain's Government Code and Cipher School (GCCS) at Bletchley Park, this was termed a *crash*. It was this feature that the British mathematician and logician Alan Turing would exploit in designing the British bombe.

A second Enigma weakness was that the plugboard connections were reciprocal, so that if A was plugged to N, then N likewise became A. It was this property that inspired mathematician Gordon Welchman at Bletchley Park to propose that a *diagonal board* be introduced into the bombe, substantially reducing the number of rotor settings that the bombe had to try.

A number of the officially-specified procedures for using Enigma also provided avenues for attack. Thus, for machines where there was a choice of more rotors than there were slots for them, a rule stipulated that no rotor should be in the same slot in the scrambler as it had been for the immediately preceding configuration. Also, no wheel order could be repeated on the monthly setting sheet. This meant that when the keys were being found on a regular basis, further economies in excluding possible wheel orders for the bombes to test, could be made.

Similarly, for some networks, the plugboard-setup rules forbade a letter being connected to an adjacent one on the alphabet.

Once detected, these constraints reduced the number of alternatives that needed to be tried.

In any case, the Germans' specified Enigma-operating procedures, and good cryptologic practice, were not adhered to by all Enigma operators.

It has been suggested by some who worked at breaking Enigma at Bletchley Park that the Enigma should have been unbreakable *in practice*, had its operating procedures been better thought out and had its operators been less ill-disciplined.

Postwar debriefings of German cryptographic specialists, conducted as part of project TICOM, tend to support this view—the Germans were well aware that Enigma was theoretically breakable, but felt that the resources required to mount a pure brute-force attack on the system would require too much effort to be worthwhile.

Had they considered the potential consequences of widespread poor operator procedure, and acted to correct the situation, it is likely that breaking Enigma on a regular basis *would* have proven impractical. To war's end, the Germans continued making improvements to the system, though they considered it to be for all practical purposes unbreakable.

Polish Breakthrough

In 1928 the German Army (German: *Heer*), Navy (German: *Reichsmarine* later *Kriegsmarine*) and Airforce (German: *Luftwaffe*) began using a 3-rotor Enigma with a 6-cable plugboard. British, French and American cryptanalysts had no success in cracking this Enigma version In Poland, however, the threat from Germany was much greater, and the Polish Cipher Bureau (*Biuro Szyfrów*) in Warsaw continued work on it. On 1 September 1932, a 27-year-old Polish mathematician, Marian Rejewski, joined the Bureau along with two somewhat younger fellow Poznan University mathematics graduates, Henryk Zygalski and Jerzy Rózycki.

In December that year, the Polish Cipher Bureau received from Captain Gustave Bertrand of French Military Intelligence two German documents and two pages of Enigma daily keys (for September and October 1932) that had been obtained by a French military intelligence agent, a German code-named *Rex*, from an agent who worked at Germany's Cipher Office in Berlin (Hans Thilo-Schmidt, whom the French code-named *Asché*). The documents were entitled *Gebrauchsanweisung für die Chiffriermaschine Enigma* (*Instructions for Using the Enigma Cipher Machine*) and

Schlüsselanleitung für die Chiffriermaschine Enigma (*Keying Instructions for the Enigma Cipher Machine*).

The tables of daily keys, Rejewski would later recall, were "a great help to me, because thanks to [them] the number of unknowns in the equations [that Rejewski had set up] was reduced, and I was able to solve [the] equations, and . . . as I was sitting there writing, the internal connections just came out in the form . . . of letters or numbers, I don't recall [which]—the internal connections ['wiring'] for the first [rotor], the one... on the far right, which always . . . revolved at every depression of a key".

Marian Rejewski told Richard Woytak that it was very important that the months happened to be September and October, in other words, periods that belonged to two different quarters [of the year. This is because . . . the key consisted of several elements [and] one element of the key was changed only once a quarter. Namely, the order of the [rotors] . . . [A]t that time they were changed once a quarter. [S]ince September and October belonged to two different quarters, in September and October the orders of the [rotors] were different. [With] the method that I had been using to find the [wiring] in a [rotor] . . . I could only solve the [far] right-hand [rotor], the one that revolved one place every time [a key was pressed]. The point is that, thanks to the keys for September, I could solve the [rotor] that was in the far right-hand position in September. And since I also had the keys for October, using the same method I was later able to find the [wiring] in the [rotor] that was at the [far] right in October. [T]he third [rotor] and . . . the [reflector] now weren't so difficult . . . I managed to find them by other methods.

Marian Rejewski about 1932, when he first broke Enigma

Marian Rejewski thus made one of the most important breakthroughs in cryptologic history by using elementary group theory to solve the Enigma wiring and rotor settings. His method made it possible to derive the rotor settings independently of the plugboard connections.

A crucial inspired guess on Rejewski's part was that the connections between the keyboard and the entry ring were in alphabetical order, rather than in the order of the keys on a German typewriter keyboard: QWERTZUIO... — the order that was used in the commercial Enigma. Britain's Dilly Knox was astonished when he learned from the Poles, in Warsaw in July 1939, that the entry-ring order was so simple.

After Rejewski had reconstructed the plugboard-equipped Enigma machine, the Poles were able to decrypt a substantial portion of German Enigma traffic through December 1938. (Thereafter they continued reading Enigma, but—due to changes in encipherment procedures—a smaller volume.)

At the time, the setting sheets specified the rotor positions in the machine, the ring settings, the plugboard connections, and the rotor settings as they appeared through the three windows on top of the machine.

The message indicator was a 6-letter sequence comprising the three letters of the message key, enciphered twice using the initial rotor position given in the ground setting (e.g., *RAO*). If the 3-letter message key chosen by the operator was *IHL*, he would encipher this after having set the rotors to *RAO*. The resultant ciphertext, say *OTUNSD*, would be transmitted, followed by the message, enciphered using message key *IHL*. The receiving operator would use the ground setting *RAO* to decipher the first six letters, yielding *IHLIHL*—assuming that there had been no distortion or *garbling* in the transmission or reception of the Morse. (It was the possibility of garbling that had led to the procedure of repeating the message key. This repetition was, however, a major security weakness that was exploited by the Poles.) The receiving operator would then decipher the message, using message key *IHL*.

CYCLOMETER

Cyclometer (mid-1930s), devised by Rejewski to catalog the cycle structure of Enigma permutations.

1. Rotor lid closed;
2. Rotor lid open;
3. Rheostat;
4. Glowlamp;
5. Switches; and
6. Letters.

The Poles set about creating a catalog of these cycle patterns. Rejewski about 1934 or 1935 devised a machine to facilitate this task, called a cyclometer, which "comprised two sets of rotors... connected by wires through which electric current could run. Rotor N in the second set was three letters out of phase with respect to rotor N in the first set, whereas rotors L and M in the second set were always set the same way as rotors L and M in the first set"

Preparation of the card catalog, using the cyclometer, was, says Rejewski, "laborious and took over a year, but when it was ready, obtaining daily keys was a question of [some fifteen] minutes"

On 1 November 1937, however, the Germans changed the Enigma reflector, necessitating the production of a new catalog—"a task which consumed, on account of our greater experience, probably somewhat less than a year's time"

On 15 September 1938 (the day that British Prime Minister Neville Chamberlain flew to the conference that led to the Munich Agreement) the indicator procedure was changed. It now comprised a 9-letter sequence. The setting, as stated in the setting sheet, no longer specified the initial rotor positions to be used. Instead the operator chose three letters, which were transmitted in clear as the first three of nine letters. These gave the key for setting the rotors for the next six letters, which constituted the 3-letter message key sent twice. This meant that the cycle-pattern method would no longer work.

Perforated Sheets

To decrypt Enigma messages, use was now made of a perforated-sheet apparatus that was devised about October 1938 by Henryk Zygalski and is therefore often called Zygalski sheets or Netz. This method depended on a message key's repetition, but also relied on the situation in which a repeated letter of the key was enciphered to the same letter of ciphertext as it had been three letters previously.

Thus, if an intercepted message had the same first and fourth, second and fifth, or third and sixth letters, it was known that some scrambler settings could be eliminated. This phenomenon was, in effect, a zero-length cycle, and details of such cycles would have been available in the catalog.

These occurrences were called samiczk (in English, females—a term later used at Bletchley Park . If the first six letters of the ciphertext were SZVSIK, this would be termed a 1-4 female; if WHOEHS, a 2-5 female; and if ASWCRW, a 3-6 female.

Demonstration of two perforated sheets at Bletchley Park MuseumThe probability of any message containing at least one female was about one in eight. Some ten females would be collected from a day's messages and subjected to the sheets apparatus.

There was a set of 26 sheets for each of the six possible sequences for inserting the three rotors into the scrambler. Each sheet related to the starting position of the left (slowest-moving) rotor. The 26 26 matrix represented the 676 possible starting positions of the middle and left rotors and was duplicated horizontally and vertically: a–z, a–y. The sheets were punched with holes in the positions that would allow a female to occur. Rejewski writes about how the perforated-sheets device was operated.

When the sheets were superposed and moved in the proper sequence and the proper manner with respect to each other, in accordance with a strictly defined program, the number of visible apertures gradually decreased. And, if a sufficient quantity of data was available, there finally remained a single aperture, probably corresponding to the right case, that is, to the solution. From the position of the aperture one could calculate the order of the rotors, the setting of their rings, and, by comparing the letters of the cipher keys with the letters in the machine, likewise permutation S; in other words, the entire cipher key.

Cryptologic Bomb

1. Rotors.
2. Electric motor.

As an alternative to the Zygalski sheets, which required about ten females, a method was developed that used only three. This required an exhaustive (brute-force) analysis of the 105,456 possible rotor settings.

If done by hand, such an analysis would have represented a vast human effort. To facilitate it, Marian Rejewski in about October 1938 invented an electro-mechanical device that was dubbed the bomba kryptologiczna or cryptologic bomb Each bomba contained six sets of Enigma rotors for the six positions of the repeated three-letter key.

In mid-November 1938, six Polish bomby (one for each rotor arrangement) were ready, and reconstruction of daily keys went on apace.

Rejewski has written about the device:

> The bomb method, invented in the fall of 1938, consisted largely in the automation and acceleration of the process of reconstructing daily keys. Each cryptologic bomb (six were built in Warsaw for the Cipher Bureau

before September 1939) essentially constituted an electrically powered aggregate of six Enigmas. It took the place of about one hundred workers and shortened the time for obtaining a key to about two hours.

On 15 December 1938, the German Army increased the complexity of its Enigma operating procedures. Previously only three rotors had been in use, and their sequence in the slots was changed daily. Now two additional rotors were introduced; three of the five would be in use at any given time. This increased the number of possible rotor arrangements in the scrambler by a factor of ten.

Other German agencies likewise received the two new rotors at the same time. Had all these organizations used the same new operating procedures as the Army, it would have nullified any chance of the Poles continuing to decrypt Enigma. However, until 1 July 1939, just two months before Germany invaded Poland, the Sicherheitsdienst (S.D.—the S.S. Security Service) continued using its machines in the old way—like the Wehrmacht prior to 15 September 1938.

The Cipher Bureau immediately exploited this incoordination between the Army and the S.D. and by about the turn of the year had reconstructed the wirings in rotors IV and V. Nevertheless, even with Rejewski's cryptologic bomb and Zygalski's perforated sheets, the new keying procedure and the increased number of rotors posed some major problems. These were exacerbated when, on New Year's Day 1939, the Germans increased the number of plug connections in the plugboard. Previously, from 1 October 1936, the number of plug connections had been variable, ranging between five and eight. Now, from 1 January 1939, the number of plug connections was increased to between seven and ten.

We quickly found the [wirings] within the [new rotors], but [their] introduction raised the number of possible sequences of [rotors] from 6 to 60 and hence also raised tenfold the work of finding the keys. Thus the change was not qualitative but quantitative. We would have had to markedly increase the personnel to operate the bombs, to produce the perforated sheets and to manipulate the sheets.

Italian Naval Enigma

During the Spanish Civil War, Italy, under Italian Fascism, was on the side of Francisco Franco's Nationalists. The Italian Navy used a version of Enigma that did not have a plugboard. In 1937 Dillwyn 'Dilly' Knox, a gifted British cryptanalyst veteran of World War I and the cryptanalytical activities of Room 40, managed to break this cipher, using a technique that he called 'buttoning up' to discover the rotor wirings and another that he called rodding to break messages This relied heavily on cribs and on crossword expertise in Italian, as it yielded a limited number of spaced-out letters at a time.

When in 1940 Dilly Knox wanted to establish whether the Italian Navy were still using the same machine, he instructed his assistants to use rodding to see whether the crib PERX (per being Italian for 'for' and X being used to indicate a space between words) worked for the first part of the message. After three months there was no success, when Mavis Laver, a 19-year-old student, found that rodding produced PERS for the first four letters. She then (against orders) tried beyond this and obtained Personale (Italian for 'personal'). This confirmed that the Italians were indeed using the same machines and procedures.

The subsequent breaking of Italian Naval Enigma ciphers led to substantial Allied successes. The cipher-breaking was disguised by sending a reconnaissance aircraft to the known location before attacking the warship, so that the Italians assumed that this was how they had been discovered. The British Royal Navy's victory at the Battle of Matapan (March 1941) was considerably helped by Ultra intelligence obtained from Italian Naval-Enigma signals.

Polish Disclosures

On 15 March 1939, German forces marched into Bohemia and Moravia. On 31 March Britain and France pledged their support for Poland in the event of any action that threatened her independence Then, on 27 April, Germany withdrew from the German-Polish Non-Aggression Pact of January 1934. The Polish General Staff, realizing the pace and direction of changes in the European political situation, decided in mid-1939 to share their work on Enigma decryption with their western allies. Rejewski later wrote:

> It was not [as Harry Hinsley suggested, cryptological] difficulties of ours that prompted us to work with the British and French, but only the deteriorating political situation. If we had had no difficulties at all we would still, or even the more so, have shared our achievements with our allies as our contribution to the struggle against Germany.

At a conference in Warsaw on 26 July 1939, the Poles revealed to the French and British that they had broken Enigma and pledged to give each a Polish-reconstructed Enigma, along with details of their Enigma-solving techniques and equipment, including Zygalski's perforated sheets and Rejewski's cryptologic bomb. Dilly Knox was a member of the British delegation. He commented on the fragility of the Polish system's reliance on the repetition in the indicator because it might, "at any moment be cancelled".

The two Enigma doubles were sent to Paris, whence Gustave Bertrand brought one to London for the British. He turned it over at Victoria Station, as he was to recall in his Enigma, to Stewart Menzies of Britain's Secret Intelligence Service.

Until then, German military Enigma traffic had defeated the French and British, and they had faced the disturbing prospect that German radio communications would remain undecipherable during the coming war. As British cryptologist Gordon Welchman has written.

Hut 6 Ultra would never have gotten off the ground if we had not learned from the Poles, in the nick of time, the details both of the German military version of the commercial Enigma machine, and of the operating procedures that were in use.

During the German invasion of Poland in September 1939, key Cipher Bureau personnel were evacuated southeast and—after the Soviets invaded eastern Poland on 17 September—into Romania, on the way destroying their cryptological equipment and documentation. Eventually, crossing Yugoslavia and still-neutral Italy, they reached France. There, at PC Bruno outside Paris, on 20 October 1939 they resumed work on German Enigma ciphers, continuing it in the subsequent Battle of France.

As late as December 1939, when Lt. Col. Gwido Langer, chief of the Polish Cipher Bureau, and French Air Force Captain Henri Braquenié, visited London and Bletchley Park, the British asked that the Polish cryptologists be turned over to them. Langer, however, took the position that the Polish team must remain where the Polish Armed Forces were being re-formed—on French soil. Actually, the mathematician-cryptologists might have reached Britain much earlier than they eventually would (that is, the two who were still alive) in 1943; but in Bucharest, Romania, when they had gone to the British Embassy, they had been brushed off by preoccupied British diplomats.

Some personnel of the Cipher Bureau's German section who had worked with Enigma, and most of the workers at the AVA Radio Company that had built Enigma doubles and cryptologic equipment for the German section, had remained in Poland. Some were interrogated by the Gestapo, but no one gave away the secret of Polish mastery of Enigma decryption.

PC Bruno and Bletchley Park worked together closely from late 1939, communicating via a telegraph teletype line secured by the use of Enigma (!). The French would close their Enigma-enciphered messages with an appreciative Heil Hitler!

In January 1940, the British cryptologist Alan Turing spent several days at PC Bruno conferring with his Polish colleagues. He had brought the Poles Zygalski sheets that had been produced at Bletchley Park by John Jeffreys using Polish-supplied information, but which were not working. It turned out that the wirings in Enigma rotors IV and V that Rejewski had worked out, had been copied down wrongly Correcting this error allowed the Poles to make, on 17 January 1940, the first break into wartime Enigma traffic—that from 28 October 1939.

During this period, until the collapse of France in June 1940, ultimately 83 per cent of the Enigma keys that were found, were solved at Bletchley Park, the remaining 17 percent at PC Bruno. Rejewski comments:

> How could it be otherwise, when there were three of us Pol[ish cryptologists] and [there were] at least several hundred British cryptologists, since about 10,000 people worked in Bletchley . . . Besides, recovery of keys also depended on the amount of intercepted cipher material, and that amount was far greater on the British side than on the French side. Finally, in France (by contrast with the work in Poland) we ourselves not only sought for the daily keys, but after finding the key also read the messages . . . One can only be surprised that the Poles had as many as 17 percent of the keys to their credit.

The inter-Allied cryptologic collaboration prevented duplication of effort and facilitated discoveries. Before fighting had started in Norway in April 1940, the Polish-French team solved an uncommonly hard three-letter code used by the Germans to communicate with fighter and bomber squadrons and for exchange of meteorological data between aircraft and land. The code had first appeared in December 1939, but the Polish cryptologists had been too preoccupied with Enigma to give the code much attention. With the German assault on the west impending, however, the breaking of the Luftwaffe code took on mounting urgency. The trail of the elusive code (whose system of letters changed every 24 hours) led back to Enigma. The first clue came from the British, who had noticed that thc code's letters did not change randomly. If A changed to P, then elsewhere P was replaced by A. The British made no further headway, but the Poles realized that what was manifesting was Enigma's exclusivity principle that they had discovered in 1932. The Germans' carelessness meant that now the Poles, having after midnight solved Enigma's daily setting, could with no further effort also read the Luftwaffe signals

The Germans, just before opening their 10 May 1940 offensive in the west that would trample Belgium, Luxemburg and Holland in order to reach the borders of France, once again changed their rding to Gustave Bertrand, "It took superhuman day-and-night effort to overcome this new difficulty: on May 20, decryption resumed.

At this stage, to break the Germans' Enigma ciphers, the cooperating particularly the cillies and the Herivel tip), as well as on some others, such as the non-uniformly-placed notches in rotor alphabet-rings that caused the rotor to the left to move one space when the first rotor reached its particular letter-notch.

At constant risk of discovery and imprisonment or worse. Whe Germany took over Vichy France in November 1942, the Poles nce again had to flee. The Cipher Bureau's chiefs, Colonel Gwido Langer and Major Maksymilian Ciezki, and some of the technical staff were captured by the Germans but, despite extensive interrogation, preserved the secret of Enigma decryption ematicians Marian Rejewski and Henryk

Zygalski, after a perilous odyssey that took them across France, into a Spanish prison, to Portugal and at last by ship to Gibraltar, finally made it to Britain. (The third mathematician, Jerzy Różycki, had perished in the sinking of a passenger ship while returning in 1942 to southern France from a tour of duty in Algeria.) In Britain, Rejewski and Zygalski were inducted into the Polish Army as privates (they would eventually be promoted to lieutenant) and put to work breaking German SS and SD hand ciphers at a Polish signals facility in Boxmoor. They were not invited to work on Enigma at Bletchley Park.

Operating Shortcomings

Apart from some less-than-ideal inherent characteristics of the Enigma, in practice the machine's greatest weakness was the way that it was used. Errors by German Army and Air Force Enigma operators were common, and the Poles had become very experienced at exploiting even very subtle cryptographic mistakes made by the Germans.

One blatant mistake made by them, Rejewski recalled, had been the inclusion, in an early Enigma manual, of a genuine plaintext and its genuine ciphertext, together with the genuine message key. When Rejewski was given this in December 1932, it "made [his reconstruction of the Enigma machine] somewhat easier".

Another German mistake described by Rejewski was the use of easily-guessed keys such as AAA or BBB, or sequences that reflected the layout of the Enigma keyboard, such as "three [typing] keys that stand next to each other [o]r diagonally [from each other]..." At Britain's Bletchley Park these would become known as cillies—either the name of a German operator's girlfriend, used as a key, or a burlesque of "sillies", for some of the foolish things that operators did despite regulations to the contrary or because one of the first message settings that was worked out at Bletchley Park, using cillies, was CIL (the word "cilli" then being a cross between CIL and "silly", describing the Bletchley Park view of such German practices) Cillies in the operation of the four-rotor Abwehr Enigma included four letter names and German obscenities.

Equally silly of the Germans, from a cryptologic perspective, was repeatedly using, in messages, the same stereotypical expressions—what Bletchley Park later would term cribs: the same standard salutations, titles and addresses. Thus, for example, Rejewski recalled that "The last phase in reconstructing daily keys was finding the settings of the rings [on the rotors]. In that phase, we relied on the fact that the greater number of messages began with the letters ANX—German for "to", followed by X as a spacer".

Another important error perpetrated by German operators, was anticipated by John Herivel soon after his arrival at Bletchley Park in January 1940 although it did not occur until after the changes of 10 May that year, during the period of close collaboration between the British, French and Poles. Some operators, after setting their Enigmas in the starting position and closing the metal lid, were selecting as the message key (Spruchschlüssel) the letters that were visible in the glass windows. These letters were often identical with, or close to, the settings on the Enigma's internal rings. As a result, they were effectively sending the ring settings almost in clear This was called Herivelismus or the Herivel tip During the first part of 1940, this meant that the French duty cryptologist could, at a few minutes past midnight, read Wehrmacht signals at the same time as their intended recipients.

One operator was in the habit of using the positions of the rotors at the end of one message (or one quite close to it), as the indicator setting for the next message.

Later in the war, a German responsible for preparing settings sheets, re-used some of the columns of wheel orders, ring settings or plugboard connections from previous months.

The resulting analytical short-cut was christened at Bletchley Park Parkerismus in honour of Reg Parker, who had, through his meticulous record-keeping, spotted this phenomenon.

Crib-based Decryption

The term 'crib' was used at Bletchley Park to denote any known plaintext or suspected plaintext at some point in an enciphered message. This cryptanalytic approach was thus effectively a known-plaintext attack. A large part of the Polish successes had relied on the repetition within the indicator; as soon as Alan Turing moved to Bletchley Park, initially joining Dilly Knox in the research section, he set about seeking methods that did not rely on this weakness, as they anticipated, correctly, that the Germans might not continue it for long.

The Poles had used an early form of crib-based decryption in the days when only six leads were used on the plugboard, leaving 14 letters self-steckered The technique became known as the Forty Weepy method for the following reason. When, on the basis of external evidence, a message was thought to be a continuation of a previous message, the plaintext would start with FORT (from Fortsetzung, meaning continuation) followed by the time of the first message. At this time numerals were represented by the letters on the top row of the Enigma keyboard.

Sources of Cribs

Cribs were a fundamental part of the British approach to breaking Enigma. Guessing the plaintext for a message was a skilled business; a special *Crib Room* was set up in 1940 by Stuart Milner-Barry.

Foremost amongst the knowledge needed for identifying cribs, was the text of previous decrypts which included German military jargon and stereotypical phrases. Meticulous traffic analysis recording, for each network: the radio frequency, the date and time of intercept, the preamble containing the *discriminant*—which identified the network, the indicator setting, the time of origin of the message and the callsign of the originating and receiving stations—allowed cross referencing of a new message with a previous one. Thus, as Derek Taunt wrote, the truism that "nothing succeeds like success" is particularly apposite here.

Stereotypical messages included *Keine besondere Ereignisse* (nothing to report), *An die Gruppe* (to the group) and a number that came from weather stations such as *Wueb null seqs null null* meaning "weather survey 0600". This was actually rendered as *WEUBYYNULLSEQSNULLNULL*. The word *WEUB* is short for *wetteruebersicht*, *YY* was used as a separator and the misspelling *sechs* as *SEQS* was a common and intentional abbreviation Field Marshall Erwin Rommel's Quatermaster started all of his messages to his commander with the same formal introduction.

Another fruitful source of cribs was re-encipherments of messages that had previously been decrypted either from another Enigma network or from a lower-level manual cipher. This happened particularly with German Naval messages being sent in a *Dockyard* cipher and repeated *verbatim* in an Enigma cipher. One German agent in Britain, code named *Treasure*, who had been *turned* to work for the British, was very verbose in her messages back to Germany, which were then re-transmitted on the *Abwehr* Enigma network. She was kept going by MI5 because of providing long cribs in this way, not because of her usefulness as an agent to feed incorrect information to the *Abwehr*.

Occasionally, when there was a particularly urgent need to break the German Naval code, such as when an Arctic convoy was about to depart, mines would be laid by the RAF in a defined position whose grid reference in the German Naval system did not contain any of the words (such as *sechs*) for which abbreviations or alternatives were sometimes used. The warning message about the mines and then the "all clear" message would be transmitted both on the dockyard network and the U-boat network. This process of *planting* a crib was called *gardening*.

Although *cillies* were not actually cribs, the *chit-chat* in clear that Enigma operators indulged in amongst themselves, often gave a clue as to the cillies that they might generate.

Mavis Lever, a member of Dilly Knox's team, recalled an occasion when there was an extraordinary message.

The one snag with Enigma of course is the fact that if you press *A*, you can get every other letter but *A*. I picked up this message and—one was so used to looking at things and making instant decisions—I thought: 'Something's gone. What has this chap done. There is not a single *L* in this message.'

My chap had been told to send out a dummy message and he had just had a fag [cigarette] and pressed the last key on the keyboard, the *L*. So that was the only letter that didn't come out. We had got the biggest crib we ever had, the encypherment was *LLLL*, right through the message and that gave us the new wiring for the wheel [rotor]. That's the sort of thing we were trained to do. Instinctively look for something that had gone wrong or someone who had done something silly and torn up the rule book.

When a captured, interrogated German Enigma operator revealed that they had been instructed to encipher numbers by spelling them out rather than using the top row of the keyboard, Alan Turing reviewed decrypted messages and determined that the number *eins* (one) appeared in 90% of messages. He automated the crib process, creating the Eins Catalogue, which assumed that *eins* was encoded at all positions in the plaintext. The catalogue included every possible rotor position, starting position, and key setting.

5

DNA Profiling

DNA profiling (also called DNA testing, DNA typing, or genetic fingerprinting) is a technique employed by forensic scientists to assist in the identification of individuals on the basis of their respective DNA profiles. DNA profiles are basically just sets of numbers that can be used as a identifier. The number set can be encrypted to a DNA indentification number. DNA profiling should thus not be confused with Full_genome_sequencing.

Although 99.9% of human DNA sequences are the same in every person, enough of the DNA is different to distinguish one individual from another. DNA profiling uses repetitive ("repeat") sequences that vary a lot, called variable number tandem repeats (VNTR). VNTRs loci are very similar between closely related humans, but so variable that unrelated individuals are extremely unlikely to have the same VNTRs.

The DNA profiling technique was first reported in 1985 by Sir Alec Jeffreys at the University of Leicester in England

and is now the basis of several national DNA databases.

DNA Profiling Process

Genetics with the extraction of an individual's DNA (typically called a "reference sample"). The most desirable method of collecting a reference sample is the use of a buccal swab, as this reduces the possibility of contamination. When this is not available (e.g. because a court order may be needed and not obtainable) other methods may need to be used to collect a sample of blood, saliva, semen, or other appropriate fluid or tissue from personal items (e.g. toothbrush, razor, etc.) or from stored samples (e.g. banked sperm or biopsy tissue). Samples obtained from blood relatives (biological relative) can provide an indication of an individual's profile, as could human remains which had been previously profiled.

A reference sample is then analysed to create the individual's DNA profile using one of a number of techniques, discussed below. The DNA profile is then compared against another sample to determine whether there is a genetic match.

RFLP Analysis

The first methods for finding out genetics used for DNA profiling involved restriction enzyme digestion, followed by Southern blot analysis. Although polymorphisms can exist in the restriction enzyme cleavage sites, more commonly the enzymes and DNA probes were used to analyze VNTR loci. However, the Southern blot technique is laborious, and requires large amounts of undegraded sample DNA. Also, Karl Brown's original technique looked at many minisatellite loci at the same time, increasing the observed variability, but making it hard to discern individual alleles (and thereby precluding parental testing). These early techniques have been supplanted by PCR-based assays.

PCR Analysis

With the invention of the polymerase chain reaction

(PCR) technique, DNA profiling took huge strides forward in both discriminating power and the ability to recover information from very small (or degraded) starting samples. PCR greatly amplifies the amounts of a specific region of DNA, using oligonucleotide primers and a thermostable DNA polymerase. Early assays such as the HLA-DQ alpha reverse dot blot strips grew to be very popular due to their ease of use, and the speed with which a result could be obtained. However they were not as discriminating as RFLP. It was also difficult to determine a DNA profile for mixed samples, such as a vaginal swab from a sexual assault victim.

Fortunately, the PCR method is readily adaptable for analyzing VNTR loci. In the United States the FBI has standardized a set of 13 VNTR assays for DNA typing, and has organized the CODIS database for forensic identification in criminal cases. Similar assays and databases have been set up in other countries. Also, commercial kits are available that analyze single nucleotide polymorphisms (SNPs). These kits use PCR to amplify specific regions with known variations and hybridize them to probes anchored on cards, which results in a colored spot corresponding to the particular sequence variation.

STR Analysis

The method of DNA profiling used today is based on PCR and uses short tandem repeats (STR). This method uses highly polymorphic regions that have short repeated sequences of DNA (the most common is 4 bases repeated, but there are other lengths in use, including 3 and 5 bases). Because different unrelated people have different numbers of repeat units, these regions of DNA can be used to discriminate between unrelated individuals. These STR loci (locations) are targeted with sequence-specific primers and are amplified using PCR. The DNA fragments that result are then separated and detected using electrophoresis. There are two common methods of separation and detection, capillary electrophoresis (CE) and gel electrophoresis.

The polymorphisms displayed at each STR region are by themselves very common, typically each polymorphism will be shared by around 5-20% of individuals. When looking at multiple loci, it is the unique combination of these polymorphisms to an individual that makes this method discriminating as an identification tool. The more STR regions that are tested in an individual the more discriminating the test becomes.

From country to country, different STR-based DNA-profiling systems are in use. In North America systems which amplify the CODIS 13 core loci are almost universal, while in the UK the SGM+ system, which is compatible with The National DNA Database in use. Whichever system is used, many of the STR regions under test are the same. These DNA-profiling systems are based around multiplex reactions, whereby many STR regions will be under test at the same time.

Capillary electrophoresis works by electrokinetically (movement through the application of an electric field) injecting the DNA fragments into a thin glass tube (the capillary) filled with polymer. The DNA is pulled through the tube by the application of an electric field, separating the fragments such that the smaller fragments travel faster through the capillary. The fragments are then detected using fluorescent dyes that were attached to the primers used in PCR. This allows multiple fragments to be amplified and run simultaneously, a procedure known as multiplexing. Sizes are assigned using labeled DNA size standards that are added to each sample, and the number of repeats are determined by comparing the size to an allelic ladder, a sample that contains all of the common possible repeat sizes. Although this method is expensive, larger capacity machines with higher throughput are being used to lower the cost/sample and reduce backlogs that exist in many government crime facilities.

Gel electrophoresis acts using similar principles as CE, but instead of using a capillary, a large polyacrylamide gel is used to separate the DNA fragments. An electric field is applied, as in

CE, but instead of running all of the samples by a detector, the smallest fragments are run close to the bottom of the gel and the entire gel is scanned into a computer. This produces an image showing all of the bands corresponding to different repeat sizes and the allelic ladder. This approach does not require the use of size standards, since the allelic ladder is run alongside the samples and serves this purpose. Visualization can either be through the use of fluorescently tagged dyes in the primers or by silver staining the gel prior to scanning. Although it is cost-effective and can be rather high throughput, silver staining kits for STRs are being discontinued. In addition, many labs are phasing out gels in favor of CE as the cost of machines becomes more manageable.

The true power of STR analysis is in its statistical power of discrimination. In the US, there are 13 core loci (DNA locations) that are currently used for discrimination in CODIS. Because these loci are independently assorted (having a certain number of repeats at one locus doesn't change the likelihood of having any number of repeats at any other locus), the product rule for probabilities can be applied. This means that if someone has the DNA type of ABC, where the three loci were independent, we can say that the probability of having that DNA type is the probability of having type A times the probability of having type B times the probability of having type C. This has resulted in the ability to generate match probabilities of 1 in a quintillion (1 with 18 zeros after it) or more. However, since there are about 12 million monozygotic twins on Earth, that theoretical probablitity is useless. For example, the actual probability that 2 random persons have the same DNA is only 1 in 3 trillion.

AmpFLP

Another technique, AmpFLP, or amplified fragment length polymorphism was also put into practice during the early 1990s. This technique was also faster than RFLP analysis and used PCR to amplify DNA samples. It relied on variable number tandem repeat (VNTR) polymorphisms to distinguish various alleles, which were separated on a polyacrylamide gel using an allelic ladder (as opposed to a molecular weight ladder). Bands could be visualized by silver staining the gel. One popular locus for fingerprinting was the D1S80 locus. As with all PCR based methods, highly degraded DNA or very small amounts of DNA may cause allelic dropout (causing a mistake in thinking a heterozygote is a homozygote) or other stochastic effects. In addition, because the analysis is done on a gel, very high number repeats may bunch together at the top of the gel, making it difficult to resolve. AmpFLP analysis can be highly automated, and allows for easy creation of phylogenetic trees based on comparing individual samples of DNA. Due to its relatively low cost and ease of set-up and operation, AmpFLP remains popular in lower income countries.

Y-chromosome Analysis

Recent innovations have included the creation of primers targeting polymorphic regions on the Y-chromosome (Y-STR), which allows resolution of a mixed DNA sample from a male and female and/or cases in which a differential extraction is not possible. Y-chromosomes are paternally inherited, so Y-STR analysis can help in the identification of paternally related males. Y-STR analysis was performed in the Sally Hemings controversy to determine if Thomas Jefferson had sired a son with one of his slaves.

Mitochondrial Analysis

For highly degraded samples, it is sometimes impossible to get a complete profile of the 13 CODIS STRs. In these situations, mitochondrial DNA (mtDNA) is sometimes typed due to there being many copies of mtDNA in a cell, while there may only be 1-2 copies of the nuclear DNA. Forensic scientists amplify the HV1 and HV2 regions of the mtDNA, then sequence each region and compare single nucleotide differences to a reference. Because mtDNA is maternally inherited, directly linked maternal relatives can be used as match references, such as one's maternal grandmother's sister's son. A difference of two or more nucleotides is generally considered to be an exclusion. Heteroplasmy and poly-C differences may throw off straight sequence comparisons, so some expertise on the part of the analyst is required. mtDNA is useful in determining unclear identities, such as those of missing persons when a maternally linked relative can be found. mtDNA testing was used in determining that Anna Anderson was not the Russian princess she had claimed to be, Anastasia Romanov.

mtDNA can be obtained from such material as hair shafts and old bones/teeth.

DNA Databases

There are now several DNA databases in existence around the world. Some are private, but most of the largest databases are government controlled. The United States maintains the largest DNA database, with the Combined DNA Index System, holding over 5 million records as of 2007 . The United Kingdom maintains the National DNA Database (NDNAD), which is of similar size. The size of this database, and its rate of growth, is giving concern to civil liberties groups in the UK, where police have wide-ranging powers to take samples and retain them even in the event of acquittal.

The U.S. Patriot Act of the United States provides a means for the U.S. government to get DNA samples from other countries if they are either a division of, or head office of, a company operating in the U.S. Under the act, the American offices of the company can't divulge to their subsidiaries/offices in other countries the reasons that these DNA samples are sought or by whom.

When a match is made from a National DNA Databank to link a crime scene to an offender who has provided a DNA Sample to a databank that link is often referred to as a *cold hit*. A cold hit is of value in referring the police agency to a specific suspect but is of less evidential value than a DNA match made from outside the DNA Databank.

Considerations when Evaluating DNA Evidence

In the early days of the use of genetic fingerprinting as criminal evidence, juries were often swayed by spurious statistical arguments by defense lawyers along these lines: given a match that had a 1 in 5 million probability of occurring by chance, the lawyer would argue that this meant that in a country of say 60 million people there were 12 people who would also match the profile. This was then translated to a 1 in 12 chance of the suspect being the guilty one. This argument is not sound unless the suspect was drawn at random from the population of the country. In fact, a jury should consider how likely it is that an individual matching the genetic profile would also have been a suspect in the case for other reasons. Another spurious statistical argument is based on the false assumption that a 1 in 5 million probability of a match automatically translates into a 1 in 5 million probability of guilt and is known as the prosecutor's fallacy.

When using RFLP, the theoretical risk of a coincidental match is 1 in 100 billion (100,000,000,000), although the practical risk is actually 1 in 1000 because monozygotic twins are 0.2% of the human population. Moreover, the rate of laboratory error is almost certainly higher than this, and often actual laboratory procedures do not reflect the theory under which the coincidence probabilities were computed. For example, the coincidence probabilities may be calculated based on the probabilities that markers in two samples have bands in *precisely* the same location, but a laboratory worker may conclude that similar—but not precisely identical—band patterns result from identical genetic samples with some imperfection in the agarose gel. However, in this case, the laboratory worker increases the coincidence risk by expanding the criteria for declaring a match. Recent studies have quoted relatively high error rates which may be cause for concern. In the early days of genetic fingerprinting, the necessary population data to accurately compute a match probability was sometimes unavailable. Between 1992 and 1996, arbitrary low ceilings were controversially put on match probabilities used in RFLP analysis rather than the higher theoretically computed ones Today, RFLP has become widely disused due to the advent of more discriminating, sensitive and easier technologies.

STRs do not suffer from such subjectivity and provide similar power of discrimination (1 in 10^13 for unrelated individuals if using a full SGM+ profile) It should be noted that figures of this magnitude are not considered to be statistically supportable by scientists in the UK, for unrelated individuals with full matching DNA profiles a match probability of 1 in a billion (one thousand million) is considered statistically supportable (Since 1998 the DNA profiling system supported by The National DNA Database in the UK is the SGM+ DNA profiling system which includes 10 STR regions and a sex indicating test. However, with any DNA technique, the cautious juror should not convict on genetic fingerprint evidence alone if other factors raise doubt. Contamination with other evidence (secondary transfer) is a key source of incorrect DNA profiles and raising doubts as to whether a sample has been adulterated is a favorite defense technique. More rarely, Chimerism is one such instance where the lack of a genetic match may unfairly exclude a suspect.

Evidence of Genetic Relationship

It's also possible to use DNA profiling as evidence of genetic relationship, but testing that shows no relationship isn't absolutely certain. While almost all individuals have a single and distinct set of genes, rare individuals, known as "chimeras", have at least two different sets of genes. There have been several cases of DNA profiling that falsely "proved" that a mother was unrelated to her children.

Fake DNA Evidence

The value of DNA evidence has to be seen in light of recent cases where criminals planted fake DNA samples at crime scenes. In one case, a criminal even planted fake DNA evidence in his own body: Dr. John Schneeberger raped one of his sedated patients in 1992 and left semen on her underwear. Police drew Schneeberger's blood and compared its DNA against the crime scene semen DNA on three occasions, never showing a match. It turned out that he had surgically inserted a Penrose drain into his arm and filled it with foreign blood and anti-coagulants.

DNA Evidence in Criminal Trials

England and Wales

Evidence from an expert who has compared DNA samples must be accompanied by evidence as to the sources of the samples and the procedures for obtaining the DNA profiles. The judge must ensure that the jury must understand the significance of DNA matches and mismatches in the profiles. The judge must also ensure that the jury does not confuse the 'match probability' (the probability that a person that is chosen at random has a matching DNA profile to the sample from the scene) with the 'likelihood ratio' (the probability that a person with matching DNA committed the crime). In *R v. Doheny*, EWCA Crim 728 (1996). Phillips LJ gave this example of a summing up, which should be carefully tailored to the particular facts in each case:

> Members of the Jury, if you accept the scientific evidence called by the Crown, this indicates that there are probably only four or five white males in the United Kingdom from whom that semen stain could have come. The Defendant is one of them. If that is the position, the decision you have to reach, on all the evidence, is whether you are sure that it was the Defendant who left that stain or whether it is possible that it was one of that other small group of men who share the same DNA characteristics.

Juries should weigh up conflicting and corroborative evidence, using their own common sense and not by using mathematical formulae, such as Bayes' theorem, so as to avoid "confusion, misunderstanding and misjudgment".

Presentation and evaluation of evidence of partial or incomplete DNA profiles

> *R* v *Bates* (2006) EWCA Crim 1395 Moore-Bick LJ said:
>
> "We can see no reason why partial profile DNA evidence should not be admissible provided that the jury are made aware of its inherent limitations and are given a sufficient explanation to enable them to evaluate it. There may be cases where the match probability in relation to all the samples tested is so great that the judge would consider its probative value to be minimal and decide to exclude the evidence in the exercise of his discretion, but this gives rise to no new question of principle and can be left for decision on a case by case basis. However, the fact that there exists in the case of all partial profile evidence the possibility that a "missing" allele might exculpate the accused altogether does not provide sufficient grounds for rejecting such evidence. In many there is a possibility (at least in theory) that evidence exists which would assist the accused and perhaps even exculpate him altogether, but that does not provide grounds for excluding relevant evidence that is available and otherwise admissible, though it does make it important to ensure that the jury are given sufficient information to enable them to evaluate that evidence properly".

Familial Searching

Familial searching is the use of family members' DNA to identify a closely related suspect in jurisdictions where large DNA databases exist, but no exact match has been found. The first successful use of the practice was in a UK case where a man was convicted of manslaughter when he threw a brick stained with his own blood into a moving car. Police could not get an exact match to the UK's DNA database because the man had no criminal convictions, but police implicated him using a close rela has proved controversial because of civil liberties concerns regarding the disproportionate representation of blacks in DNA databases.

Surreptitious DNA Collecting

Police forces may collect DNA samples without the suspects' knwledge, and use it as evidence. Legality of this mode of proceeding has been questioned in Australia.

In the United States, it has been accepted, courts often claiming tht there was no expectation of privacy, citing California v. Greenwood (1985), during which the Supreme Court held that the Fourth Amendment does not prohibit the warrantless search and seizure of garbage left for collection outside the curtilage of a home. Critics of this practice underline the fact that this analogy ignores that "most people have no idea that they risk surrendering their genetic identity to the police by, for instance, failing to destroy a used coffee cup. Moreover, even if they do realize it, there is no way to avoid abandoning one's DNA in public".

In the UK, the Human Tissue Act of 2004 prohibited private individuals from covertly collecting biological samples (hair, fingernails, etc.) for DNA analysis, but excluded medical and criminal investigations from the offense.

Cases

- In the 1950s, Anna Anderson claimed that she was Grand Duchess Anastasia Nikolaevna of Russia; in the 1980s after her death, samples of her tissue that had been stored at a Charlottesville, Virginia hospital following a medical procedure were tested using DNA fingerprinting and showed that she bore no relation to the Romanovs.
- In 1987, British baker Colin Pitchfork was the first

criminal caught using DNA fingerprinting in Leicester, the city where it was first discovered.

- In 1987, Florida rapist Tommy Lee Andrews was the first person in the United States to be convicted as a result of DNA evidence, for raping a woman during a burglary; he was convicted on 6 November 1987 and sentenced to 22 years in prison.
- In 1988, Timothy Spencer was the first man in Virginia to be sentenced to death through DNA Testing for several rape and murder charges, He was dubbed "The South Side Strangler" because he killed victims on the southside of Richmond, Virginia. He was later charged with rape and 1st degree murder and was sentenced to death. He was executed on April 27, 1994. David Vasquez, initially convicted of one of Spencer's crimes, became the first man in America exonerated based on DNA evidence.
- In 1989, Chicago man Gary Dotson was the first person whose conviction was overturned using DNA evidence.
- In 1991, Allan Legere was the first Canadian to be convicted as a result of DNA evidence, for four murders he had committed while an escaped prisoner in 1989. During his trial, his defense argued that the relatively shallow gene pool of the region could lead to false positives.
- In 1992, DNA evidence was used to prove that Nazi doctor Josef Mengele was buried in Brazil under the name Wolfgang Gerhard.
- In 1993, Kirk Bloodsworth was the first person to have been convicted of murder and sentenced to death, whose conviction was overturned using DNA evidence.
- The 1993 rape and murder of Mia Zapata, lead singer for the Seattle punk band The Gits was unsolved 9 years after the murder. A database search in 2001 failed, but

the killer's DNA was collected when he was arrested in Florida for burglary and domestic abuse in 2002.

- The science was made famous in the United States in 1994 when prosecutors heavily relied on — and through expert witnesses exhaustively presented and explained — DNA evidence allegedly linking O.J. Simpson to a double murder. The case also brought to light the laboratory difficulties and handling procedure mishaps which can cause such evidence to be significantly doubted.
- In 1994, RCMP detectives successfully tested hairs from a cat known as Snowball, and used the test to link a man to the murder of his wife, thus marking for the first time in forensic history the use of non-human DNA to identify a criminal.
- In 1998, Dr. Richard J. Schmidt was convicted of attempted second-degree murder when it was shown that there was a link between the viral DNA of the human immunodeficiency virus (HIV) he had been accused of injecting in his girlfriend and viral DNA from one of his patients with full-blown AIDS. This was the first time viral DNA fingerprinting had been used as evidence in a criminal trial.
- In 1999, Raymond Easton a disabled man from Swindon, England was arrested and detained for 7 hours in connection with a burglary due to an inaccurrate DNA match. His DNA had been retained on file after an unrelated domestic incident some time previously.
- In 2001, Wayne Butler was convicted for the murder of Celia Douty. It was the first murder in Australia to be solved using DNA profiling.
- In 2002, DNA testing was used to exonerate Douglas Echols, a man who was wrongfully convicted in a 1986 rape case. Echols was the 114th person to be exonerated through post-conviction DNA testing.

- In August 2002, Annalisa Vincenzi was shot dead in Tuscany. Some time later, Bartender Peter Hamkin, 23, was arrested in Merseyside in March 2003 on an extradition warrant heard at Bow Street Magistrates' Court in London to establish whether he should be taken to Italy to face a murder charge. DNA "proved" he shot her, but he was cleared on other evidence.
- In 2003, Welshman Jeffrey Gafoor was convicted of the 1988 murder of Lynette White, when crime scene evidence collected 12 years earlier was re-examined using STR techniques, resulting in a match with his nephew This may be the first known example of the DNA of an innocent yet related individual being used to identify the actual criminal, via "familial searching".
- In June 2003, because of new DNA evidence, Dennis Halstead, John Kogut and John Restivo won a re-trial on their murder conviction. The three men had already served eighteen years of their thirty-plus-year sentences.
- The trial of Robert Pickton is notable in that DNA evidence is being used primarily to identify the *victims*, and in many cases to prove their existence.
- In March 2003, Josiah Sutton was released from prison after serving four years of a twelve-year sentence for a sexual assault charge. Questionable DNA samples taken from Sutton were retested in the wake of the Houston Police Department's crime lab scandal of mishandling DNA evidence.
- In 2004, DNA testing shed new light into the mysterious 1912 disappearance of Bobby Dunbar, a four-year-old boy who vanished during a fishing trip. He was allegedly found alive eight months later in the custody of William Cantwell Walters, but another woman claimed that the boy was her son, Bruce Anderson,

whom she had entrusted in Walters' custody. The courts disbelieved her claim and convicted Walters for the kidnapping. The boy was raised and known as Bobby Dunbar throughout the rest of his life. However, DNA tests on Dunbar's son and nephew revealed the two were not related, thus establishing that the boy found in 1912 was not Bobby Dunbar, whose real fate remains unknown.

- In 2005, Gary Leiterman was convicted of the 1969 murder of Jane Mixer, a law student at the University of Michigan, after DNA found on Mixer's pantyhose was matched to Leiterman. DNA in a drop of blood on Mixer's hand was matched to John Ruelas, who was only four years old in 1969 and was never successfully connected to the case in any other way. Leiterman's defense unsuccessfully argued that the unexplained match of the blood spot to Ruelas pointed to cross-contamination and raised doubts about the reliability of the lab's identification of Leiterman.

GENEALOGICAL DNA TEST

A genealogical DNA test examines the nucleotides at specific locations on a person's DNA for genetic genealogy purposes. The test results are not meant to have any informative medical value and do not determine specific genetic diseases or disorders; they are intended only to give genealogical information. Genealogical DNA tests generally involve comparing the results of living individuals as opposed to obtaining samples from deceased people.

Procedure

The general procedure for taking a genealogical DNA test involves taking a painless cheek-scraping (also known as a buccal swab) at home and mailing the sample to a genetic genealogy laboratory for testing. Some laboratories use mouth wash or chewing gum instead of cheek swabs. Some laboratories, such as the Human Origins Genotyping Laboratory (HOGL) at the University of Arizona, offer to store DNA samples for ease of future testing. All United States laboratories will destroy the DNA sample upon request by the customer, guaranteeing that a sample is not available for further analysis.

Types of Tests

The most popular ancestry tests are Y chromosome (Y-DNA) testing and mitochondrial DNA (mtDNA) testing. Other tests attempt to determine a person's comprehensive genetic history and/or ethnic origins.

Y Chromosome (Y-DNA) Testing

A man's paternal ancestry can be traced using the DNA on his Y chromosome (Y-DNA) through Y-STR testing. This is useful because the Y chromosome, like many European surnames, passes from father to son, and can be used to help study surnames. Women who wish to determine their paternal ancestry can ask their father, brother, paternal uncle, paternal grandfather, or a cousin who shares the same paternal lineage to take a test for them.

What gets tested

Y-DNA testing involves looking at segments of DNA on the Y chromosome (found only in males). The segments which are examined are referred to as genetic markers and occur in what is considered "junk" DNA.

STR Markers

A chromosome contains sequences of repeating nucleotides known as *short tandem repeats* (STRs). The number of repetitions varies from one person to another and a particular number of repetitions is known as an allele of the marker. An STR on the Y chromosome is designated by a DYS number (DNA Y-chromosome Segment number). The example below shows the allele of Rumpelstiltskin's DYS393 marker is 12. That means that sequence of nucleotides repeats 12 times — with a DNA sequence of [AGAT].

SNP Markers

A *single nucleotide polymorphism* (SNP) is a change to a single nucleotide in a DNA sequence. The relative mutation rate for an SNP is extremely low. This makes them ideal for marking the history of the human genetic tree. SNPs are named with a letter code and a number. The letter indicates the lab or research team that discovered the SNP. The number indicates the order in which it was discovered. For example M173 is the 173rd SNP documented by the group who uses the letter M.

Understanding Test Results

Y-DNA tests generally examine 10-67 STR markers on the Y chromosome but over 100 markers are available. STR test results provide the personal haplotype. SNP results indicate the haplogroup.

Haplotype

A Y-DNA haplotype is the numbered results of a genealogical Y-DNA test. Each allele value has a distinctive frequency within a population. For example, at DYS455, the results will show 8, 9, 10, 11 or 12 repeats, with 11 being most common For high marker tests the allele frequencies provide a signature for a Mitochondrial DNA (mtDNA) testing.

Microchondial DNA (mDNA) Testing

A person's maternal ancestry can be traced using his or her *mitochondrial* DNA (*mtDNA*). The DNA in the human mitochondria is passed down by the mother unchanged. One exception, which was linked to infertility, has been shown. Additionally, some people cite paternal mtDNA transmission as invalidating mtDNA testing but this is not considered problematic in scholarly population genetics studies or genetic genealogy.

What gets tested

mtDNA by current conventions is divided into three regions. They are the coding region and two Hyper Variable Regions (HVR1 and HVR2). All test results are compared to the mtDNA of a European in Haplogroup H2a2. This sample is known as the Cambridge Reference Sequence (CRS). A list of single nucleotide polymorphisms (SNPs) is returned. Any "mutations" or "transitions" that are found are simply differences from the CRS.

The test results are compared to another person's results to determine the time frame in which the two people shared a most recent common ancestor (MRCA). The two most common mtDNA tests are a sequence of HVR1 and a sequence of both HVR1 and HVR2. Some people are now choosing to have a full sequence performed. This is still somewhat controversial as it may reveal medical information.

Understanding Test Results

The most basic of mtDNA tests will sequence Hyper Variable Region 1 (HVR1). HVR1 nucleotides are numbered 16001-16569. Some test reports might omit the 16 prefix from HVR1 results. ie 519C and not 16519C.

Geographic Origin Tests

Autosomal tests that test the recombining chromosomes are available. These attempt to measure an individual's mixed geographic heritage by identifying particular markers, called ancestry informative markers or AIM, that are associated with populations of specific geographical areas. The tests' validity and reliability have been called into question but they continue to be popular. Anomalous findings most often result from databases too small to associate markers with all the areas where they occur in indigenous populations.

Biogeographical Ancestry

Autosomal DNA testing purports either to determine the "genetic percentages" of a person's ancestry from particular continents/regions or list the countries and "tribes" of origin on an overall basis. Admixture tests arrive at percentages by examining SNPs, which are locations on the DNA where one nucleotide has "mutated" or "switched" to a different nucleotide. Tests listing geographical places of ancestry use alleles — individual and family variations on various chromosomes across the genome analyzed with the aid of population databases. One line of tests is designed to tell what percentages of Native American, European and Near Eastern, East Asian, and Sub-Saharan African ancestry a person has. The second type of test concentrates on standard identity markers such as the CODIS profile combined with databases like OmniPop, ENFSI and proprietary adaptations of published studies.

One company describes four biogeographic groups as follows:

- *Native American:* Populations that migrated from Asia to inhabit North, South and Central America.
- *European:* European, Middle Eastern and South Asian populations from the Indian subcontinent, including India, Pakistan and Sri Lanka.
- *East Asian:* Japanese, Chinese, Mongolian, Korean, Southeast Asian and Pacific Islander populations, including populations native to the Philippines.
- *African:* Populations from Sub-Saharan Africa such as Nigeria and Congo region.

Based on customer feedback, the company in June 2007 introduced a new version of its EURO DNA test with a more limited range of countries that promises to have more meaningful clues to one's European ancestry. Both tests — the four-part ethnicity estimate and EURO DNA test — use a high number of so-called Ancestry Informative Markers whose genetic distance between populations reflects the populations' geographic distance from each other. The location and variation of these AIMs are proprietary to the company and have never been published.

In 2006, another company developed an autosomal DNA ancestry-tracing product that combined the traditional CODIS markers used by law enforcement officers and the judicial system with OmniPop, a population database developed by San Diego detective Brian Burritt. Customers received matches to their profile's frequency of occurrence in world populations as well as a breakout for European ancestry based on the European Network of Forensic Science Institutes, or ENFSI As a public service, the company has supported the expansion of OmniPop, which currently encompasses over 360 populations, double that of its first release. The ENFSI calculator uses data from 24 European populations (5700 profiles). The two databases must be searched separately, because they are based on two different sets of markers. The company sells its product as the DNA Fingerprint Test. The 16 markers incorporated in its results are: D8S1179, D21S11, D7S820, CSFIPO, D3S1358, THO1, D13S317, D16S539, D2S1338, D19S433, VWA, TPOX, D18S51, D5S818, and FGA.

The theory behind using a forensic profile for ancestry tracing is that the alleles' respective frequency of occurrence develops over generations with equal input of the two parents since for each location we take one value from our mother and one from our father. It thus serves as a window into a person's total ancestral composition. The configuration of scores reflects inherited changes from all previous generations, all ancestral lines, and can predict an individual's unique probable ethnic matches based on the profile's commonness or rarity in different populations.

To give an idea of the inclusiveness of the latest version of OmniPop, the following are the last populations that have been added.

Greek,

Sikkim (India),

Bhutia (India),

Italian,

Argentinian (Misiones),

Hungarian (E. Romani),

Hungarian (Ashkenazim),

Romanian (Szekler),

Romanian (Csango),

Tibet (Luoba).

As studies from more and more populations are included, the accuracy of results should improve, leading to a more informative picture of one's ancestry.

Along the same lines, yet another company identifies the indigenous and diaspora populations in which an individual's autosomal STR profile is most common. This test examines autosomal STRs, which are locations on a chromosome where a pattern of two or more nucleotides is repeated and the repetitions are directly adjacent to each other. The populations in which the individual's profile is most common are identified and assigned a likelihood score. The individual's profile is assigned a likelihood of membership in each of thirty-four world regions:

- Caucasian
    - European
        - Eastern European: The Slavic speaking region of Eastern Europe.
        - Finno-Ugrian: The Uralic speaking region of North-eastern Europe.
        - Mediterranean: The Romance speaking region of Southwestern Europe.
        - Northwest European: The Celtic and Germanic speaking region of Northwestern Europe.

- Near Eastern
  - Arabian: The Arabian Peninsula.
  - North African: Populations of the Atlas Mountains and Sahara Desert.
  - Mesopotamian: The historical "Cradle of Western Civilization" including modern Iran, Iraq and nearby territories.
  - Aegean: Anatolia region, modern territories of Southern Italy and Sicily, Greece, and Turkey.
  - Levantine: Populations along the coast of the eastern Mediterranean Sea.
- Asian
  - Central and South Asian Regions:
    - Altaian
    - Eastern India
    - North India
    - South India
  - East Asian Regions:
    - Japanese
    - Malay Archipelago
    - North Chinese
    - South Chinese
    - Southeast Asian
    - Tibetan
  - Sub-Saharan African Regions:
    - East African
    - Southern African
    - West African

- American Indians
  - Native North American Regions:
    * Arctic: Inuit (Eskimo) peoples of Alaska.
    * Athabaskan: Athabaskan speaking Dine peoples of western North America.
    * Mexican: Native peoples of Mexico, including the historical territories of the Aztec Empire.
    * North Amerindian: Native peoples of the Great Plains region of North America.
    * Ojibwa (East Algonquian): Eastern Algonquian speaking peoples of northeastern North America.
    * Salishan: Salish of the Pacific Northwest.
  - Native Central and South American Regions:
    * Amazonian
    * Andean
    * Central American
    * Mayan
    * Patagonian
  - Pacific Regions:
    * Australian: Aboriginal peoples of Australia and Papua New Guinea.
    * Polynesian

The *STR analysis* measures the frequency of a person's DNA profile within major world regions. Unlike SNP admixture tests, this analysis is based on objectively identified world regions and does not depend on any system of presumed biogeographic classifications. As most STR analysis examines markers chosen for their high intra-group variation, the utility of these particular STR markers to access inter-group relationships may be greatly diminished.

United States Native American Ancestry

Autosomal testing, Y-DNA, and mtDNA testing can be conducted to determine Amerindian ancestry. A mitochondrial Haplogroup determination test based on mutations in Hypervariable Region 1 and 2 may establish whether a person's direct female line belongs to one of the canonical Native American Haplogroups, A, B, C, D or X. If one's DNA belonged to one of those groups the implication would be that he or she is, in whole or part, Native American. Comparison with tribal-specific haplotypes is at times possible. Significantly, however, the U.S. government does not consider DNA as admissible evidence for enrollment in any federally recognized tribe. Tribes, after all, are political constructs, not genetic populations. Membership in a federally recognized entity is based on the record of names of one's direct ancestors on tribal-specific Native American censuses (or final rolls) prepared during treaty-making and relocation to reservations in the 1800s.

Complicating factors in identification are the Native American name controversy and recent evidence that indigenous North American Mitochondrial Haplogroups may not be limited to the five named. The vast majority of Native American individuals do belong to one of the five identified mtDNA Haplogroups. Many Americans are just discovering their Native roots, however. The small chance of belonging to one of the acknowledged lineages, particularly in the case of male lines, which were almost entirely eradicated by the process of history, does not deter some from attempting to validate their heritage with the goal of gaining admittance into a tribe. These tests, moreover, are ideal for adoptees with Native American ancestry. There are many such adoptees or their descendants in U.S. and Canadian society because of past policies of assimilation.

United States African Ancestry

Y-DNA and mtDNA testing can determine with which present-day African country a person shares a direct line of part of his or her ancestry. Testing company African Ancestry maintains an "African Lineage Database" of African lineages from 30 countries and over 160 ethnic groups. Due to joint long histories in the US, approximately 30% of African American males have a European Y chromosome haplogroup Some Native American ancestry is evident in modern-day African Americans as well. By the early 19th century, substantial families of Free Persons of Color had been established who were related to people free during the colonial period; most of those have been documented as descended from white women (servant or free) and African men (servant, slave or free).

As for the mitochondrial haplotypes, African Ancestry lists approximately 300 tribal affiliations and seeks to assign, within a certain measure of likelihood, an African tribe to individuals who are tested. This is how Oprah Winfrey discovered one direct line of maternal ancestry. When Oprah had her DNA tested, the results suggested her most likely match in direct matrilineal ancestry was to the Kpelle people of Liberia. According to authorities like Salas, nearly three-quarters of the ancestors of African Americans taken in slavery came from West Africa.

The African-American movement to discover and identify with ancestral tribes has burgeoned since DNA testing. Often members of African-American churches take the test as groups. African Americans cannot easily trace their ancestry during the years of slavery through surname research, census and property records, and other traditional means. Genealogical DNA testing gives them at least one distinct tie to African heritage.

Cohanim Ancestry

The Cohanim (or Kohanim) is a patrilineal priestly descent in Judaism. According to the *Bible*, the ancestor of the Cohanim is Aaron, brother of Moses. Many believe that descent from Aaron is verifiable with a Y-DNA test: the first published study of all in genealogical Y chromosome DNA testing found that very many of the Cohens did indeed have distinctively similar DNA, rather more so than general Jewish or Middle Eastern populations. These Cohens tended to belong to Haplogroup J, with Y-STR values clustered unusually closely around a haplotype known as the Cohen Modal Haplotype (CMH). This could indeed be consistent with a shared common ancestor, or with the hereditary priesthood having originally been founded from members of a single closely related clan.

It should be noted that the original studies tested only six Y-STR markers, now considered a very low-resolution test. Such a test simply does not have the resolution to prove relatedness, nor to estimate reliably the time to a common ancestor. The Cohen Modal Haplotype (CMH), while notably frequent among Cohens, also appears in the general populations of haplogroups J1 and J2 with no particular link to the Cohen ancestry. So while many Cohens have haplotypes close to the CMH, a far larger number of such haplotypes worldwide belong to people with no likely Cohen connection at all. According to researchers (Hammer), it is only the CMH that is found in J1 that is to be attributed to the Aaron lineage, not the CMH in J2. It is not possible for Jews with the CMH in both J1 and J2 to all be descended from one man who lived approximately 3300 years ago, because J1 diverged from J2 10,000 years ago, significantly before the postulated time of Aaron.

There are a high percentage of Arabs in haplogroup J1 with the CMH: for example, 20% of men in Oman. There are also Arab men with one-step mutations from the CMH, such as Galilee Modal Haplotype and Negev Bedouin Haplotype (Coffman study 2005). Some of them claim a Cohen connection to the MCRA (most recent common ancestor) before Aaron, which is Abraham, who supposedly lived 500 years earlier than Aaron.

To some extent one could increase resolution by testing more than six Y-STR markers. For some this could certainly help to establish relatedness to particular recent Cohen clusters. For many it is likely that testing would still be unable to distinguish definitively shared Cohen ancestry from the more general population distribution. So far there is no openly published research to indicate what extended Y-STR haplotype distributions appear to be characteristic of Cohens. Although some high-resolution testing has certainly been done, to date the results are held as closely guarded secrets. There have been no reports as to whether the high-resolution testing that has been done tends to confirm or tends to call into question the basic hypothesis of a majority of Cohens' sharing a recent common ancestry back to a Y-chromosomal Aaron at an appropriate date. This is a basic problem with the "for-profit" DNA companies now trying to sell their products: they have published no research proving their claims that the 37-marker test can prove relatedness to a mathematical degree of certainty within a genealogical time frame.

European Testing

For people with European maternal ancestry, mtDNA tests are offered to determine which of eight European maternal "clans" the direct-line maternal ancestor belonged to. This is simply an mtDNA haplotype test based on the research in the book *The Seven Daughters of Eve.*

SNP testing may enable mostly European individuals to determine to which Sub-European population they belong:

- Northern European subgroup (NOR) - mostly Northern and Southwestern European.
- Southeastern European (Mediterranean) subgroup (MED) - mostly Southeastern Europeans (Greeks or Turks).
- Middle Eastern subgroup (MIDEAS) - mostly Middle Eastern.
- South Asian subgroup (SA) - mostly South Asian from the Indian sub-continent (i.e. Indian).

Hindu Testing

The 49 established *gotras* are clans or families whose members trace their descent to a common ancestor, usually a sage of ancient times. The gotra proclaims a person's identity and a "gotraspeak" is required to be presented at Hindu ceremonies. People of the same gotra are not allowed to marry.

One company says it can use a 37-marker Y-DNA test to "verify genetic relatedness and historical gotra genealogies for Hindu and Buddhist engagements, marriages and business partnerships." Any Y-DNA test can be used to compare results with another person whose gotra is known.

United States Melungeon Testing

Several efforts, including a number of ongoing studies, have examined the genetic makeup of families historically identified as Melungeon. Most results point primarily to a mixture of European and African, with a very small amount of Native American lineages (none in one study). Though some companies provide additional Melungeon research materials with Y-DNA and mtDNA tests, any test will allow comparisons with the results of current and past Melungeon DNA studies.

Genealogical DNA tests have become popular due to the ease of testing at home and the various additions they make to genealogical research. Genealogical DNA tests allow for an individual to determine with 99.9% certainty whether he or she is related to another person within a certain time frame, or with 100% certainty that he or she is not related. DNA tests are perceived as more scientific, conclusive and expeditious than research alternatives, although they are limited by restrictions on lines which may be studied.

The above results are theoretical and are the best case results. For example, the 12/12 marker test match gives a 50% likelihood in 7 generations. The probability is for the most recent common ancestor. When having a 36 of 37 marker match, it gives a 90% likehood in eight generations.

Benefits

Genealogical DNA test have become popular due to the ease of testing at home and the various additions they make to genealogical research. Genealogical DNA tests allow for an individual to determine with high accuracy whether he or she is related to another person within a certain time frame, or with certainty that he or she is not related. DNA tests are perceived as more scientific, conclusive and expeditious than searching the civil records. However, they are limited by restrictions on lines which may be studied. Also, the civil records are always only as accurate as the individual who provided or wrote the information.

The earlier Y-DNA testing results are normally stated as probabilities: For example, a perfect 12/12 marker test match gives a 50% likelihood of the most recent common ancestor (MRCA) being within 7 generations back, while a 67 of 67 marker gives a 95% likelihood of the MRCA being within 6 generations back.

As presented above in mtDNA testing, if a perfect match is found the mtDNA test results can be similarly helpful, in spite of the extra difficulty in *traditional genealogy* itself due to the lack of matrilineal surname information in most cultures.

Drawbacks

Common concerns about genealogical DNA test are cost and privacy issues (some testing companies electing to retain samples and results for their own use without a privacy agreement with subjects). The most common complaint from DNA test customers is the failure of the company to make results understandable and meaningful to them. According to an earlier survey, 1 in 6 Americans (16.6%) said they were aware of the ancestry-tracing capability of a home DNA test but when probed, most knew little about the details, reliability, or differences between tests.

The Y-DNA lineage from father to son can have complications including unusual mutations, secret adoptions, and false paternity (i.e. the father in one generation is not the father in birth records, a discovery that might upset some people). Maternal DNA is hard to correlate with surnames because surnames are not generally passed on from women. A further drawback, at least with autosomal tests, is their present state of imperfection and large margin of error (up to 15%, according to some genomics experts), with significant blind spots, such as confusion of Mongolian ancestry with Native American.

Medical Information

Though genealogical DNA tests results generally have no informative medical value and are not intended to determine genetic diseases or disorders, there has been a correlation established between a lack of DYS464 markers and infertility, and a correlation between mtDNA haplogroup H and protection from sepsis. Certain haplogroups have been linked to longevity.

The testing of full mtDNA sequences is still somewhat controversial as it may reveal medical information. The field of linkage disequilibrium, unequal association of genetic disorders with a certain mitochondrial lineage, is in its infancy, but those mitochondrial mutations that have been linked are searchable in the genome database Mitomap The National Human Genome Research Institute operates the Genetic And Rare Disease Information Center that can assist consumers in identifying an appropriate screening test and help locate a nearby medical center that offers such.

DNA in Genealogy Software

Some genealogy software programs now allow recording DNA marker test results, allowing for tracking of both Y-chromosome and Mitochrondrial DNA tests and results for relatives. Also DNA wall charts are available.

GENETIC GENEALOGY

Genetic genealogy is the application of genetics to traditional genealogy. Genetic genealogy involves the use of genealogical DNA testing to determine the level of genetic relationship between individuals.

History

The investigation of surnames in genetics can be said to go back to George Darwin, a son of Charles Darwin. In 1875, George Darwin used surnames to estimate the frequency of first-cousin marriages and calculated the expected incidence of marriage between people of the same surname (isonymy) He arrived at a figure between 2.25% and 4.5% for cousin-marriage in the population of Great Britain, with the upper classes being on the high end and the general rural population on the low end. (His parents, Charles Darwin and Emma Wedgwood, were first cousins.) This simple study was innovative for its era. The next stimulus toward using genetics to study family history had to wait until the 1990s, when certain locations on the Y chromosome were identified as being useful for tracing male-to-male inheritance.

Dr. Karl Skorecki, a Canadian nephrologist of Ashkenazi parentage, noticed that a Sephardic fellow-congregant who was a Kohen like himself had completely different physical features. According to Jewish tradition, all Kohanim are descended from the priest Aaron, brother of Moses. Skorecki reasoned that if Kohanim were indeed the descendants of only one man, they should have a common set of genetic markers and should perhaps preserve some family resemblance to each other.

To test that hypothesis, he contacted Professor Michael Hammer of the University of Arizona, a researcher in molecular genetics and pioneer in Y chromosome research. Their report in the *Nature* in 1997 sent shock waves through the worlds of science and religion. A particular marker was indeed more likely to be present in Jewish men from the priestly tradition than in the general Jewish population. It was apparently true that a common descent had been strictly preserved for thousands of years. (See *Y-chromosomal Aaron*). Moreover, the data showed that there were very few "non-paternity events".

The first to test the new methodology in general surname research was Bryan Sykes, a molecular biologist at Oxford University. His study of the Sykes surname obtained valid results by looking at only four markers on the male chromosome. It pointed the way to genetics becoming a valuable assistant in the service of genealogy and history. In 2001, Sykes went on to write the popular book *The Seven Daughters of Eve*, which described the seven major haplogroups of European ancestors.

In the wake of that book's success, and the growing availability and affordability of genealogical DNA tests, genetic genealogy as a field began growing rapidly. By 2003, the field of DNA testing of surnames was declared officially to have "arrived" in an article by Jobling and Tyler-Smith in *Nature Reviews Genetics*. The number of firms offering tests, and the number of consumers ordering them, had risen dramatically.

Another milestone in the acceptance of genetic genealogy is the Genographic Project. The Genographic Project is a five-year research partnership launched by the National Geographic Society and IBM in 2005. Although its goals are primarily anthropological, not genealogical, the project's sale by October 2007 of over 225,000 of its public participation testing kits, which test the general public for either twelve STR markers on the Y chromosome or the HVR1 region of the mtDNA, has helped increase the visibility of genetic genealogy.

More state-of-the-art commercial laboratories now recommend testing at least 25 markers, since the more markers tested, the more discriminating and powerful the results will be. A 12-marker STR test is usually not discriminating enough to provide conclusive results for a common surname. Genetic laboratories such as Genebase and Family Tree DNA give the option of testing 67 Y-DNA Markers.

Annual sales of genetic genealogical tests for all companies, including the laboratories that support them, are estimated to be in the area of $60 million.

Interpretation

Since the year 2000, dozens of relevant academic papers have been published, and thousands of private test results organised by surname study groups have been made available on the internet. The comparison of results may be complicated by the fact that some laboratories use different testing methods. Apparently differing results from two sources may in fact be identical, and vice-versa.

Uses

Paternal and Maternal Lineages

The two most common types of genetic genealogy tests are Y-DNA (paternal line) and mtDNA (maternal line) genealogical DNA tests.

These tests involve the comparison of certain sequences of DNA pairs of individuals in order to estimate the probability that they share a common ancestor in a genealogical time frame and, through the use of a Bayesian model published by Bruce Walsh, to estimate the number of generations separating the two individuals from their most recent common ancestor.

Y-DNA research involves short tandem repeat (STR) and, sometimes, single nucleotide polymorphism (SNP) testing of the Y-chromosome. The Y-chromosome is present only in males and reveals information on the strict paternal line. These tests can provide insight in the recent (via STRs) and ancient (via SNPs) genetic ancestry. A Y-chromosome STR test will reveal a haplotype, which should be similar among all male descendants of a male ancestor. SNP tests are used to assign people to a paternal haplogroup, which defines a genetic population.

mtDNA research involves sequencing the HVR-1 region, HVR-2 region or both. A mtDNA test can also be used to assign people to a maternal haplogroup.

Either Y-DNA or mtDNA test results can be compared to the results of others via private or public DNA databases.

Biogeographical and Ethnic Origins

Additional DNA tests exist for determining biogeographical and ethnic origin, but these tests have less relevance for traditional genealogy.

Genetic genealogy has revealed astonishing links between peoples. For instance, it has shown that the ancient Phoenician people were ancestors of much of the present-day population of the island of Malta. Preliminary results from a study by Pierre Zalloua of the American University of Beirut and Spencer Wells, supported by a grant from National Geographic's Committee for Research and Exploration, were published in the October 2004 issue of *National Geographic*. One of the conclusions is that "more than half of the Y chromosome lineages that we see in today's Maltese population could have come in with the Phoenicians.

Human Migration

Genealogical DNA testing methods are also being used on a longer time scale to trace human migratory patterns. For example, they have been used to determine when the first humans came to North America and what path they followed.

For several years, a number of researchers and laboratories from around the world have been sampling indigenous populations from around the globe in an effort to map historical human migration patterns. Recently, several projects have been created that are aimed at bringing this science to the public. One example is the National Geographic Society's Genographic Project, which aims to map historical human migration patterns by collecting and analyzing DNA samples from over 100,000 people across five continents. Another example is the DNA Clans Genetic Ancestry Analysis, which measures a person's precise genetic connections to indigenous ethnic groups from around the world.

Typical Customers and Interest Groups

Male DNA testing customers most often start with a Y chromosome test to determine their father's paternal ancestry. Females generally begin with a mitochondrial test to trace their ancient maternal lineage, which males often have tested for the same purpose.

A common consumer goal in purchasing DNA testing services is to acquire quantified, scientific linkage to a specific ancestral group. A compelling example of this motive is found in the expressed desires of some consumers to be proven to have Viking paternal ancestry. In keeping with this marketplace demand, one British DNA testing service, Oxford Ancestors, offers a Y chromosome test purporting to assess whether given males are of "Viking stock." Those whose DNA falls into the designated haplogroup are issued Viking Descendant certificates by the testing service. The same DNA testing company participated in producing a televised documentary, "The Blood of the Vikings," in conjunction with the BBC, which showed how DNA testing could reveal Viking ancestry.

The Rootsweb DNA-Genealogy Internet discussion group has a membership of 750 subscribers from around the world. Some subscribers have had various DNA tests performed and are seeking advice and guidance in interpreting their results. The list also includes administrators of DNA projects that examine surnames, geographic regions, or ethnic groups. The sophistication of subscribers ranges from expert to novice. In some cases, subscribers have been credited with making useful and novel contributions to knowledge in the field of genetic genealogy.

Paternal and Maternal Lineages

Mitochondria are small *organelles* that lie in the *cytoplasm* of eucaryotic cells, such as those of humans. Their primary purpose is to provide energy to the cell. Mitochondria are thought to be the vestigial remains of symbiotic bacteria that were once free living. One indication that mitochondria were once free living is that they contain a relatively small circular segment of DNA, called mitochondrial DNA (mtDNA). The overwhelming majority of a human's DNA is contained in chromosomes in the nucleus of the cell, but mtDNA is an exception. An individual inherits their cytoplasm and the organelles it contains exclusively from their mother, as these are derived from the ovum (egg cell), sperm only carry chromosomal DNA due to the necessity of maintaining motility. When a mutation arises in mtDNA molecule, the mutation is therefore passed in a direct female line of descent. These mutations are derived from copying mistakes, when the DNA is copied it is possible that a single mistake occurs in the DNA sequence, these single mistakes are called single nucleotide polymorphisms (SNPs).

Human *Y chromosomes* are male-specific sex chromosomes; nearly all humans that possess a Y chromosome will be morphologically male. Y chromosomes are therefore passed from father to son; although Y chromosomes are situated in the cell nucleus, they only recombine with the X chromosome at the ends of the Y chromosome; the vast majority of the Y chromosome (95%) does not recombine. When mutations (SNPs) arise in the Y chromosome, they are passed on directly from father to son in a direct male line of descent. The Y chromosome and mtDNA therefore share certain properties.

Other chromosomes, autosomes and X chromosomes in women, share their genetic material (called crossing over leading to recombination) during meiosis (a special type of cell division that occurs for the purposes of sexual reproduction). Effectively this means that the genetic material from these chromosomes gets mixed up in every generation, and so any new mutations are passed down randomly from parents to offspring.

The special feature that both Y chromosomes and mtDNA display is that mutations can accrue along a certain segment of both molecules and these mutations remain fixed in place on the DNA. Furthermore the historical sequence of these mutations can also be inferred. For example, if a set of ten Y chromosomes (derived from ten different men) contains a mutation, A, but only five of these chromosomes contain a second mutation, B, it must be the case that mutation B occurred after mutation A. Furthermore all ten men who carry the chromosome with mutation A are the direct male line descendants of the same man who was the first person to carry this mutation. The first man to carry mutation B was also a direct male line descendant of this man, but is also the direct male line ancestor of all men carrying mutation B. Series of mutations such as this form molecular lineages. Furthermore each mutation defines a set of specific Y chromosomes called a haplogroup. All men carrying mutation A form a single haplogroup, all men carrying mutation B are part of this haplogroup, but mutation B also defines a more recent haplogroup (which is a subgroup or subclade) of its own which men carrying only mutation A do not belong to. Both mtDNA and Y chromosomes are grouped into lineages and haplogroups; these are often presented as tree like diagrams.

Benefits

Genetic genealogy gives genealogists a means to check or supplement the historical record with information from genetic data. A positive test match with another individual may:

- provide locations for further genealogical research
- help determine ancestral home land

- discover living relatives
- validate existing research
- confirm or deny suspected connections between families
- prove or disprove theories regarding ancestry

Drawbacks

People who resist testing may cite one of the following concerns:

- Cost
- Quality of testing
- Concerns over privacy issues
- Loss of ethnic identity

Finally, Y-DNA and mtDNA tests each only trace a single lineage (one's father's father's father's etc. lineage or one's mother's mother's mother's etc. lineage). At 10 generations back, an individual has up to 1024 unique ancestors (fewer if ancestor cousins interbred) and a Y-DNA or mtDNA test is only studying one of those ancestors, as well as their descendants and siblings (same sexed siblings for Y-DNA or all siblings for mtDNA). However, most genealogists maintain contact with many cousins (1st, 2nd, 3rd, etc., with different surnames) whose Y-DNA and mtDNA are different, and thus can be encouraged to be tested to find additional ancestral DNA lineages.

Expected Growth

Genetic genealogy is a rapidly growing field. As the cost of testing continues to drop, the number of people being tested continues to increase. The probability of finding a genetic match among the DNA databases should continue to improve. Laboratories and testing firms are engaging in active research and development that will allow for higher confidence intervals and better results interpretation, including historical interpretive reports and customized research.

6

Capillary Electrophoresis

Capillary electrophoresis (CE), also known as capillary zone electrophoresis (CZE), can be used to separate ionic species by their charge and frictional forces. In traditional electrophoresis, electrically charged analytes move in a conductive liquid medium under the influence of an electric field. Introduced in the 1960s, the technique of capillary electrophoresis (CE) was designed to separate species based on their size to charge ratio in the interior of a small capillary filled with an electrolyte.

Instrumentation

The instrumentation needed to perform capillary electrophoresis is relatively simple. A basic schematic of a capillary electrophoresis system is shown in figure 6.1. The system's main components are a sample vial, source and destination vials, a capillary, electrodes, a high-voltage power supply, a detector, and a data output and handling device. The source vial, destination vial and capillary are filled with an electrolyte such as an aqueous buffer solution. To introduce the sample, the capillary inlet is placed into a vial containing the

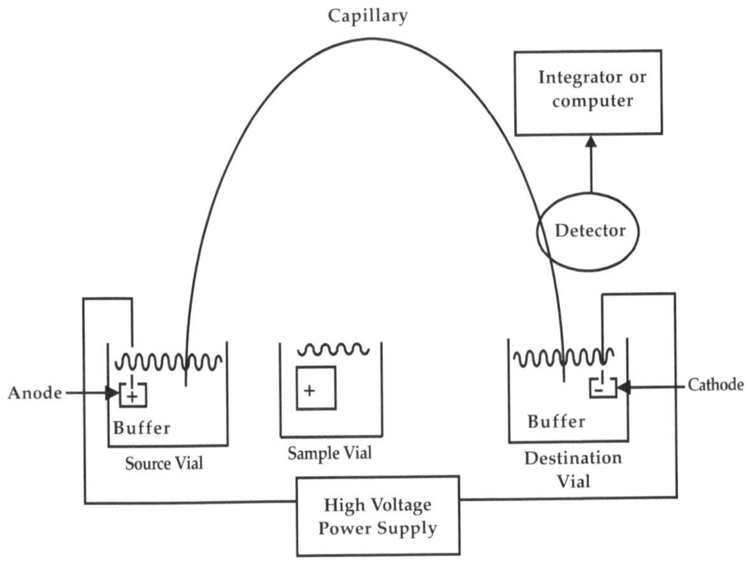

Fig. 6.1: **Diagram of Capillary Electrophoresis System**

sample and then returned to the source vial (sample is introduced into the capillary via capillary action, pressure, or siphoning). The migration of the analytes is then initiated by an electric field that is applied between the source and destination vials and is supplied to the electrodes by the high-voltage power supply. It is important to note that all ions, positive or negative, are pulled through the capillary in the same direction by electroosmotic flow, as will be explained. The analytes separate as they migrate due to their electrophoretic mobility, as will be explained, and are detected near the outlet end of the capillary. The output of the detector is sent to a data output and handling device such as an integrator or computer. The data is then displayed as an electropherogram, which reports detector response as a function of time. Separated chemical compounds appear as peaks with different retention times in an electropherogram.

Detection

Separation by capillary electrophoresis can be detected by several detection devices. The majority of commercial systems use UV or UV-Vis absorbance as their primary mode of detection. In these systems, a section of the capillary itself is used as the detection cell. The use of on-tube detection enables detection of separated analytes with no loss of resolution. In general, capillaries used in capillary electrophoresis are coated with a polymer for increased stability. The portion of the capillary used for UV detection, however, must be optically transparent. Bare capillaries can break relatively easily and, as a result, capillaries with transparent coatings are available to increase the stability of the cell window. The path length of the detection cell in capillary electrophoresis (~ 50 micrometers) is far less than that of a traditional UV cell (~ 1 cm). According to the Beer-Lambert law, the sensitivity of the detector is proportional to the path length of the cell. To improve the sensitivity, the path length can be increased, though this results in a loss of resolution. The capillary tube itself can be expanded at the detection point, creating a "bubble cell" with a longer path length or additional tubing can be added at the detection point as shown in fig. 6.2. Both of these methods, however, will decrease the resolution of the separation.

Fluorescence detection can also be used in capillary electrophoresis for samples that naturally fluoresce or are chemically modified to contain fluorescent tags. This mode of detection offers high sensitivity and improved selectivity for these samples, but cannot be utilized for samples that do not fluoresce. The set-up for fluorescence detection in a capillary electrophoresis system can be complicated. The method requires that the light beam be focused on the capillary, which can be difficult for many light sources. Laser-induced fluorescence has been used in CE systems with detection limits as low as 10-18 to 10-21 mol. The sensitivity

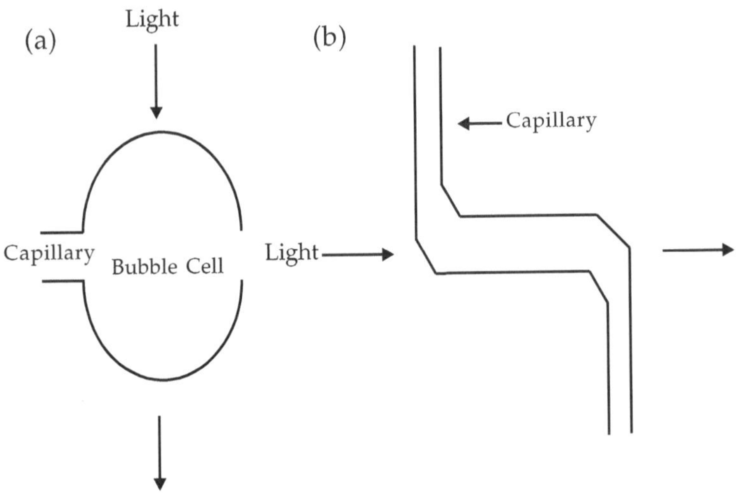

Fig. 6.2: **Techniques for Interesting the Path Length of the Capillary (a) Bubble cell and (b) z-cell (additional tubing)**

of the technique is attributed to the high intensity of the incident light and the ability to accurately focus the light on the capillary.

In order to obtain the identity of sample components, capillary electrophoresis can be directly coupled with mass spectrometers or Surface Enhanced Raman Spectroscopy (SERS). In most systems, the capillary outlet is introduced into an ion source that utilizes electrospray ionization (ESI). The resulting ions are then analyzed by the mass spectrometer. This set-up requires volatile buffer solutions, which will affect the range of separation modes that can be employed and the degree of resolution that can be achieved. The measurement and analysis are mostly done with a specialized gel analysis software.

For CE-SERS, capillary electrophoresis eluants can be deposited onto a SERS-active substrate. Analyte retention times can be translated into spatial distance by moving the SERS-active substrate at a constant rate during capillary electrophoresis. This allows the subsequent spectroscopic technique to be applied to specific eluants for identification with high sensitivity. SERS-active substrates can be chosen that do not interfere with the spectrum of the analytes.

Modes of Separation

The separation of compounds by capillary electrophoresis is dependent on the differential migration of analytes in an applied electric field. The electrophoretic migration velocity (u_p) of an analyte toward the electrode of opposite charge is:

$$u_p = \mu_p E$$

where μ_p is the electrophoretic mobility and E is the electric field strength. The electrophoretic mobility is proportional to the ionic charge of a sample and inversely proportional to any frictional forces present in the buffer. When two species in a sample have different charges or experience different frictional forces, they will separate from one another as they migrate through a buffer solution. The frictional forces experienced by an analyte ion depend on the viscosity (?) of the medium and the size and shape of the ion Accordingly, the electrophoretic mobility of an analyte at a given pH is given by:

$$\mu_p = \frac{z}{6\pi\eta r}$$

where z is the net charge of the analyte and *r* is the Stokes radius of the analyte. The Stokes radius is given by:

$$r = \frac{kBT}{6\pi\eta D}$$

where k_B is the Boltzmann constant, and *T* is the temperature, D is the diffusion coefficient. These equations indicate that the electrophoretic mobility of the analyte is proportional to the charge of the analyte and inversely proportional to its radius. The electrophoretic mobility can be determined experimentally from the migration time and the field strength:

$$\mu_p = \left(\frac{L}{t_r}\right)\left(\frac{Lt}{V}\right)$$

where L is the distance from the inlet to the detection point, tr is the time required for the analyte to reach the detection point (migration time), V is the applied voltage (field strength), and Lt is the total length of the capillary. Since only charged ions are affected by the electric field, neutral analytes are poorly separated by capillary electrophoresis.

The velocity of migration of an analyte in capillary electrophoresis will also depend upon the rate of electroosmotic flow (EOF) of the buffer solution. In a typical system, the electroosmotic flow is directed toward the negatively charged cathode so that the buffer flows through the capillary from the source vial to the destination vial. Separated by differing electrophoretic mobilities, analytes migrate toward the electrode of opposite charge As a result, negatively charged analytes are attracted to the positively charged anode, counter to the EOF, while positively charged analytes are attracted to the cathode, in agreement with the EOF as depicted in fig. 6.3.

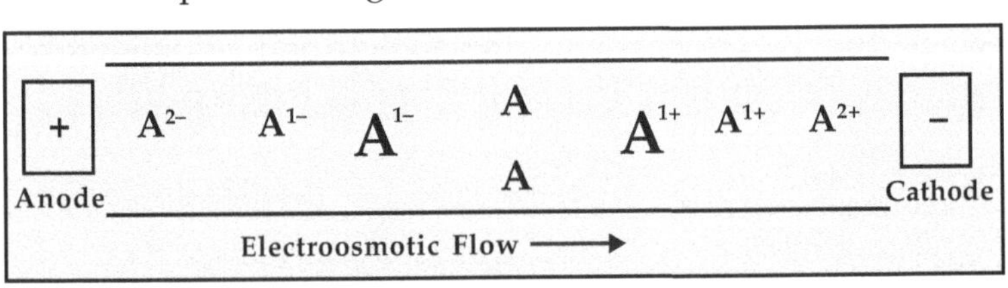

Fig. 6.3: **Diagram of the separation of charged and neutral analytes (A) according to their respective electrophoretic and electroosmotic flow mobilities**

The velocity of the electroosmotic flow, u_o can be written as:

$$u_o = \mu_o E$$

where μ_o is the electroosmotic mobility, which is defined as:

$$\mu_0 = \frac{\varepsilon\varsigma}{\eta}$$

where ? is the zeta potential of the capillary wall, and e is the relative permittivity of the buffer solution. Experimentally, the electroosmotic mobility can be determined by measuring the retention time of a neutral analyte. The velocity (u) of an analyte in an electric field can then be defined as:

$$u_p + u_o = (\mu_p + \mu_o)E$$

Since the electroosmotic flow of the buffer solution is generally greater than that of the electrophoretic flow of the analytes, all analytes are carried along with the buffer solution toward the cathode. Even small, triply charged anions can be redirected to the cathode by the relatively powerful EOF of the buffer solution. Negatively charged analytes are retained longer in the capilliary due to their conflicting electrophoretic mobilities. The order of migration seen by the detector is shown in fig. 6.3 small multiply charged cations migrate quickly and small multiply charged anions are retained strongly.

Electroosmotic flow is observed when an electric field is applied to a solution in a capillary that has fixed charges on its interior wall. Charge is accumulated on the inner surface of a capillary when a buffer solution is placed inside the capillary. In a fused-silica capillary, silanol (Si-OH) groups attached to the interior wall of the capillary are ionized to negatively charged silanoate ($Si\text{-}O^-$) groups at pH values greater than three. Thc ionization of the capillary wall can be enhanced by first running a basic solution, such as NaOH or KOH through the capillary prior to introducing the buffer solution. Attracted to the negatively charged silanoate groups, the positively charged cations of the buffer solution will form two inner layers of cations (called the diffuse double layer or the electrical double layer) on the capillary wall as shown in figure 6.4. The first layer is referred to as the fixed layer because it is held tightly to the silanoate groups. The outer layer, called the mobile layer, is farther from the silanoate groups. The mobile cation layer is pulled in the direction of the negatively charged cathode when an electric field is applied. Since these cations are solvated, the bulk buffer solution migrates with the mobile layer, causing the electroosmotic flow of the buffer solution. Other capillaries including Teflon capillaries also exhibit electroosmotic flow. The EOF of these capillaries is probably the result of adsorption of the electrically charged ions of the buffer onto the capillary walls The rate of EOF is dependent on the field strength and the charge density of the capillary wall. The wall's charge density is proportional to the pH of the buffer solution. The electroosmotic flow will increase with pH until all of the available silanols lining the wall of the capillary are fully ionized.

Efficiency and Resolution

The number of theoretical plates, or separation efficiency, in capillary electrophoresis is given by:

$$N = \frac{\mu V}{2D_m}$$

where N is the number of theoretical plates, μ is the apparent mobility in the separation medium and Dm is the diffusion coefficient of the analyte. According to this equation, the efficiency of separation is only limited by diffusion and is proportional to the strength of the electric field. The efficiency of capillary electrophoresis separations is typically much higher than the efficiency of other separation techniques like HPLC. Unlike HPLC, in capillary electrophoresis there is no mass transfer between phases. In addition, the flow profile in EOF-driven systems is flat, rather than the rounded laminar flow profile characteristic of the pressure-driven flow in chromatography columns as shown in figure 6.5. As a result, EOF does not significantly contribute to band broadening as in pressure-driven chromatography. Capillary electrophoresis separations can have several hundred thousand theoretical plates.

The resolution (R_s) of capillary electrophoresis separations can be written as:

$$R_s = \frac{1}{4}\left(\frac{\Delta\mu_p\sqrt{N}}{\mu_p + \mu_o}\right)$$

According to this equation, maximum resolution is reached when the electrophoretic and electroosmotic mobilities are similar in magnitude and opposite in sign. In addition, it can be seen that high resolution requires lower velocity and, correspondingly, increased analysis time.

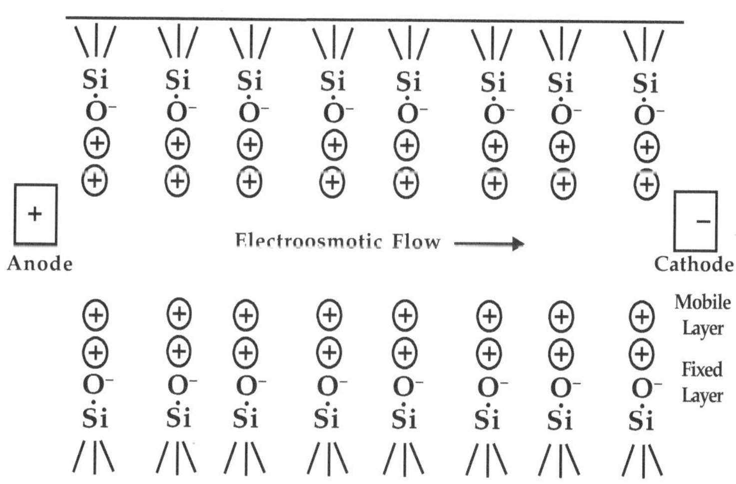

Fig. 6.4: **Depiction of the interior of a fused silica gel capillary in the presence of buffer solution**

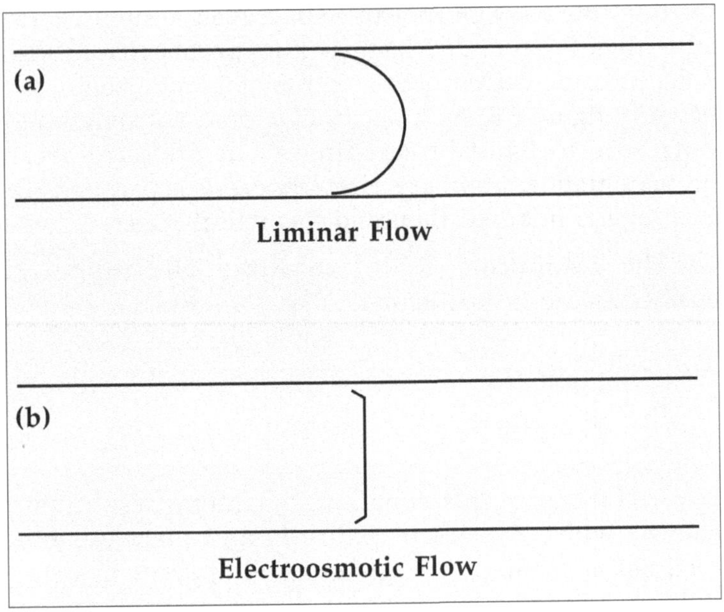

Fig. 6.5: **Flow profiles of laminar and electroosmotic flow**

Related Techniques

As discussed above, separations in a capillary electrophoresis system are typically dependent on the analytes having different electrophoretic mobilities. However, some classes of analyte cannot be separated by this effect because they are neutral (uncharged) or because they may not differ significantly in electrophoretic mobility. However, there are several techniques that can help separate such analytes with a capillary electrophoresis system. Adding a surfactant to the electrolyte can facilitate the separation of neutral compounds by micellar electrokinetic chromatography. Charged polymers such as DNA can be separated by filling the capillary with a gel matrix that retards longer strands more than shorter strands. This is called capillary gel electrophoresis. This is a high-resolution alternative to slab gel electrophoresis. Some capillary electrophoresis systems can also be used for microscale liquid chromatography or capillary electrochromatography. A capillary electrophoresis system can also be used for isotachophoresis, isoelectric focusing, and affinity electrophoreis.

7

Questioned Document Examination

Questioned document examination (QDE) is the forensic science discipline pertaining to documents that are (or may be) in dispute in a court of law. The primary purpose of questioned/forensic document examination is to answer questions about a disputed document using a variety of scientific processes and methods. Many examinations involve a comparison of the questioned document, or components of the document, to a set of known standards. The most common type of examination involves handwriting wherein the examiner tries to address concerns about potential authorship.

A document examiner is often asked to determine if a questioned item originated from the same source as the known item(s), then present their opinion on the matter in court as an expert witness. Other common tasks include determining what has happened to a document, determining when a document was produced, or deciphering information on the document that has been obscured, obliterated or erased.

The discipline is known by many names including forensic document examination, document examination, diplomatics, handwriting examination, or sometimes handwriting analysis, although the latter term is not often used as it may be confused with graphology. Likewise a forensic document examiner is not to be confused with a graphologist, and *vice versa*.

Many document examiners receive extensive training in all of the different aspects of the discipline. As a result they are competent to address a wide variety of questions about document evidence. However, this "broad specialization" approach has not been universally adopted.

In some locales, a clear distinction is made between the terms forensic document examiner and a forensic handwriting expert/examiner. In such cases, the former term refers to examiners who focus on non-handwriting examination types while the latter refers to those trained exclusively to do handwriting examinations. Even in places where the more general meaning is common, such as North American or Australia, there are many individuals who have specialized training only in certain relatively limited areas. As the terminology varies from jurisdiction to jurisdiction, it is important to clarify the meaning of the title used by any given individual professing to be a "forensic document examiner".

Scope of Document Examination

A forensic document examiner is intimately linked to the legal system as a forensic scientist. Forensic science is the application of science to address issues under consideration in the legal system.

Common criminal charges involved in a document examination case fall into the "white-collar crime" category. These include identity theft, forgery, counterfeiting, fraud, or uttering a forged document. Questioned documents are often important in other contexts simply because documents are used in so many different contexts and for so many different purposes. For example, a person may commit murder and forge a suicide note. This is an example wherein a document is produced directly as a fundamental part of a crime. More often a questioned document is simply the by-product of normal day-to-day business or personal activities.

A forensic document examiner deals with items that form part of a case which may or may not come before a court of law. The many types of possible examinations include the following:

- Handwriting (cursive/printing) and Signatures.
- Typewriters, Photocopiers, Laser printers, Ink Jet Printers, Fax machines.
- Chequewriters, Rubber stamps, Price markers, Label makers.
- Printing Processes.
- Ink, Pencil, Paper.
- Alterations, additions, erasures, obliterations.
- Indentations.
- Sequence of Strokes.
- Physical Matching.

ASTM (American Society for Testing and Material) Standard E444-98 (Standard Description of Scope of Work Relating to Forensic Document Examination) indicates there are four components to the work of a forensic document examiner. It states that an examiner "makes scientific examinations, comparisons, and analyses of documents in order to:

- establish genuineness or nongenuineness, or to expose forgery, or to reveal alterations, additions or deletions;
- identify or eliminate persons as the source of handwriting;

- identify or eliminate the source of typewriting or other impression, marks, or relative evidence; and
- write reports or give testimony, when needed, to aid the users of the examiner's services in understanding the examiner's findings."

Some forensic document examiners limit their work to the examination and comparison of handwriting but most inspect and examine the whole document in accordance with this ASTM standard.

What sort of documents are examined?

Documents feature prominently in all manner of business and personal affairs. Almost any type of document may become disputed in an investigation or litigation. For example, a questioned document may be a sheet of paper bearing handwriting or mechanically-produced text such as a ransom note, a forged cheque or a business contract. Or it may be some material not normally thought of as a 'document'. Forensic document examiners define the word "document" in a very broad sense as being any material bearing marks, signs or symbols intended to convey a message or meaning to someone. This encompasses traditional paper documents but also includes things like graffiti on a wall, stamp impressions on meat products, or covert markings hidden in a written letter, among other things.

Historical Cases

- The National Archives forgeries (aka Martin Allen forgeries or Himmler forged documents) (2005)
- The Killian memos (2004)
- The Martha Stewart trial (2004)
- The Yellowcake Forgery (2003)
- Nina Wang and the Teddy Wang will forgery (2002)

- The JonBenét Ramsey murder (1996)
- The Paul Jennings Hill murders (1994)
- The Hitler Diaries (1983)
- The Mark Hofmann forgeries and murders (1980-84)
- The Mormon Will (1978)
- Clifford Irving and the Howard Hughes biography (1972)
- The Zodiac Killer (1969)
- The Lindbergh kidnapping (1934) where comparison of the ransom note and Hauptman's handwriting was crucial
- The Howland will forgery trial (1868)

Although the crimes were committed some time before the discipline of document examination was firmly established, the letters of the Jack the Ripper case have since been examined in great detail.

Candidacy

A person who desires to enter a career of forensic document examination must possess certain traits and abilities. First and foremost, excellent eyesight is required in order to see fine details that are otherwise inconspicuous. The aspirant must also pass a form blindness test in order to ensure that the aspirant does not suffer from the condition of being unable to tell apart two similarly-appearing, yet different, items. Similarly successful completion of a test for color perception is normal. A bachelor of science degree is also typically required, as it gives the aspirant a scientific background with which to approach the work in an objective manner, as well as bestowing necessary biological, physical, and chemical knowledge sometimes called upon. ASTM Standard E2388-05 (Standard Guide for Minimum Training Requirements for Forensic Document Examiners) has "an earned baccalaureate degree or equivalent" as one of several requirements. Additional desirable skills would include knowledge of paper, ink, printing processes, or handwriting.

Training

There are three possible methods of instruction for an aspiring document examiner:

- Self-education is the way in which the pioneers of the field began, as there was no other method of instruction.
- Apprenticeship has become the widespread manner in which many examiners are now taught. In fact, this is the method that is recommended by ASTM in Standard E2388-05. To conform with the ASTM standard such training "shall be the equivalent of a minimum of 24 months full-time training under the supervision of a principal trainer" and "the training program shall be successfully completed in a period not to exceed four years". The training program must also include an extensive list of specific syllabus topics outlined in ASTM Standard E2388-05.
- College and/or university programs are very limited at this time. This is due, in part, to the relatively limited demand for forensic document examiners. It also relates to the need for extensive practical experience; particularly with respect to handwriting examination. It is difficult to include this degree of practical experience in a normal academic program. Nonetheless, a few academic programs directly related to forensic document examination are:
  - Universidad Autonoma de Barcelona (Cataluña, España)
  - Oklahoma State University Grad Program in Forensic Science

- L'Université de Lausanne Institut de Police Scientifique (Lausanne, Switzerland)
- University of Central Lancashire, MSc in Document Analysis (Lancashire, UK)
- Institut fur Schrift- und Urkundenuntersuchung (Mannheim, Germany

A more extensive listing relating to forensic training may be viewed at the website for the Canadian Society of Forensic Science.

There are some distance learning courses available as well. These are taught through a virtual reality classroom and may include an apprenticeship and/or a correspondence course.

A forensic document examination trainee must learn how to present evidence before the court in clear, forceful testimony. Fledgling examiners in the later stages of training can get a glimpse into the legal process as well as a better sense of this aspect of their work through participation in a mock trial or by attending actual court hearings to observe the testimony of qualified examiners.

Examination

Handwriting Examinations

The examination of handwriting to assess potential authorship proceeds from the principle of identification which can be expressed as: "Two writings are the product of one person if the similarities, when taken in combination, are sufficiently individual and there are no fundamental unexplainable differences."

Generally, there are three stages in the process of examination In brief, they are:

- *Analysis:* The questioned and the known items are analyzed and broken down to directly perceptible characteristics.

- *Comparison:* The characteristics of the questioned item are then compared against the known standard.
- *Evaluation:* Similarities and/or differences in the compared properties are evaluated and this determines which ones are valuable for a conclusion. This depends on the uniqueness and frequency of occurrence in the items.
- Optionally, the procedure may involve a fourth step consisting of validation or peer review.

ASTM International has published a standard guide for the examination of handwriting entitled "E2290-03: Examination of Handwritten Items". Note: some of the guides listed under "Other Examinations" also apply to forensic handwriting comparisons (eg. E444 or E1658).

An alternative examination method for handwriting and signatures has been developed by the Forensic Expertise Profiling Laboratory (School of Human Biosciences, La Trobe University, Victoria, Australia).

Visit the European Network of Forensic Handwriting Experts (ENFHEX) website for information pertaining to methods endorsed by this group.

Other Examinations

Aside from E2290 mentioned above, many standard guides pertaining to the examination of questioned documents have been published by ASTM International. They include the following:

- E444-06 Scope of Work Relating to Forensic Document Examiners.
- E2195-02 Terminology: Examination of Questioned Documents.
- E1658-04 Terminology: Expressing Conclusions of Forensic Document Examiners.

- E1422-05 Test Methods for Forensic Writing Ink Comparison.
- E1789-04 Writing Ink Identification.
- E2285-03 Examination of Mechanical Checkwriter Impressions.
- E2286-03 Examination of Dry Seal Impressions.
- E2287-03 Examination of Fracture Patterns and Paper Fibre Impressions on Single-Strike Film Ribbons and Typed Text.
- E2288-03 Physical Match of Paper Cuts, Tears, and Perforations in Forensic Document Examinations.
- E2289-03 Examination of Rubber Stamp Impressions.
- E2291-03 Indentation Examinations.
- E2325-05 Non-destructive Examination of Paper.
- E2331-04 Examination of Altered Documents.
- E2388-05 Minimum Training Requirements for Forensic Document Examiners.
- E2389-05 Examination of Documents Produced with Liquid Ink Jet Technology.
- E2390-06 Examination of Documents Produced with Toner Technology.

Common Tools of the Trade

- Excellent Eyesight
- Handlens/Loupe
- Stereomicroscope
- Electrostatic Detection Apparatus (ESDA)
- Video Spectral Comparator (VSC)

Professional Organizations

- American Society of Questioned Document Examiners (ASQDE) - USA

- American Academy of Forensic Science (AAFS) - USA
- Australasian Society of Forensic Document Examiners (ASFDE) - Australia/Asia
- ASOCIACIÓN PROFESIONAL DE PERITOS CALÍGRAFOS DE CATALUÑA (España)
- Canadian Society of Forensic Science (CSFS) - Canada
- European Network of Forensic Science Institutes (ENFSI) - Europe
- European Network of Forensic Handwriting Experts (ENFHEX)
- European Document Experts Working Group (EDEWG)
- Southwestern Association of Forensic Document Examiners (SWAFDE) - Southwest USA
- Southeastern Association of Forensic Document Examiners (SAFDE) - Southeast USA
- Forensic Science Society (FSS) - United Kingdom
- International Association for Identification (IAI)
- Gesellschaft für Forensische Schriftuntersuchung (GFS) - Frankfurt (Germany)
- National Association of Document Examiners (NADE)
- Association of Forensic Document Examiners (AFDE)
- Mid-Atlantic Association of Forensic Scientists (MAAFS)

Certification

ABFDE

A document examiner may be certified by the American Board of Forensic Document Examiners, Inc. (ABFDE), which was formed in 1977 with a grant from the U.S. Department of Justice. The ABFDE is one of two bodies accredited and recognized by the Forensic Specialties

Accreditation Board, Inc (FSAB) to carry out certification of forensic document examiners. To date, there is no federal licensing involved in the discipline. However, the court has recognized the ABFDE as reputable in the case of U.S. v. Buck, 1987, in denying a motion that claimed that handwriting comparisons were unreliable.

An applicant to the ABFDE for certification must meet the following requirements:

— they must be of good moral character, high integrity and good repute; and possess high ethical and professional standing;

— the programme is limited to permanent residents of the USA, Canada and Mexico;

— must possess a bachelor degree (or higher) from an accredited academic institution, or equivalent;

— must successfully have completed a full-time training program of at least 2 years duration in a forensic laboratory recognized by the Board;

— must provide three references from forensic document examiners certified or recognized by the Board;

— must be actively engaged in the full-time practise of forensic document examination; and

— must demonstrate a record of appropriate professional activity in forensic document examination.

In addition to meeting the basic requirements listed above, an applicant must also pass comprehensive written, practical and oral examinations that explore the wide range of problems encountered in document examination.

Certificates issued by the ABFDE are valid for five years, and can be renewed. During that five-year renewal period, the diplomate must earn at least 40 continuing education credits. Credits are awarded for a variety of related activities, such as attendance and participation at

ABFDE recognized forensic meeting and programs, and publication of articles in journals recognized by the Board. Individuals holding a valid Certificate of Qualification issued by the ABFDE will use the designation "Diplomate of the American Board of Forensic Document Examiners."

ABFDE History

John J. Harris sat as the inaugural chairman in 1977, and in the following year, the Committee of Certification was created. The board states its objectives as "to establish, maintain and enhance standards of qualification for those who practice forensic document examination, and to certify applicants who comply with ABFDE requirements for qualified specialists."

Backed by the American Society of Questioned Document Examiners (ASQDE), Canadian Society of Forensic Science (CSFS), and the American Academy of Forensic Science (AAFS), the ABFDE ensures that the applicant satisfies a number of standardized requirements with regular testing to ensure that the examiner performs at the same high level of professionalism, as do the other people in the trade. More-so than merely denoting the attainment of certain academic and minimum standards, board certification indicates that the examiner cares enough about the profession to spend time and effort to adequately prepare himself or herself to properly serve the public. Courts must assess the credibility of the document examiner as an expert witness and to do this they will often rely upon the examiner's reputation in the profession together with his or her affiliations with credible professional organizations.

8

Crime

Societies define crime as the breach of one or more rules or laws for which some governing authority or force may ultimately prescribe a punishment.

The word *'crime'* originates from the Latin word *crimen* (genitive: *criminis*), reflecting the Latin root *cerno* = "I decide, I give judgement". Originally the Latin word *crimen* meant "charge (in law), guilt, accusation".

When society deems informal relationships and sanctions insufficient to establish and maintain a desired social order, there may result more formalized systems of social control imposed by a government, or more broadly, by a State. With the institutional and legal machinery at their disposal, agents of the State can compel individuals to conform to behavioral codes, and can punish those that do not.

Authorities employ various mechanisms to regulate behaviour, including rules codified into laws, policing people to ensure they comply with those laws, and other policies and practices designed to prevent crime. In addition, authorities provide remedies and sanctions, and collectively these constitute a criminal justice system. Not all breaches of the law, however, are considered crimes, for example, breaches of contract and other civil law offences.

The label of "crime" and the accompanying social stigma normally confine their scope to those activities seen as injurious to the general population or the State, including some that cause serious loss or damage to individuals. The label is intended to assert an hegemony of a dominant population, or to reflect a consensus of condemnation for the identified behavior and to justify a punishment imposed by the State, in the event that an accused person is tried and convicted of a crime. Usually, the perpetrator of the crime is a natural person, but in some jurisdictions and in some moral environments, legal persons are also considered to have the capability of committing crimes.

Definition

A normative definition views crime as deviant behavior that violates prevailing norms – cultural standards prescribing how humans ought to behave normally. This approach considers the complex realities surrounding the concept of crime and seeks to understand how changing social, political, psychological, and economic conditions may affect the current definitions of crime and the form of the legal, law-enforcement, and penal responses made by society.

These structural realities remain fluid and often contentious. For example: as cultures change and the political environment shifts, societies may criminalise or decriminalise certain behaviours, which will directly affect the statistical crime rates, determine the allocation of resources for the enforcement of laws, and (re-)influence the general public opinion.

Similarly, changes in the collection and/or calculation of data on crime may affect the public perceptions of the extent of any given "crime problem". All such adjustments to crime statistics, allied with the experience of people in their everyday lives, shape attitudes on the extent to which the State should use law to enforce any particular social norm. There are many ways in which behaviour can be controlled without having to resort to the criminal justice system.

Indeed, in those cases where no clear consensus exists on a given norm, the use of criminal law by the group in power to prohibit the behaviour of another group may count as an improper limitation of the second group's freedom, and the ordinary members of society may lose some of their respect for the law in general — whether the disputed law is actively enforced or not.

Legislatures pass laws (called *mala prohibita*) that define crimes which violate social norms. These laws vary from time to time and from place to place: note variations in gambling laws, for example. Other crimes, called *mala in se*, count as outlawed in almost all societies, (murder, theft and rape, for example).

Criminalization

One can view criminalization as a procedure intended as a pre-emptive, harm-reduction device, using the threat of punishment as a deterrent to those proposing to engage in the behavior causing harm. The State becomes involved because they usually believe costs of not criminalizing (i.e. allowing the harms to continue unabated) outweigh the costs of criminalizing it (i.e. restricting individual liberty in order to minimize harm to others).

Criminalization may provide future harm-reduction even after a crime, assuming those incarcerated for committing crimes are more likely to cause harm in the future.

Criminalization might be intended as a way to make potential criminals pay for their crimes. In this case, criminalization is a way to set the price that one must pay (to society) for certain actions that are considered detrimental to society as a whole. In this sense criminalization can be viewed as nothing more than State-sanctioned revenge.

States control the process of criminalization because:

- Even if victims recognize their own role as victims, they may not have the resources to investigate and seek legal redress for the injuries suffered: the enforcers formally appointed by the State have the expertise and the resources.
- The victims may only want compensation for the injuries suffered, while remaining indifferent to a possible desire for deterrence on the fundamental divergence between the private and the social motivation for using the legal system).
- Fear of retaliation may deter victims or witnesses of crimes from taking any action. Even in policed societies, fear may inhibit reporting or co-operation in a trial.
- Victims, on their own, may lack the economies of scale which might allow them to administer a penal system, let alone to collect any fines levied by a court Garoupa & Klerman (2002) warn that a rent-seeking government has as its primary motivation to maximize revenue and so, if offenders have sufficient wealth, a rent-seeking government will act more aggressively than a social-welfare-maximizing government in enforcing laws against minor crimes (usually with a fixed penalty such as parking and routine traffic violations), but more laxly in enforcing laws against major crimes.
- As a result of the crime, victims may die or become incapacitated.

History

The idea of crime has a long history. Some religious communities regard sin as a crime; some may even highlight the crime of sin very early in legendary or mythological accounts of origins — note the tale of Adam and Eve and the theory of original sin. What one group considers a crime may cause or ignite war or conflict. However, the earliest known civilizations had codes of law, containing both civil and penal rules mixed together, though not always in recorded form.

The Sumerians produced the earliest surviving written codes Urukagina had an early code that does not survive; a later king, Ur-Nammu, left the earliest extant written law-system, the Code of Ur-Nammu, which prescribed a formal system of penalties for specific cases in 57 articles. The Sumerians later issued other codes, including the "code of Lipit-Ishtar". This code, from the 20th century BCE, contains some fifty articles, and has been reconstructed by comparison among several sources.

> The Sumerian was deeply conscious of his personal rights and resented any encroachment on them, whether by his King, his superior, or his equal. No wonder that the Sumerians were the first to compile laws and law codes.

Successive legal codes in Babylon, including the code of Hammurabi, reflected Mesopotamian society's belief that law derived from the will of the gods Many states at this time functioned as theocracies, with codes of conduct largely religious in origin or reference.

Sir Henry Maine (1861) studied the ancient codes available in his day, and failed to find any criminal law in the "modern" sense of the word. While modern systems distinguish between offences against the "State" or "Community", and offences against the "Individual", the so-called penal law of ancient communities did not deal with "crimes" (Latin: *crimina*), but with "wrongs" (Latin: *delicta*). Thus the Hellenic laws treated all forms of theft, assault, rape, and murder as private wrongs, and left action for enforcement up to the victims or their survivors. The earliest systems seem to have lacked formal courts.

The Romans systematized law and applied it across the Roman Empire. Again, the initial rules of Roman Law regarded assaults as a matter of private compensation. The most significant Roman Law concept involved *dominion* The *pater familias* owned all the family and its property (including slaves); the *pater* enforced matters involving interference with any property. The *Commentaries* of Gaius on the Twelve Tables treated *furtum* (in modern parlance: theft) as a tort.

Similarly, assault and violent robbery involved trespass as to the *pater's* property (so, for example, the rape of a slave could become the subject of compensation to the *pater* as having trespassed on his "property"), and breach of such laws created a *vinculum juris* (an obligation of law) that only the payment of monetary compensation (modern "damages") could discharge. Similarly, the consolidated Teutonic laws of the Germanic tribes ncluded a complex system of monetary compensations for what courts would now consider the complete range of criminal offences against the person, from murder down.

Even though Rome abandoned its Britannic provinces sometime around 400 AD, the Germanic mercenaries – who had largely become instrumental in enforcing Roman rule in Britannia – acquired ownership of land there and continued to use a mixture of Roman and Teutonic Law, with much written down under the early Anglo-Saxon Kings. But only when a more centralized English monarchy emerged following the Norman invasion, and the kings of England attempted to assert power over the land and its peoples, did the modern concept emerge, namely of a crime not only as an offence against the "individual", but also as a wrong against the "State".

This idea came from common law, and the earliest conception of a criminal act involved events of such major significance that the "State" had to usurp the usual functions of the civil tribunals, and direct a special law or *privilegium* against the perpetrator. All the earliest English criminal trials involved wholly extraordinary and arbitrary courts without any settled law to apply, whereas the civil (delictual) law operated in a highly developed and consistent manner (except where a King wanted to raise money by selling a new form of writ). The development of the idea that the "State" dispenses justice in a court only emerges in parallel with or after the emergence of the concept of sovereignty.

In continental Europe, Roman law persisted, but with a stronger influence from the Church Coupled with the more diffuse political structure based on smaller State units, various different legal traditions emerged, remaining more strongly rooted in Roman jurisprudence modified to meet the prevailing political climate.

In Scandinavia the effect of Roman law did not become apparent until the 17th century, and the courts grew out of the *things* — the assemblies of the people. The people decided the cases (usually with largest freeholders dominating). This system later gradually developed into a system with a royal judge nominating a number of most esteemed men of the parish as his board, fulfilling the function of "the people" of yore.

From the Hellenic system onwards, the policy rationale for requiring the payment of monetary compensation for wrongs committed has involved the avoidance of feuding between clans and families If compensation could mollify families' feelings, this would help to keep the peace. On the other hand, the threat of feudal warfare was played down also by the institution of oaths. Both in archaic Greece and in medieval Scandinavia, the accused was released if he could get a sufficient number of male relatives to swear him unguilty. This may be compared with the United Nations Security Council where the veto power of the permanent members ensures that the organization is not drawn into crises where it could not enforce its decisions.

These means of restraining private feuds did not always work, and sometimes prevented the fulfillment of justice. But in the earliest times the "state" did not always provide an independent police force. Thus criminal law grew out of what is now tort; and, in real terms, many acts and omissions classified as crimes actually overlap with civil-law concepts.

The development of sociological thought from the 19th century onwards prompted some fresh views on crime and criminality, and fostered the beginnings of criminology as a study of crime in society. Nietzsche noted a link between crime and creativity – in *The Birth of Tragedy* he asserted: "The best and brightest that man can acquire he must obtain by crime". In the 20th century Michel Foucault in *Discipline and Punish* made a study of criminalization as a coercive method of state control.

Natural-law Theory

Justifying the State's use of force to coerce compliance with its laws has proven a consistent theoretical problem. One of the earliest justifications involved the theory of natural law. This posits that the nature of the world or of human beings underlies the standards of morality or constructs them. Thomas Aquinas said: "the rule and measure of human acts is the reason, which is the first principle of human acts" (Aquinas, ST I-II, Q.90, A.I), i.e. since people are by nature rational beings, it is morally appropriate that they should behave in a way that conforms to their rational nature. Thus, to be valid, any law must conform to natural law and coercing people to conform to that law is morally acceptable. William Blackstone (1979: 41) describes the thesis:

> "This law of nature, being co-eval with mankind and dictated by God himself, is of course superior in obligation to any other. It is binding over all the globe, in all countries, and at all times: no human laws are of any validity, if contrary to this; and such of them as are valid derive all their force, and all their authority, mediately or immediately, from this original."

But John Austin (1790-1859), an early positivist, applied utilitarianism in accepting the calculating nature of human beings and the existence of an objective morality, but denied that the legal validity of a norm depends on whether its content conforms to morality. Thus in Austinian terms a moral code can objectively determine what people ought to do, the law can embody whatever norms the legislature decrees to achieve social utility, but every individual remains free to choose what he or she will do. Similarly, Hart (1961) saw the law as an aspect of sovereignty, with lawmakers able to adopt any law as a means to a moral end.

Thus the necessary and sufficient conditions for the truth of a proposition of law simply involved internal logic and consistency, and that the state's agents used state power with responsibility. Dworkin (2005) rejects Hart's theory and argues that fundamental among political rights is the right of each individual to the equal respect and concern of those who govern him. He offers a theory of compliance overlaid by a theory of deference (the citizen's duty to obey the law) and a theory of enforcement, which identifies the legitimate goals of enforcement and punishment. Legislation must conform to a theory of legitimacy, which describes the circumstances under which a particular person or group is entitled to make law, and a theory of legislative justice, which describes the law they are entitled or obliged to make.

Indeed, despite everything, the majority of natural-law theorists have accepted the idea of enforcing the prevailing morality as a primary function of the law. This view entails the problem that it makes any moral criticism of the law impossible in that, if conformity with natural law forms a necessary condition for legal validity, all valid law must, by definition, be morally just. Thus, on this line of reasoning, the legal validity of a norm necessarily entails its moral justice.

One can solve this problem by granting some degree of moral relativism and accepting that norms may evolve over time and, therefore, one can criticize the continued enforcement of old laws in the light of the current norms. People may find such law acceptable, but the use of State power to coerce citizens to comply with that law is not morally justified. In more modern conceptions of the theory, crime is characterized as the violation of individual rights.

Since society considers so many rights as natural (hence the term "right") rather than man-made, what constitutes a crime is also natural, in contrast to laws (which are man-made). Adam Smith illustrates this view, saying that a smuggler would be an excellent citizen, "...had not the laws of his country made that a crime which nature never meant to be so."

Natural-law theory therefore distinguishes between "criminality" (which derives from human nature) and "illegality" (which originates with the interests of those in power). Lawyers sometimes express the two concepts with the phrases *malum in se* and *malum prohibitum* respectively. They regard a crime *malum in se* as inherently criminal; whereas a crime *malum prohibitum* (the argument goes) counts as criminal only because the law has decreed it so.

This view leads to a seeming paradox: an act can be illegal that is no crime, while a criminal act could be perfectly legal. Many Enlightenment thinkers (such as Adam Smith and the American Founding Fathers) subscribed to this view to some extent, and it remains influential among so-called classical liberals and libertarians

Distinctions

Governments criminalise antisocial behaviour — and treat it within a system of offences against society — in order to justify the imposition of punishment. Authorities make a series of distinctions depending on the passive subject of the crime (the victim), or on the offended interest(s), in crimes against:

- Honour
- Administration of justice

- Law and order
- Patrimony
- the person
- Personality of the State
- Personality rights
- Public administration
- Public economy, industry, and commerce
- Public morality
- religious sentiment and faith
- Rights of the citizen.

Or one can categorise crimes depending on the related punishment, with sentencing tariffs prescribed in line with the perceived seriousness of the offence. Thus fines and noncustodial sentences may address the least serious crimes, and lengthy imprisonment or (in some States) capital punishment the most serious.

Types

Researchers and commentators may classify crime into categories, including:

- property crime
- public order crime
- violent crime

Analysts can also group crimes by severity, some common category-terms including:

- felonies (US and previously UK)
- indictable offences (UK)
- infractions
- misdemeanors (US and previously UK)
- summary offences (UK)

U.S. Classification

In the United States since 1930, the FBI has tabulated Uniform Crime Reports (UCR) annually from crime data submitted by law enforcement agencies across the United States. Officials compile this data at the city, county, and state levels into the Uniform crime reports (UCR). They classify violations of laws which derive from common law as Part I (index) crimes in UCR data, further categorised as violent or property crimes. Part I violent crimes include murder and criminal homicide (voluntary manslaughter), forcible rape, aggravated assault, and robbery; while Part I property crimes include burglary, arson, larceny/theft, and motor-vehicle theft. All other crimes count as Part II crimes.

For convenience, such lists usually include infractions although, in the U.S., they may come into the sphere not of the criminal law, but rather of the civil law. Compare tortfeasance.

Booking arrests requires detention for a time-frame ranging 1 to 24 hours.

Crimes in International Law

Crimes defined by treaty as crimes against international law include:

- crimes against peace
- crimes of apartheid
- genocide
- piracy
- the slave trade
- waging a war of aggression war crimes

From the point of view of State-centric law, extraordinary procedures (usually international courts) may prosecute such crimes. Note the role of the International Criminal Court at The Hague in the Netherlands.

Popular opinion often associates international law with the concept of opposing terrorism — seen as a crime as distinct from warfare.

Religion and Crime

Socially accepted or imposed religious morality has influenced secular jurisdictions on issues that may otherwise concern only an individual's conscience. Activities sometimes criminalized on religious grounds include (for example) alcohol-consumption (prohibition), abortion and stem-cell research. In various historical and present-day societies institutionalized religions have established systems of earthly justice which punish crimes against the divine will and specific devotional, organizational and other rules under specific codes, such as Islamic sharia or Roman Catholic canon law.

Military Jurisdictions and States of Emergency

In the military sphere, authorities can prosecute both regular crimes and specific acts (such as mutiny or desertion) under martial-law codes that either supplant or extend civil codes in times of war.

Many constitutions contain provisions to curtail freedoms and criminalize otherwise tolerated behaviors under a state of emergency in the event of war, natural disaster or civil unrest. Such undesired activities may include assembly in the streets, violation of curfew, or possession of firearms.

Employee Crime

Two common types of employee crime exist: embezzlement and sabotage.

The complexity and anonymity of computers may help criminal employees camouflage their operations. The victims of the most costly scams include banks, brokerage houses.

Most people guilty of embezzlement do not have criminal histories Embezzlers tend to have a gripe against their employer, have financial problems, or simply an inability to resist the temptation of a loop-hole they have found.[*citation needed*] Screening and background checks on perspective employees can help in prevention; however, many laws make some types of screening difficult or even illegal. Fired or disgruntled employees sometimes sabotage their company's computer system as a form of 'pay back' This sabotage may take the form of a Logic bomb, a computer virus, or creating general havoc.

Some places of employment have developed measures in an attempt to combat and prevent employee crime. Places of employment sometimes implement security measures such as cameras, fingerprint records of employees, and background checks. Although privacy-advocates have questioned such methods, they serve the interests of the organisations using them. Not only do these methods help prevent employee crime, but they protect the company from punishment and/or lawsuits for negligent hiring.

Criminal Procedure

Criminal procedure refers to the legal process for adjudicating claims that someone has violated criminal law.

Differences Between Civil Law and Common Law Systems

- The majority of civil law jurisdictions follow an inquisitorial system of adjudication, in which judges undertake an active investigation of the claims by examining the evidence and preparing reports.
- In common law systems, the trial judge, the investigators, and the prosecution are separate functions. After an investigation has been completed and charges lodged, the trial judge presides over proceedings grounded in the adversarial system of dispute resolution, where both the prosecution and the defense prepare arguments to be presented before the court. Some civil law systems have adopted adversarial procedures.

Proponents of either system tend to consider that their system defends best the rights of the innocent. There is a tendency in common law countries to believe that civil law/ inquisitorial systems do not have the so-called "presumption of innocence", and do not provide the defense with adequate rights. Conversely, there is a tendency in countries with an inquisitorial system to believe that accusatorial proceedings unduly favour rich defendants who can afford large legal teams, and are very harsh on poorer defendants.

Basic Rights

Currently, in many countries with a democratic system and the rule of law, criminal procedure puts the burden of proof on the prosecution – that is, it is up to the prosecution to prove that the defendant is guilty, as opposed to having the defense prove that s/he is innocent, and any doubt is resolved in favor of the defendant. This provision, known as the presumption of innocence, is required, for example, in the 46 countries that are members of the Council of Europe, under Article 6 of the European Convention on Human Rights, and it is included in other human rights documents. However, in practice it operates somewhat differently in different countries.

Similarly, all such jurisdictions allow the defendant the right to legal counsel and provide any defendant who cannot afford their own lawyer with a lawyer paid for at the public expense (which is in some countries called a "court-appointed lawyer"). Again, the efficiency of this system depends greatly on the jurisdictions. In some jurisdictions, the lawyers provided to indigent defendants are often overworked or less competent, or may not take much interest in the cases they have to defend.

Difference in Criminal and Civil Procedures

Most countries make a rather clear distinction between civil and criminal procedures. For example, an English criminal court may force a defendant to pay a fine as punishment for his crime, and he may sometimes have to pay the legal costs of the prosecution. But the victim of the crime pursues his claim for compensation in a civil, not a criminal, action In France, Italy, and many countries besides, the victim of a crime (known as the "injured party") may be awarded damages by a criminal court judge.

The standards of proof are higher in a criminal action than in a civil one since the loser risks not only financial penalties but also being sent to prison (or, in some countries, executed). In English law the prosecution must prove the guilt of a criminal "beyond reasonable doubt"; but the plaintiff in a civil action is required to prove his case "on the balance of probabilities" Thus, in a criminal case a crime cannot be proven if the person or persons judging it doubt the guilt of the suspect and have a reason (not just a feeling or intuition) for this doubt. In a civil case, however, the court weighs the evidence and decides what is most probable.

Criminal and civil procedure are different. Although some systems, including the English, allow a private citizen to bring a criminal prosecution against another citizen, criminal actions are nearly always started by the state. Civil actions, on the other hand, are usually started by individuals.

In Anglo-American law, the party bringing a criminal action (that is, in most cases, the state) is called the prosecution, but the party bringing a civil action is the plaintiff. In both kinds of action the other party is known as the defendant. A criminal case against a person called Ms. Sanchez would be described as "The People vs. (=versus, or against) Sanchez" in the United States and "R. (Regina, that is, the Queen) vs. Sanchez" in England. But a civil action between Ms. Sanchez and a Mr. Smith would be "Sanchez vs. Smith" if started by Sanchez, and "Smith vs. Sanchez" if started by Mr. Smith.

Evidence from a criminal trial is not necessarily admissible as evidence in a civil action about the same matter. For example, the victim of a road accident does not directly benefit if the driver who injured him is found guilty of the crime of careless driving. He still has to prove his case in a civil action In fact he may be able to prove his civil case even when the driver is found not guilty in the criminal trial.

Once the plaintiff has shown that the defendant is liable, the main argument in a civil court is about the amount of money, or damages, which the defendant should pay to the plaintiff.

9
Fingerprint

A fingerprint is an impression of the friction ridges on all parts of the finger A friction ridge is a raised portion of the epidermis on the palmar (palm) or digits (fingers and toes) or plantar (sole) skin, consisting of one or more connected ridge units of friction ridge skin These are sometimes known as "dermal ridges" or "dermal papillae". These ridges assist in gripping objects and may also serve to amplify vibrations triggered when fingertips brush across an uneven surface, better transmitting the signals to sensory nerves involved in fine texture perception.

Fingerprints may be deposited in natural secretions from the eccrine glands present in friction ridge skin (secretions consisting primarily of water) or they may be made by ink or other contaminants transferred from the peaks of friction skin ridges to a relatively smooth surface such as a fingerprint card The term fingerprint normally refers to impressions transferred from the pad on the last joint of fingers and thumbs, though fingerprint cards also typically record portions of lower joint areas of the fingers (which are also used to make identifications).

Fingerprints used for Identification

Fingerprint identification (sometimes referred to as *dactyloscopy* or palm print identification is the process of comparing questioned and known friction skin ridge impressions from fingers or palms or even toes to determine if the impressions are from the same finger or palm. The flexibility of friction ridge skin means that no two finger or palm prints are ever exactly alike (never identical in every detail), even two impressions recorded immediately after each other. Fingerprint identification (also referred to as individualization) occurs when an expert (or an expert computer system operating under threshold scoring rules) determines that two friction ridge impressions originated from the same finger or palm (or toe, sole) to the exclusion of all others.

A known print is the intentional recording of the friction ridges, usually with black printers ink rolled across a contrasting white background, typically a white card. Friction ridges can also be recorded digitally using a technique called Live-Scan. A latent print is the chance reproduction of the friction ridges deposited on the surface of an item. Latent prints are often fragmentary and may require chemical methods, powder, or alternative light sources in order to be visualized.

When friction ridges come in contact with a surface that is receptive to a print, material on the ridges, such as perspiration, oil, grease, ink, etc. can be transferred to the item. The factors which affect friction ridge impressions are numerous, thereby requiring examiners to undergo extensive and objective study in order to be trained to competency. Pliability of the skin, deposition pressure, slippage, the matrix, the surface, and the development medium are just some of the various factors which can cause a latent print to appear differently from the known recording of the same friction ridges. Indeed, the conditions of friction ridge deposition are unique and never duplicated. This is another reason why extensive and objective study is necessary for examiners to achieve competency.

Fingerprint Types

Latent Prints

Although the word latent means hidden or invisible, in modern usage for forensic science the term latent prints means any chance of accidental impression left by friction ridge skin on a surface, regardless of whether it is visible or invisible at the time of deposition. Electronic, chemical and physical processing techniques permit visualization of invisible latent print residue whether they are from natural secretions of the eccrine glands present on friction ridge skin (which produce palmar sweat, consisting primarily of water with various salts and organic compounds in solution), or whether the impression is in a contaminant such as motor oil, blood, paint, ink, etc.

Latent prints may exhibit only a small portion of the surface of the finger and may be smudged, distorted, overlapping, or any combination, depending on how they were deposited. For these reasons, latent prints are an "inevitable source of error in making comparisons," as they generally "contain less clarity, less content, and less undistorted information than a fingerprint taken under controlled conditions, and much, much less detail compared to the actual patterns of ridges and grooves of a finger."

Patent Prints

These are friction ridge impressions of unknown origins which are obvious to the human eye and are caused by a transfer of foreign material on the finger, onto a surface. Because they are already visible they need no enhancement, and are generally photographed instead of being lifted in the same manner as latent prints Finger deposits can include materials such as ink, dirt, or blood onto a surface.

Plastic Prints

A plastic print is a friction ridge impression from a finger or palm (or toe/foot) deposited in a material that retains the shape of the ridge detail Commonly encountered examples are melted candle wax, putty removed from the perimeter of window panes and thick grease deposits on car parts. Such prints are already visible and need no enhancement, but investigators must not overlook the potential that invisible latent prints deposited by accomplices may also be on such surfaces. After photographically recording such prints, attempts should be made to develop other non-plastic impressions deposited at natural finger/palm secretions (eccrine gland secretions) or contaminates.

Fingerprint Capture and Detection

Livescan Devices

Fingerprint image acquisition is considered the most critical step of an automated fingerprint authentication system, as it determines the final fingerprint image quality, which has drastic effects on the overall system performance. There are different types of fingerprint readers on the market, but the basic idea behind each capture approach is to measure in some way the physical difference between ridges and valleys. All the proposed methods can be grouped in two major families: solid-state fingerprint readers and optical fingerprint readers. The procedure for capturing a fingerprint using a sensor consists of rolling or touching with the finger onto a sensing area, which according to the physical principle in use (capacitive, optical, thermal, acoustic, etc.) captures the difference between valleys and ridges. When a finger touches or rolls onto a surface, the elastic skin deforms. The quantity and direction of the pressure applied by the user, the skin conditions and the projection of an irregular 3D object (the finger) onto a 2D flat plane introduce distortions, noise and inconsistencies in the captured fingerprint image. These problems result in inconsistent, irreproducible and non-uniform contacts and, during each acquisition, their effects on the same fingerprint results are different and uncontrollable. The representation of the same fingerprint changes every time the finger is placed on the sensor platen, increasing the complexity of the fingerprint matching, impairing the system performance, and consequently limiting the widespread use of this biometric technology.

Methods of Fingerprint Detection

Since the late nineteenth century, fingerprint identification methods have been used by police agencies around the world to identify both suspected criminals as well as the victims of crime. The basis of the traditional fingerprinting technique is simple. The skin on the palmar surface of the hands and feet forms ridges, so-called papillary ridges, in patterns that are unique to each individual and which do not change over time. Even identical twins (who share their DNA) do not have identical fingerprints. Fingerprints on surfaces may be described as patent or latent. Patent fingerprints are left when a substance (such as paint, oil or blood) is transferred from the finger to a surface and are easily photographed without further processing. Latent fingerprints, in contrast, occur when the natural secretions of the skin are deposited on a surface through fingertip contact, and are usually not readily visible. The best way to render latent fingerprints visible, so that they can be photographed, is complex and depends, for example, on the type of surface involved. It is generally necessary to use a 'developer', usually a powder or chemical reagent, to produce a high degree of visual contrast between the ridge patterns and the surface on which the fingerprint was left.

Developing agents depend on the presence of organic materials or inorganic salts for their effectiveness although the water deposited may also take a key role. Fingerprints are typically formed from the aqueous based secretions of the eccrine glands of the fingers and palms with additional material from sebaceous glands primarily from the forehead. The latter contamination results from the common human behaviors of touching the face and hair.

The resulting latent fingerprints consist usually of a substantial proportion of water with small traces of amino acids, chlorides etc mixed with a fatty, sebaceous component which contains a number of fatty acids, triglycerides etc Detection of the small proportion of reactive organic material such as urea and amino acids is far from easy.

Crime scene fingerprints may be detected by simple powders, or some chemicals applied at the crime scene; or more complex, usually chemical techniques applied in specialist laboratories to appropriate articles removed from the crime scene. With advances in these more sophisticated techniques some of the more advanced crime scene investigation services from around the world are now reporting that 50% or more of the total crime scene fingerprints result from these laboratory based techniques.

Although there are hundreds of reported techniques for fingerprint detection many are only of academic interest and there are only around 20 really effective methods which are currently in use in the more advanced fingerprint laboratories around the world. Some of these techniques such as Ninhydrin, Diazofluorenone, and Vacuum Metal Deposition show quite surprising sensitivity and are used operationally to great effect. Some fingerprint reagents are specific, for example Ninhydrin or Diazo-fluorenone reacting with amino acids. Others such as ethyl cyanoacrylate polymerisation, work apparently by water based catalysis and polymer growth. Vacuum metal deposition using gold and zinc has been shown to be non-specific but detect fat layers as thin as one molecule. More mundane methods such as application of fine powders work by adhesion to sebaceous deposits and possibly aqueous deposits for fresh fingerprints. The aqueous component whilst initially sometimes making up over 90% of the weight of the fingerprint can evaporate quite quickly and most may be gone in after 24 hours. After work by Duff and Menzel on the use of Argon Ion lasers for fingerprint detection a wide range of fluorescence techniques have been introduced, primarily for the enhancement of chemically developed fingerprints but also some detection of inherent fluorescence of the latent fingerprints.

The International Fingerprint Research Group (IFRG) which meets biennially, consisting of members of the leading fingerprint research groups from Europe, the US, Canada, Australia and Israel leads the way in the development, assessment and implementation of new techniques for operational fingerprint detection.

One problem is the fact that the organic component of any deposited material is readily destroyed by heat, such as occurs when a gun is fired or a bomb is detonated, when the temperature may reach as high as 500 °C. In contrast, the non-volatile, inorganic component of eccrine secretion remains intact even when exposed to temperatures as high as 600 °C.

Within the Materials Research Centre, University of Swansea, UK University of Swansea, UK, Professor Neil McMurray and Dr Geraint Williams have developed a technique that enables fingerprints to be visualised on metallic and electrically conductive surfaces without the need to develop the prints first. The technique involves the use of an instrument called a scanning Kelvin probe (SKP), which measures the voltage, or electrical potential, at pre-set intervals over the surface of an object on which a fingerprint may have been deposited. These measurements can then be mapped to produce an image of the fingerprint. A higher resolution image can be obtained by increasing the number of points sampled, but at the expense of the time taken for the process. A sampling frequency of 20 points per mm is high enough to visualise a fingerprint in sufficient detail for identification purposes and produces a voltage map in 2–3 hours. So far the technique has been shown to work effectively on a wide range of forensically important metal surfaces including iron, steel and aluminum. While initial experiments were performed on planar, i.e. flat, surfaces, the technique has been further developed to cope with severely non-planar surfaces, such as the warped cylindrical surface of fired cartridge cases. The very latest research from the department has found that physically removing a fingerprint from a metal surface, e.g. by rubbing with a tissue, does not necessarily result in the loss of all fingerprint information. The reason for this is that the differences in potential that are the basis of the visualisation are caused by the interaction of inorganic salts in the fingerprint deposit and the metal surface and begin to occur as soon as the finger comes into contact with the metal, resulting in the formation of metal – ion complexes that cannot easily be removed.

Currently, in crime scene investigations, a decision has to be made at an early stage whether to attempt to retrieve fingerprints through the use of developers or whether to swab surfaces in an attempt to salvage material for DNA fingerprinting. The two processes are mutually incompatible, as fingerprint developers destroy material that could potentially be used for DNA analysis, and swabbing is likely to make fingerprint identification impossible.

The application of the new SKP fingerprinting technique, which is non-contact and does not require the use of developers, has the potential to allow fingerprints to be retrieved while still leaving intact any material that could subsequently be subjected to DNA analysis. The University of Swansea group hope to have a forensically usable prototype in the near future and it is intended that eventually the instrument will be manufactured in sufficiently large numbers that it will be widely used by forensic teams on the frontline.

There has recently been significant worldwide interest in the technique with articles appearing in/on BBC.co.uk Sky News S4C news, The Daily Mail, FHM magazine, AOL, Yahoo news, Telegraph.co.uk, The Hindu, Taipei times, Sydney Morning Herald, San Francisco Gate, The Mercury (South Africa), Brisbane Courier Mail and many others. There has also been significant interest from the Home Office and a number of different police forces across the UK.

More information about the technique has been published in a number of scientific journals.

Classifying Fingerprints

Before computerization replaced manual filing systems in large fingerprint operations, manual fingerprint classification systems were used to categorize fingerprints based on general ridge formations (such as the presence or absence of circular patterns in various fingers), thus permitting filing and retrieval of paper records in large collections based on friction ridge patterns independent of name, birth date and other biographic data that persons may misrepresent. The most popular ten-print classification systems include the Roscher system, the Vucetich system, and the Henry Classification System. Of these systems, the Roscher system was developed in Germany and implemented in both Germany and Japan, the Vucetich system was developed in Argentina and implemented throughout South America, and the Henry system was developed in India and implemented in most English-speaking countries.

In the Henry system of classification, there are three basic fingerprint patterns: Arch, Loop and Whorl There are also more complex classification systems that further break down patterns to plain arches or tented arches Loops may be radial or ulnar, depending on the side of the hand the tail points towards. Whorls also have sub-group classifications including plain whorls, accidental whorls, double loop whorls, peacock's eye, accidental, composite, and central pocket loop whorls.

Footprints

Friction ridge skin present on the soles of the feet and toes (plantar surfaces) is as unique as ridge detail on the fingers and palms (palmar surfaces). When recovered at crime scenes or on items of evidence, sole and toe impressions are used in the same manner as finger and palm prints to effect identifications. Footprint (toe and sole friction ridge skin) evidence has been admitted in U.S. courts since 1934.

Footprints of infants, along with thumb or index finger prints of mothers, are still commonly recorded in hospitals to assist in verifying the identity of infants. Often, the only identifiable ridge detail in such impressions is from the large toe or adjacent to the large toe, due to the difficulty of recording such fine detail. When legible ridge detail is lacking, DNA is normally effective (except in instances of chimaerism) for indirectly identifying infants by confirming maternity and paternity of an infant's parents.

It is not uncommon for military records of flight personnel to include bare foot inked impressions. Friction ridge skin protected inside flight boots tends to survive the trauma of a plane crash (and accompanying fire) better than fingers. Even though the U.S. Armed Forces DNA Identification Laboratory (AFDIL) stores refrigerated DNA samples from all current active duty and reserve personnel, almost all casualty identifications are effected using fingerprints from military ID card records (live scan fingerprints are recorded at the time such cards are issued). When friction ridge skin is not available from deceased military personnel, DNA and dental records are used to confirm identity.

Lifestyle Information

The secretions, skin oils and dead cells in the fingerprint contain residues of various chemicals and their metabolites present in the body. These can be detected and used for forensic purposes. For example the fingerprints of tobacco smokers contain traces of cotinine, a nicotine metabolite; they also contain traces of nicotine itself; however that may be ambiguous as its presence may be caused by mere contact of the finger with a tobacco product. By treating the fingerprint with gold nanoparticles with attached cotinine antibodies, and then subsequently with fluorescent agent attached to cotinine antibody antibodies, a fingerprint of a smoker becomes fluorescent; non-smoker's fingerprint stays dark. The same approach is investigated to be used for identifying heavy coffee drinkers, cannabis smokers, and users of various other drugs.

U.S. Databases and Compression

The FBI manages a fingerprint identification system and database called IAFIS, which currently holds the fingerprints and criminal records of over fifty-one million criminal record subjects, and over 1.5 million civil (non-criminal) fingerprint records. U.S. Visit currently holds a repository of over 50 million persons, primarily in the form of two-finger records (by 2008, U.S. Visit is transforming to a system recording FBI-standard tenprint records).

Most American law enforcement agencies use Wavelet Scalar Quantization (WSQ), a wavelet-based system for efficient storage of compressed fingerprint images at 500 pixels per inch (ppi). WSQ was developed by the FBI, the Los Alamos National Lab, and the National Institute for Standards and Technology (NIST). For fingerprints recorded at 1000 ppi spatial resolution, law enforcement (including the FBI) uses JPEG 2000 instead of WSQ.

History of Fingerprinting for Identification

Fingerprints have been found on ancient Babylonian clay tablets, seals, and pottery They have also been found on the walls of Egyptian tombs and on Minoan, Greek, and Chinese pottery — as well as on bricks and tiles in Babylon and Rome. Some of these fingerprints were deposited unintentionally by workers during fabrication; sometimes the fingerprints served as decoration. However, on some pottery, fingerprints were impressed so deeply that they were likely intended to serve as the equivalent of a brand label.

Fingerprints were also used as substitutes for signatures. In Babylon from 1885-1913 B.C.E., in order to protect against forg the clay tablet on which the contract had been written. By 246 B.C.E., Chinese officials impressed their fingerprints in clay seals, which were used to seal documents. With the advent of silk and paper in China, parties to a legal contract impressed their handprints on the document. Sometime before 851 C.E., an Arab merchant in China, Abu Zayd Hasan, witnessed Chinese merchants using fingerprints to authenticate loans. By 702 C.E., Japan had adopted the Chinese practice of sealing contracts with fingerprints.

Although the ancient peoples probably did not realize that fingerprints could identify individuals, references from the age of the law officials fingerprinted people who had been arrested. In China around 300 C.E. handprints were used as evidence in a trial for theft. In 650 C.E., the Chinese historian Kia Kung-Yen remarked that fingerprints could be used as a means of authentication. In his *Jami al-Tawarikh*, Persian official and physician Rashid-al-Din Hamadani (a.k.a. "Rashideddin") (1247-1318) comments on the Chinese practice of identifying people via their fingerprints: "Experience shows that no two individuals have fingers exactly alike. Supposedly, in Persia at this time, government documents were authenticated with thumbprints.

Time Lane

A list of significant modern dates documenting the use of fingerprints for positive identification are as follows:

- 1684: Nehemiah Grew (1641-1712, English physician, botanist, and microscopist) published the first paper on the ridge structure of skin of the fingers and palms. In 1685, Govard Bidloo (1649-1713, Dutch physician) and Marcello Malpighi (1628-1694, Italian physician) published books on anatomy which also illustrated the ridge structure of the fingers.
- 1788: Johann Christoph Andreas Mayer (1747-1801, German anatomist) recognized that fingerprints are unique to each individual.
- 1823: Jan Evangelista Purkyne, a professor of anatomy at the University of Breslau, published his thesis

discussing 9 fingerprint patterns, but he did not mention the use of fingerprints to identify persons.

- 1853: Georg von Meissner (1829-1905, German anatomist) studied friction ridges.
- 1858: Sir William James Herschel (1833-1918, English magistrate) initiated fingerprinting in India.
- 1880: Dr. Henry Faulds published his first paper on the subject in the scientific journal *Nature* in 1880. Returning to the UK in 1886, he offered the concept to the Metropolitan Police in London but it was dismissed.
- 1892: Sir Francis Galton published a detailed statistical model of fingerprint analysis and identification and encouraged its use in forensic science in his book *Finger Prints*.
- 1892: Juan Vucetich, an Argentine police officer who had been studying Galton pattern types for a year, made the first criminal fingerprint identification. He successfully proved Francisca Rojas guilty of murder after showing that the bloody fingerprint found at the crime scene was hers, and could only be hers.
- 1897: The world's first Fingerprint Bureau opened in Calcutta (Kolkata), India after the Council of the Governor General approved a committee report that fingerprints should be used for classification of criminal records. Working in the Calcutta Anthropometric Bureau (before it became the Fingerprint Bureau) were Azizul Haque and Hem Chandra Bose. Haque and Bose were the Indian fingerprint experts credited with primary development of the fingerprint classification system eventually named after their supervisor, Sir Edward Richard Henry.
- 1901: The first United Kingdom Fingerprint Bureau was founded in Scotland Yard. The Henry Classification System, devised by Sir Edward Richard Henry with the help of Haque and Bose was accepted in England and Wales.

- 1902: Dr. Henry P. DeForrest used fingerprinting in the New York Civil Service.
- 1906: New York City Police Department Deputy Commissioner Joseph A. Faurot introduced fingerprinting of criminals to the United States.

Validity of Fingerprinting for Identification

The validity of forensic fingerprint evidence has recently been challenged by academics, judges and the media. While fingerprint identification was an improvement over earlier anthropometric systems, the subjective nature of matching, despite a very low error rate, has made this forensic practice controversial.

Certain specific criticisms are now being accepted by some leaders of the forensic fingerprint community, providing an incentive to improve training and procedures. Glenn Langenburg who is a Forensic Scientist, Latent Print Examiner for the Minnesota Bureau of Criminal Apprehension, is such an individual, having written an article that responds to the most active academic critics.

Criticism

The words "reliability" and "validity" have specific meanings to the scientific community. Reliability means successive tests bring the same results. Validity means that the results accurately reflect the external criteria being measured.

> Although experts are often more comfortable relying on their instincts, this reliance does not always translate into superior predictive ability. For example, in the popular Analysis, Comparison, Evaluation, and Verification (ACE-V) paradigm for fingerprint identification, the verification stage, in which a second examiner confirms the assessment of the original examiner, may increase the consistency of the

assessments. But while the verification stage has implications for the reliability of latent print comparisons, it does not assure their validity.

The few tests of validity of forensic fingerprinting have not been supportive of the method.

> Despite the absence of objective standards, scientific validation, and adequate statistical studies, a natural question to ask is how well fingerprint examiners actually perform. Proficiency tests do not validate a procedure per se, but they can provide some insight into error rates. In 1995, the Collaborative Testing Service (CTS) administered a proficiency test that, for the first time, was "designed, assembled, and reviewed" by the International Association for Identification (IAI).The results were disappointing. Four suspect cards with prints of all ten fingers were provided together with seven latents. Of 156 people taking the test, only 68 (44%) correctly classified all seven latents. Overall, the tests contained a total of 48 incorrect identifications. David Grieve, the editor of the Journal of Forensic Identification, describes the reaction of the forensic community to the results of the CTS test as ranging from "shock to disbelief," and added:
>
> Errors of this magnitude within a discipline singularly admired and respected for its touted absolute certainty as an identification process have produced chilling and mind- numbing realities. Thirty-four participants, an incredible 22% of those involved, substituted presumed but false certainty for truth. By any measure, this represents a profile of practice that is unacceptable and thus demands positive action by the entire community.
>
> What is striking about these comments is that they do not come from a critic of the fingerprint community, but from the editor of one of its premier publications.

Defense

Fingerprints collected at a crime scene, or on items of evidence from a crime, can be used in forensic science to identify suspects, victims and other persons who touched a surface. Fingerprint identification emerged as an important system within police agencies in the late 19th century, when it replaced anthropometric measurements as a more reliable method for identifying persons having a prior record, often under an alias name, in a criminal record repository.

The science of fingerprint identification can assert its standing amongst forensic sciences for many reasons, including the following:

- Has served all governments worldwide during the past 100 years to provide accurate identification of criminals. No two fingerprints have ever been found identical in many billions of human and automated computer comparisons. Fingerprints are the very basis for criminal history foundation at every police agency.
- Established the first forensic professional organization, the International Association for Identification (IAI), in 1915.
- Established the first professional certification program for forensic scientists, the IAI's Certified Latent Print Examiner program (in 1977), issuing certification to those meeting stringent criteria and revoking certification for serious errors such as erroneous identifications.
- Remains the most commonly used forensic evidence worldwide—in most jurisdictions fingerprint examination cases match or outnumber all other forensic examination casework combined.
- Continues to expand as the premier method for identifying persons, with tens of thousands of persons added to fingerprint repositories daily in America alone—far outdistancing similar databases in growth.

- Is claimed to outperform DNA and all other human identification systems (fingerprints are said to solve ten times more unknown suspect cases than DNA in most jurisdictions).
- Fingerprint identification was the first forensic discipline (in 1977) to formally institute a professional certification program for individual experts, including a procedure for decertifying those making errors. Other forensic disciplines later followed suit in establishing certification programs whereby certification could be revoked for error. Fingerprint identification effects far more positive identifications of persons worldwide daily than any other human identification procedure. Some of the discontent over fingerprint evidence may be due to the desire to push the conclusiveness of fingerprint examinations to the same level of certitude as that of DNA analysis. DNA is probability-based inasmuch as an individual is genetically half from the mother's contribution and half from the father's contribution. These genetic contributions are passed down from generation to generation. While pattern type (arch, loops, and whorls) may be inherited, the details of the friction ridges are not. For example, it cannot be concluded that a person inherited a certain bifurcation from their mother and an ending ridge from their father as the development of these features are completely random. Further, fingerprints as an analogy of uniqueness has been widely scientifically accepted. For example, chemists often use the term "fingerprint region" to describe an area of a chemical that can be used to identify it.

Another criticism sometimes leveled at fingerprint practice is that it is a "closed discipline". However, practitioners in the scientific community are generally specialized and may not extend to other areas of science; in this respect, fingerprint scientists are no different from the rest of the scientific community. The fingerprint community asserts that it maintains the need for objectivity and continued research in the area of friction ridge analysis.

Errors in Identification or Processing

Bele cases involved misfiling of fingerprints or suspect profiling which slanted interpretation, rather than faults by objective matches from fingerprint search technology.

William West

A story that some regard as apocryphal circulates about events occurring in the early 20th century when a man was spotted in the, the incoming prisoner claimed to be named Will West, while the existing prisoner was named William West. According to their Bertillon measurements, they were essentially indistinguishable. Only their fingerprints could readily identify them, and the Bertillon Method was discredited.

There is evidence that men named Will and William West were both imprisoned in the Federal Penitentiary in Leavenworth, Kansas, between 1903 and 1909. However, the details of the case are suspicious, especially since they differ between retells, and the story did not appear in print until 1918. Today, people familiar with the story differ on whether the story was accurate, a case of people (possibly separated twins) who bore a striking resemblance, a case of known twins, or complete fiction. The story of Will West is mentioned on page 167 of Forensic Uses of Digital Imaging by John C. Russ, with mug shots of "the two Will Wests" on page 168.

It should be noted that the West case is not a case of fingerprint error, but an error in the method of anthropometry, which the fingerprint science replaced.

Brandon Mayfield and Madrid Bombing

Brandon Mayfield is an Oregon lawyer who was identified as a participant in the Madrid bombing based on a so-called fingerprint match by the FBI. The FBI Latent Print Unit ran the print collected in Madrid and reported a match against one of 20 fingerprint candidates returned in a search response from their IAFIS — Integrated Automated Fingerprint Identification System. The FBI initially called the match "100 percent positive" and an "absolutely incontrovertible match". The Spanish National Police examiners concluded the prints did not match Mayfield, and after two weeks identified another man who matched. The FBI acknowledged the error, and a judge released Mayfield after two weeks in May 2004 In January of 2006, a U.S. Justice Department report was released which faulted the FBI for sloppy work but exonerated them of more serious allegations. The report found that misidentification was due to misapplication of methodology by the examiners involved: Mayfield is an American-born convert to Islam and his wife is an Egyptian immigrant not factors that affect fingerprint search technology.

On 29 November 2006, the FBI agreed to pay Brandon Mayfield the sum of US$2 million The judicial settlement allows Mayfield to continue a suit regarding certain other government practices surrounding his arrest and detention. The formal apology stated that the FBI, which erroneously linked him to the 2004 Madrid bombing through a fingerprinting mistake, had taken steps to "ensure that what happened to Mr. Mayfield and the Mayfield family does not happen again.

René Ramón Sánchez

Error in "Clerical" processing. René Ramón Sánchez, a legal Dominican Republic immigrant was booked on a DUI charge on July 15, 1995. He had his fingerprints affixed on a card containing the name, Social Security number and other data for Leo Rosario, who was being processed at the same time. Leo Rosario was arrested for selling cocaine to an undercover police officer. In August of 1998, Sanchez was stopped again by police officers, for DUI in Manhattan. René was then identified as Leo

Rosario on October 11, 2000, while returning from a visit to relatives in the Dominican Republic. He was arrested at Kennedy International Airport. Even though he did not match the physical description of Rosario, the fingerprints were considered more reliable

Shirley McKie

Error in identification. Shirley McKie was a police detective in 1997 when she was accused of leaving her thumb print inside a house in Kilmarnock, Scotland where Marion Ross had been murdered. Although detective constable McKie denied having been inside the house, she was arrested in a dawn raid the following year and charged with perjury. The only evidence was the thumb print allegedly found at the murder scene. Two American experts testified on her behalf at her trial in May 1999 and she was found not guilty. The Scottish Criminal Record Office (SCRO) would not admit any error, but Scottish first minister Jack McConnell later said there had been an "honest mistake".

On February 7, 2006, McKie was awarded £750,000 in compensation from the Scottish Executive and the SCRO. Controversy continues to surround the McKie case with calls for the resignations of Scottish ministers and for either a public or a judicial inquiry into the matter

Stephan Cowans

Error in identification. Stephan Cowans (d. 2007-10-25)[39] was convicted of attempted murder in 1997 after he was accused of the shooting of a police officer while fleeing a robbery in Roxbury, Massachusetts. He was implicated in the crime by the testimony of two witnesses, one of whom was the victim. The other evidence was a fingerprint on a glass mug that the assailant drank water from, and experts testified that the fingerprint belonged to him. He was found guilty and sent to prison with a sentence of 35 years. While in prison he earned money cleaning up biohazards until he could afford to have the evidence tested for DNA. The DNA did not match his, but he had already served six years in prison before he was released.

Privacy Issues

Fingerprinting of Children

Various schools have implemented fingerprint locks or registered children's fingerprints. This happened in the United Kingdom (fingerprint lock in the Holland Park School in London databases, etc in Belgium (école Marie-José in Liège , in France, in Italy, etc. The NGO Privacy International has alerted that tens of thousands of UK school children were being fingerprinted by schools, often without the knowledge or consent of their parents In 2002, the supplier Micro Librarian Systems, which use a technology similar to US prisons and German military, estimated that 350 schools through-out Britain were using such systems, to replace library cards In 2007, it is estimated that 3 500 schools (ten times more) are using such systems Under the Data Protection Act (DPA), schools in the UK do not have to ask parental consent for such practices. Parents opposed to such practices may only bring individual complaints against schools.

In Belgium, this practice gave rise to a question in Parliament on February 6, 2007 by Michel de La Motte (Humanist Democratic Centre) to the Education Minister Marie Arena, who replied that they were legal insofar as the school did not use them for external purposes nor to survey the private life of children. Such practices have also been used in France (Angers, Carqueiranne college in the Var — the latter won the Big Brother Award of 2005, etc.) although the CNIL, official organisation in charge of protection of privacy, has declared them "disproportionate."

In March 2007, the British government was considering fingerprinting of children aged 11 to 15 as part of new passport and ID card (the latter having been recently implemented in the UK), also lifting opposition for privacy concerns. All fingerprints taken would be cross-checked against prints from 900,000 unsolved crimes. Shadow Home secretary David Davis called the plan "sinister."

Recently, serious concerns about the security implications of using conventional biometric templates in schools have been raised by a number of leading IT security experts, including Kim Cameron, architect of identity and access in the connected systems division at Microsoft, who cites research by Cavoukian and Stoianov to back up his assertion that "it is absolutely premature to begin using 'conventional biometrics' in schools".

Biometric vendors claim benefits to schools such as improved reading skills, decreased wait times in lunch lines and increased revenues They do not cite independent research to support this. Educationalist Dr Sandra Leaton Gray of Homerton College, Cambridge stated in early 2007 that "I have not been able to find a single piece of published research which suggests that the use of biometrics in schools promotes healthy eating or improves reading skills amongst children... There is absolutely no evidence for such claims".

The Ottawa Police in Canada advised parents who fear that their children may be kidnapped to have their fingerprints taken.

Other Uses

Locks and Other Applications

In the 2000s, electronic fingerprint readers have been introduced for security applications such as identification of computer users (log-in authentication). However, early devices have been discovered to be vulnerable to quite simple methods of deception, such as fake fingerprints cast in gels. In 2006, fingerprint sensors gained popularity in the notebook PC market. Built-in sensors in ThinkPads, VAIO laptops, and others also double as motion detectors for document scrolling, like the scroll wheel.

Another recent use of fingerprints in a day-to-day setting has been the increasing reliance on biometrics in schools where fingerprints and, to a lesser extent, iris scans are used to validate electronic registration, cashless catering, and library access. This practice is particularly widespread in the UK, where more than 3500 schools currently use such technology, though it is also starting to be adopted in some states in the US.

Fingerprints in Other Species

Some other animals, including many primates, koalas, and fishers have their own unique prints. According to one study, even with an electron microscope, it can be quite difficult to distinguish between the fingerprints of a koala and a human.

10

Fingerprint Recognition

Fingerprint recognition or fingerprint authentication refers to the automated method of verifying a match between two human fingerprints. Fingerprints are one of many forms of biometrics used to identify an individual and verify their identity. This article touches on two major classes of algorithms (minutia and pattern) and four sensor designs (optical, ultrasonic, passive capacitance, and active capacitance).

Background

The analysis of fingerprints for matching purposes generally requires the comparison of several features of the print pattern. These include patterns, which are aggregate characteristics of ridges, and minutia points, which are unique features found within the patterns. It is also necessary to know the structure and properties of human skin in order to successfully employ some of the imaging technologies.

Patterns

The three basic patterns of fingerprint ridges are the arch (*Fig. 10.1*), loop (*Fig. 10.2*), and whorl (*Fig. 10.3*). An arch is a pattern where the ridges enter from one side of the finger, rise in the center forming an arc, and then exit the other side of the finger. The loop is a pattern where the ridges enter from one side of a finger, form a curve, and tend to exit from the same side they enter. In the whorl pattern, ridges form circularly around a central point on the finger. Scientists have found that family members often share the same general fingerprint patterns, leading to the belief that these patterns are inherited.

Fig. 10.1: **Picture of an arch *fingerprint* pattern**

Minutia Features

The major Minutia features of fingerprint ridges are: ridge ending, bifurcation, and short ridge (or dot). The ridge ending is the point at which a ridge terminates. Bifurcations are points at which a single ridge splits into two ridges. Short ridges (or dots) are ridges which are significantly shorter than the average ridge length on the fingerprint. Minutiae and patterns are very important in the analysis of fingerprints since no two fingers have been shown to be identical.

Fig. 10.2: Picture of the loop fingerprint pattern

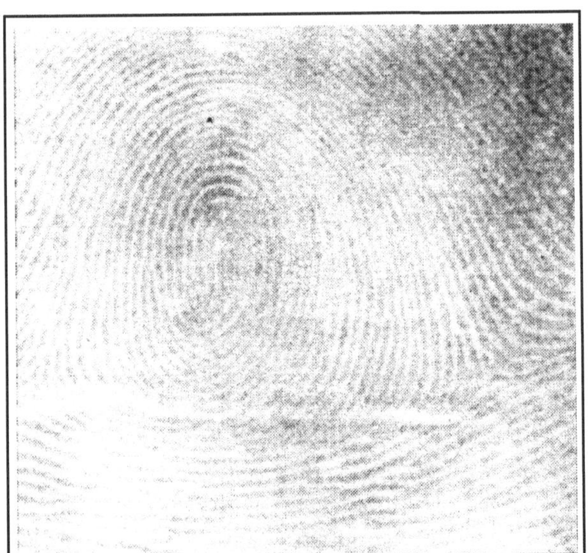

Fig. 10.3: Picture of a whorl fingerprint pattern

Fingerprint Sensors

A fingerprint sensor is an electronic device used to capture a digital image of the fingerprint pattern. The captured image is called a live scan. This live scan is digitally processed to create a biometric template (a collection of extracted features) which is stored and used for matching. This is an overview of some of the more commonly used fingerprint sensor technologies.

Optical

Optical fingerprint imaging involves capturing a digital image of the print using visible light. This type of sensor is, in essence, a specialized digital camera. The top layer of the sensor, where the finger is placed, is known as the touch surface. Beneath this layer is a light-emitting phosphor layer which illuminates the surface of the finger. The light reflected from the finger passes through the phosphor layer to an array of solid state pixels (a charge-coupled device) which captures a visual image of the fingerprint. A scratched or dirty touch surface can cause a bad image of the fingerprint. A disadvantage of this type of sensor is the fact that the imaging capabilities are affected by the quality of skin on the finger. For instance, a dirty or marked finger is difficult to image properly. Also, it is possible for an individual to erode the outer layer of skin on the fingertips to the point where the fingerprint is no longer visible. It can also be easily fooled by an image of a fingerprint if not coupled with a "live finger" detector. However, unlike capacitive sensors, this sensor technology is not susceptible to electrostatic discharge damage.

Ultrasonic

Ultrasonic sensors make use of the principles of medical ultrasonography in order to create visual images of the fingerprint. Unlike optical imaging, ultrasonic sensors use very high frequency sound waves to penetrate the epidermal layer of skin. The sound waves are generated using piezoelectric transducers and reflected energy is also measured using piezoelectric materials. Since the dermal skin layer exhibits the same characteristic pattern of the fingerprint, the reflected wave measurements can be used to form an image of the fingerprint. This eliminates the need for clean, undamaged epidermal skin and a clean sensing surface.

Capacitance

Capacitance sensors utilize the principles associated with capacitance in order to form fingerprint images. The two equations used in this type of imaging are:

$$C = \frac{Q}{v}$$

$$C = \varepsilon_0 \varepsilon_\tau \frac{A}{d}$$

where

C is the capacitance in farads

Q is the charge in coulombs

V is the potential in volts.

e_0 is the permittivity of free space, measured in farad per metre.

e_r is the dielectric constant of the insulator used

A is the area of each plane electrode, measured in square metres

d is the separation between the electrodes, measured in metres

In this method of imaging, the sensor array pixels each act as one plate of a parallel-plate capacitor, the dermal layer (which is electrically conductive) acts as the other plate, and the non-conductive epidermal layer acts as a dielectric.

Passive Capacitance

A passive capacitance sensor uses the principle outlined above to form an image of the fingerprint patterns on the dermal layer of skin. Each sensor pixel is used to measure the capacitance at that point of the array. The capacitance varies between the ridges and valleys of the fingerprint due to the fact that the volume between the dermal layer and sensing element in valleys contains an air gap. The dielectric constant of the epidermis and the area of the sensing element are known values. The measured capacitance values are then used to distinguish between fingerprint ridges and valleys.

Active Capacitance

Active capacitance sensors use a charging cycle to apply a voltage to the skin before measurement takes place. The application of voltage charges the effective capacitor. The electric field between the finger and sensor follows the pattern of the ridges in the dermal skin layer. On the discharge cycle, the voltage across the dermal layer and sensing element is compared against a reference voltage in order to calculate the capacitance. The distance values are then calculated mathematically, using the above equations, and used to form an image of the fingerprint. Active capacitance sensors measure the ridge patterns of the dermal layer like the ultrasonic method. Again, this eliminates the need for clean, undamaged epidermal skin and a clean sensing surface.

Algorithms

Matching algorithms are used to compare previously stored templates of fingerprints against candidate fingerprints for authentication purposes. In order to do this either the original image must be directly compared with the candidate image or certain features must be compared.

Pattern-based (or Image-based) Algorithms

Pattern based algorithms compare the basic fingerprint patterns (arch, whorl, and loop) between a previously stored template and a candidate fingerprint. This requires that the images be aligned in the same orientation. To do this, the algorithm finds a central point in the fingerprint image and centers on that. In a pattern-based algorithm, the template contains the type, size, and orientation of patterns within the aligned fingerprint image. The candidate fingerprint image is graphically compared with the template to determine the degree to which they match.

FINGERPRINT VERIFICATION COMPETITION

Fingerprint Verification Competition (FVC) is an international competition focused on fingerprint verification software assessment. A subset of fingerprint impressions acquired with various sensors was provided to registered participants, to allow them to adjust the parameters of their algorithms. Participants were requested to provide enroll and match executable files of their algorithms; the evaluation was conducted at the organizers' facilities using the submitted executable files on a sequestered database, acquired with the same sensors as the training set.

The Organizers of FVC are:

- Biometric System Laboratory (University of Bologna)
- Pattern Recognition and Image Processing Laboratory (Michigan State University)
- Biometric Test Center (San Jose State University)
- Biometric Recognition Group - ATVS (Universidad Autonoma de Madrid)

Each participant can submit up to one algorithm to the open and light categories.

The first, second and third international competitions on fingerprint verification (FVC2000, FVC2002 and FVC2004) were organized in 2000, 2002 and 2004, respectively. These events received great attention both from academic and industrial biometric communities. They established a common benchmark, allowing developers to unambiguously compare their algorithms, and provided an overview of the state-of-the-art in fingerprint recognition. Based on the response of the biometrics community, FVC2000, FVC2002 and FVC2004 were undoubtedly successful initiatives. The interest shown in previous editions by the biometrics research community has prompted the organizers to schedule a new competition for the year 2006.

In 2006 we had:

- Four new databases (three real and one synthetic)
- Two categories (Open Category and Light Category)
- 53 participants (27 industrial, 13 academic, and 13 independent developers)
- 70 algorithms submitted (44 in the Open Category and 26 in the Light Category)

Aim

- Continuous advances in the field of biometric systems and, in particular, in fingerprint-based systems (both in matching techniques and sensing devices) require that performance evaluation of biometric systems be carried out at regular intervals.
- The aim of FVC2006 is to track recent advances in fingerprint verification, for both academia and industry, and to benchmark the state-of-the-art in fingerprint technology.
- Further testing, on interoperability and quality related issues, will be performed in a second stage, after the competition is completed.
- This competition should not be viewed as an "official" performance certification of biometric systems, since

only parts of the system software will be evaluated by using images from sensors not native to each system. Nonetheless, the results of this competition will give a useful overview of the state-of-the-art in this field and will provide guidance to the participants for improving their algorithms.

Categories

- Two different sub-competitions (Open category and Light category) will be organized using the same databases.
- Each participant is allowed to submit only one algorithm to each category.
- The Open category has no limits on memory requirements and template size. For practical testing reasons, the maximum response time of the algorithms is limited as follows: the maximum time for each enrollment is 5 seconds, the maximum time for each matching is 3 seconds. The test will be executed under Windows XP Professional O.S. on PC INTEL PENTIUM 4 - 3.20 GHz - 1.00 GB RAM.
- The Light category is intended for algorithms conceived for light architectures and therefore characterized by low computing needs, limited memory usage and small template size. The maximum time for enrollment is 0.3 seconds and the maximum time for matching is 0.1 seconds. The test will be executed under Windows XP Professional O.S. on PC INTEL PENTIUM 4 - 3.20 GHz - 1.00 GB RAM. The maximum memory that can be allocated by the processes is 4 MB. The maximum template size is 2 kB. A utility will be made available to the participants to test if their executables comply with the memory requirement.

Databases

One of the most important and time-consuming tasks of any biometric system evaluation is the data collection. We have created a multi-database, containing four disjoint fingerprint databases, each collected with a different sensor/ technology.

- Four distinct databases, provided by the organizers, will constitute the benchmark: DB1, DB2, DB3 and DB4. Each database is 150 fingers wide and 12 samples per finger in depth (i.e., it consists of 1800 fingerprint images). Each database will be partitioned in two disjoint subsets A and B.
  - subsets DB1-A, DB2-A, DB3-A and DB4-A, which contain the first 140 fingers (1680 images) of DB1, DB2, DB3 and DB4, respectively, will be used for the algorithm performance evaluation.
  - subsets DB1-B, DB2-B, DB3-B and DB4-B, containing the last 10 fingers (120 images) of DB1, DB2, DB3 and DB4, respectively, will be made available to the participants as a development set to allow parameter tuning before the submission.
- During performance evaluation, fingerprints belonging to the same database will be matched against each other.
- The image format is BMP, 256 gray-levels, uncompressed.
- The image size and resolution vary depending on the database (detailed information will be available to the participants).
- Data collection in FVC2006 was performed without deliberately introducing difficulties such as exaggerated distortion, large amounts of rotation and displacement, wet/dry impressions, etc. (as it was done in the previous editions), but the population is more heterogeneous and also includes manual workers and elderly people. The volunteers were simply asked to put their fingers naturally on the acquisition device, but no constraints were enforced to guarantee a minimum

quality in the acquired images. The final datasets were selected from a larger database by choosing the most difficult fingers according to a quality index, to make the benchmark sufficiently difficult for a technology evaluation.

11

Biometrics

Biometrics refers to methods for uniquely recognizing humans based upon one or more intrinsic physical or behavioral traits. In information technology, in particular, biometrics is used as a form of identity access management and access control. It is also used to identify individuals in groups that are under surveillance.

Biometric characteristics can be divided in two main classes:

- **Physiological** are related to the shape of the body. Examples include, but are not limited to fingerprint, face recognition, DNA, hand and palm geometry, iris recognition, which has largely replaced retina, and odor/scent.
- **Behavioural** are related to the behavior of a person. Examples include, but are not limited to typing rhythm, gait, and voice. Some researchers have coined the term behaviometrics for this class of biometrics.

Strictly speaking, *voice* is also a physiological trait because every person has a different pitch, but voice recognition is mainly based on the study of the way a person speaks, commonly classified as behavioural.

Introduction

It is possible to understand if a human characteristic can be used for biometrics in terms of the following parameters:

- **Universality** – each person should have the characteristic.
- **Uniqueness** – is how well the biometric separates individually from another.
- **Permanence** – measures how well a biometric resists aging.
- **Collectability** – ease of acquisition for measurement.
- **Performance** – accuracy, speed, and robustness of technology used.
- **Acceptability** – degree of approval of a technology.
- **Circumvention** – ease of use of a substitute.

A biometric system can provide the following two functions:

- **Verification** – Authenticates its users in conjunction with a smart card, username or ID number. The biometric template captured is compared with that stored against the registered user either on a smart card or database for verification.
- **Identification** – Authenticates its users from the biometric characteristic alone without the use of smart cards, usernames or ID numbers. The biometric template is compared to all records within the database and a closest match score is returned. The closest match within the allowed threshold is deemed the individual and authenticated.

The main operations a system can perform are enrollment and test. During the enrollment, biometric information from an individual is stored. During the test, biometric information is detected and compared with the stored information. Note that it is crucial that storage and retrieval of such systems themselves be secure if the biometric system is to be robust. The first block (sensor) is the interface between the real world and our system; it has to acquire all the necessary data. Most of the times it is an image acquisition system, but it can change according to the characteristics desired. The second block performs all the necessary pre-processing: it has to remove artifacts from the sensor, to enhance the input (e.g. removing background noise), to use some kind of normalization, etc. In the third block features needed are extracted. This step is an important step as the correct features need to be extracted and the optimal way. A vector of numbers or an image with particular properties is used to create a *template*. A template is a synthesis of all the characteristics extracted from the source, in the optimal size to allow for adequate identifiability.

If enrolment is being performed the template is simply stored somewhere (on a card or within a database or both). If a matching phase is being performed, the obtained template is passed to a matcher that compares it with other existing templates, estimating the distance between them using any algorithm (e.g. Hamming distance). The matching program will analyze the template with the input. This will then be output for any specified use or purpose (e.g. entrance in a restricted area).

Performance

The following are used as performance metrics for biometric systems:

- **false accept rate or false match rate (FAR or FMR)** – the probability that the system incorrectly declares a successful match between the input pattern and a non-matching pattern in the database. It measures the percent of invalid matches. These systems are critical since they are commonly used to forbid certain actions by disallowed people.

- **false reject rate or false non-match rate (FRR or FNMR)** – the probability that the system incorrectly declares failure of match between the input pattern and the matching template in the database. It measures the percent of valid inputs being rejected.
- **receiver operating characteristic or relative operating characteristic (ROC)** – In general, the matching algorithm performs a decision using some parameters (e.g. a threshold). In biometric systems the FAR and FRR can typically be traded off against each other by changing those parameters. The ROC plot is obtained by graphing the values of FAR and FRR, changing the variables implicitly. A common variation is the Detection error trade-off (DET), which is obtained using normal deviate scales on both axes. This more linear graph illuminates the differences for higher performances (rarer errors).
- **equal error rate or crossover error rate (EER or CER)** – the rate at which both accept and reject errors are equal. ROC or DET plotting is used because how FAR and FRR can be changed, is shown clearly. When quick comparison of two systems is required, the EER is commonly used. Obtained from the ROC plot by taking the point where FAR and FRR have the same value. The lower the EER, the more accurate the system is considered to be.
- **failure to enroll rate (FTE or FER)** – the percentage of data input is considered invalid and fails to input into the system. Failure to enroll happens when the data obtained by the sensor are considered invalid or of poor quality.
- **failure to capture rate (FTC)** – Within automatic systems, the probability that the system fails to detect a biometric characteristic when presented correctly.

- **template capacity** – the maximum number of sets of data which can be input into the system.

As the sensitivity of biometric devices increases, it decreases the FAR but increases the FRR.

One simple but artificial way to judge a system is by EER, but not all the authors provided it. Moreover, there are two particular values of FAR and FRR to show how one parameter can change depending on the other. For fingerprint there are two different results, the one from 2003 is older but it was performed on a huge set of people, while in 2004 far fewer people were involved but stricter conditions have been applied. For iris, both references belong to the same year, but one was performed on more people, the other one is the result of a competition between several universities so, even if the sample is much smaller, it could reflect better the state of art of the field.

Issues and Concerns

Privacy

One common concern is how a person's biometric, once collected, can be protected. Australia has therefore introduced a Biometrics Institute Privacy Code in order to protect consumer personal data beyond the current protections offered by the Australian Privacy Act.

Another concern is that if the system is used at more than one location, a person's movements may be tracked as with any non-anonymous authentication system. An example of this would be posted security cameras linked to a facial recognition system, or a public transportation system requiring the use of biometry or registered identification card.

Discrimination

There are concerns whether our personal information taken through biometric methods can be misused, e.g. by the government to determine unwanted traits in humans for global population control. Also, the data obtained using biometrics can be used in unauthorized ways without the individual's consent.

Danger to Owners of Secured Items

When thieves cannot get access to secure properties, there is a chance that the thieves will stalk and assault the property owner to gain access. If the item is secured with a biometric device, the damage to the owner could be irreversible, and potentially cost more than the secured property. For example, in 2005, Malaysian car thieves cut off the finger of a Mercedes-Benz S-Class owner when attempting to steal the car.

Cancelable Biometrics

Physical features, such as face, fingerprint, iris, retina, hand, or behavioral features, such as signature, voice, gait, must fulfill a certain criteria to qualify for use in recognition. They must be unique, universal, acceptable, collectible and convenient to the person, in addition, to reliability at recognition, performance and circumvention. Most importantly, however, permanence is a key feature for biometrics. They must retain all the above features in particular the uniqueness unchanged, or acceptably changed, over the lifetime of the individual. On the other hand, this fundamental feature has brought biometrics to challenge a new risk. If biometric data is obtained, for example compromised from a database, by unauthorized users, the genuine owner will lose control over them forever and lose his/her identity.

Countries Applying Biometrics

United States

The United States government has become a strong advocate of biometrics with the increase in fear of terrorism since September 11, 2001.

The FBI is currently spending $1 billion to create a new biometric database, which will store DNA, fingerprints, and other biometric data. The computers running the database will be contained in an underground facility about the size of a football field.

Both the Department of Homeland Security and DARPA are heavily funding research into facial recognition systems The Information Processing Technology Office, ran a program known as Human Identification at a Distance which developed technologies that are capable of identifying a person at up to 500 ft by their facial features.

Bush issued a presidential directive (NSPD 59, HSPD 24 in 2008 which requires increased capability for sharing and interoperability in "collection, storage, use, analysis, and sharing of biometric and associated biographic and contextual information of individuals" among the departments and agencies of the executive branch of the U.S. federal government.

Starting in 2005, US passports with facial (image-based) biometric data were scheduled to be produced. Privacy activists in many countries have criticized the technology's use for the potential harm to civil liberties, privacy, and the risk of identity theft. Currently, there is some apprehension in the United States (and the European Union) that the information can be "skimmed" and identify people's citizenship remotely for criminal intent, such as kidnapping.

The US Department of Defense (DoD) Common Access Card, is an ID card issued to all US Service personnel and contractors on US Military sites. This card contains biometric data and digitized photographs. It also has laser-etched photographs and holograms to add security and reduce the risk of falsification. There have been over 10 million of these cards issued.

According to Jim Wayman, director of the National Biometric Test Center at San Jose State University, Walt

Disney World is the nation's largest single commercial application of biometrics However, the US-VISIT program will very soon surpass Walt Disney World for biometrics deployment.

Short Form of Currency

Germany

The biometrics market in Germany will experience enormous growth until 2009. "The market size will increase from approximately 12 million {(2004) to 377 million} (2009). "The federal government will be a major contributor to this development" In particular, the biometric procedures of fingerprint and facial recognition can profit from the government project. In May 2005 the German Upper House of Parliament approved the implementation of the ePass, a passport issued to all German citizens which contain biometric technology. The ePass has been in circulation since November 2005, and contains a chip that holds a digital photograph and one fingerprint from each hand, usually of the index fingers, though others may be used if these fingers are missing or have extremely distorted prints. "A third biometric identifier – iris scans – could be added at a later stage" An increase in the prevalence of biometric technology in Germany is an effort to not only keep citizens safe within German borders but also to comply with the current US deadline for visa-waiver countries to introduce biometric passports. In addition to producing biometric passports for German citizens, the German government has put in place new requirements for visitors to apply for visas within the country. "Only applicants for long-term visas, which allow more than three months' residence, will be affected by the planned biometric registration program. The new work visas will also include fingerprinting, iris scanning, and digital photos".

Germany is also one of the first countries to implement biometric technology at the Olympic Games to protect

German athletes. "The Olympic Games is always a diplomatically tense affair and previous events have been rocked by terrorist attacks - most notably when Germany last held the Games in Munich in 1972 and 11 Israeli athletes were killed".

Biometric technology was first used at the Olympic Summer Games in Athens, Greece in 2004. "On registering with the scheme, accredited visitors will receive an ID card containing their fingerprint biometrics data that will enable them to access the 'German House'. Accredited visitors will include athletes, coaching staff, team management and members of the media". gainst the increasing use of biometric data, the influential hacker group Chaos Computer Club published a fingerprint of German Minister of the Interior Wolfgang Schäuble in the March 2008 edition of its magazine *Datenschleuder*. The magazine also included the fingerprint on a film that readers could use to fool fingerprint readers.

Brazil

Since the beginning of the 20th century, Brazilian citizens have had user ID cards. The decision by the Brazilian government to adopt fingerprint-based biometrics was spearheaded by Dr. Felix Pacheco at Rio de Janeiro, at that time capital of the Federative Republic. Dr. Pacheco was a friend of Dr. Juan Vucetich, who invented one of the most complete tenprint classification systems in existence. The Vucetich system was adopted not only in Brazil, but also by most of the other South American countries. The oldest and most traditional ID Institute in Brazil (Instituto de Identificação Félix Pacheco) was integrated at DETRAN (Brazilian equivalent to DMV) into the civil and criminal AFIS system in 1999.

Each state in Brazil is allowed to print its own ID card, but the layout and data are the same for all of them. The ID cards printed in Rio de Janeiro are fully digitized using a 2D bar code with information which can be matched against its owner off-line. The 2D bar code encodes a color photo, a signature, two fingerprints, and other citizen data. This technology was developed in 2000 in order to enhance the safety of the Brazilian ID cards.

By the end of 2005, the Brazilian government started the development of its new passport. The new documents started to be released by the beginning of 2007, in Brasilia. The new passport included several security features, like Laser perforation, UV hidden symbols, security layer over variable data and etc. Brazilian citizens will have their signature, photo, and 10 rolled fingerprints collected during passport requests. All of the data is planned to be stored in ICAO E-passport standard. This allows for contactless electronic reading of the passport content and Citizens ID verification since fingerprint templates and token facial images will be available for automatic recognition.

Iraq

Biometrics are being used extensively in Iraq to catalogue as many Iraqis as possible providing Iraqis with a verifiable identification card, immune to forgery. During account creation, the collected biometrics information is logged into a central database which then allows a user profile to be created. Even if an Iraqi has lost their ID card, their identification can be found and verified by using their unique biometric information. Additional information can also be added to each account record, such as individual personal history. This can help American forces determine whether someone has been causing trouble in the past. One major system in use in Iraq is called BISA This system uses a smartcard and a user's biometrics (fingerpint, iris, and face photos) to ensure they are authorized access to a base or facility. Another is called BAT for Biometric Automated Toolset.

Japan

Several banks in Japan have adopted either palm vein authentication or finger vein authentication technology on their ATMs. Palm vein authentication technology which was developed by Fujitsu, among other companies, proved to have a false acceptance rate of 0.01177% and a false rejection rate of 4.23%. Finger vein authentication technology, developed by Hitachi, has a false acceptance rate of 0.0100% and a false rejection rate of 1.26% Finger vein authentication technology has so far been adopted by banks such as Sumitomo Mitsui Financial Group, Mizuho Financial Group and Japan Post Bank. Palm vein authentication technology has been adopted by banks such as the Bank of Tokyo-Mitsubishi UFJ.

United Kingdom

Fingerprint scanners used in some schools to facilitate the subtraction of funds from an account financed by parents for the payment of school dinners. By using such a system nutritional reports can be produced for parents to surveil a child's intake. This has raised questions from liberty groups as taking away the liberty of choice from the youth of society. Other concerns arise from the possibility of data leaking from the providers of school meals to interest groups that provide health services such as the NHS and insurance groups that may end up having a detrimental effect on the ability of individuals to enjoy equality of access to services.

Australia

Visitors intending to visit Australia may soon have to submit to biometric authentication as part of the Smartgate system, linking individuals to their visas and passports. Biometric data are already collected from some visa applicants by Immigration. Australia is the first country to introduce a Biometrics Privacy Code, which is established and administered by the Biometrics Institute. The Biometrics Institute Privacy Code Biometrics Institute forms part of Australian privacy legislation. The Code includes privacy standards that are at least equivalent to the Australian National Privacy Principles (NPPs) in the Privacy Act and also incorporates higher standards of privacy protection in relation to certain acts and practices. Only members of the Biometrics Institute are eligible to subscribe to this Code. Biometrics Institute membership, and thus subscription to this Code, is voluntary.

FACIAL RECOGNITION SYSTEM

A facial recognition system is a computer application for automatically identifying or verifying a person from a digital image or a video frame from a video source. One of the ways to do this is by comparing selected facial features from the image and a facial database.

It is typically used in security systems and can be compared to other biometrics such as fingerprint or eye iris recognition systems.

Techniques

Traditional

Some facial recognition algorithms identify faces by extracting landmarks, or features, from an image of the subject's face. For example, an algorithm may analyze the relative position, size, and/or shape of the eyes, nose, cheekbones, and jaw. These features are then used to search for other images with matching features. Other algorithms normalize a gallery of face images and then compress the face data, only saving the data in the image that is useful for face detection. A probe image is then compared with the face data One of the earliest, successful systems is based on template matching techniques applied to a set of salient facial features, providing a sort of compressed face representation.

Popular recognition algorithms include eigenface, fisherface, the Hidden Markov model, and the neuronal motivated dynamic link matching.

3-D

A newly emerging trend, claimed to achieve previously unseen accuracies, is three-dimensional face recognition. This technique uses 3-D sensors to capture information about the shape of a face. This information is then used to identify distinctive features on the surface of a face, such as the contour of the eye sockets, nose, and chin.

One advantage of 3-D facial recognition is that it is not affected by changes in lighting like other techniques. It can also identify a face from a range of viewing angles, including a profile view.

Skin Texture Analysis

Another emerging trend uses the visual details of the skin, as captured in standard digital or scanned images. This technique, called skin texture analysis, turns the unique lines, patterns, and spots apparent in a person's skin into a mathematical space.

Tests have shown that with the addition of skin texture analysis, performance in recognizing faces can increase 20 to 25 percent.

Notable Users and Deployments

The London Borough of Newham, in the UK, previously trialled a facial recognition system built into their borough-wide CCTV system.

The German Federal Police use a facial recognition system to allow voluntary subscribers to pass fully automated border controls at Frankfurt Rhein-Main international airport. Subscribers need to be European Union or Swiss citizens Recognition system are also used by casinos to catch card counters and other blacklisted individuals.

The Australian Customs Service has an automated border processing system called SmartGate that uses facial recognition. The system compares the face of the individual with the image in the e-passport microchip, certifying that the holder of the passport is the rightful owner.

Pennsylvania Justice Network searches crime scene photographs and CCTV footage in the mugshot database of previous arrests. A number of cold cases have been resolved since the system became operational in 2005. Other law enforcement agencies in the USA and abroad use arrest mugshot databases in their forensic investigative work.

U.S. Department of State operates one of the largest face recognition systems in the world with over 75 million photographs that is actively used for visa processing.

Spaceship Earth in EPCOT uses this for the touch screen part of the ride.

Additional Uses

In addition to being used for security systems, authorities have found a number of other applications for facial recognition systems. While earlier post 9/11 deployments were well publicized trials, more recent deployments are rarely written about due to their covert nature.

At *Super Bowl XXXV* in January 2001, police in Tampa Bay, Florida, used Identix's facial recognition software, FaceIt, to search for potential criminals and terrorists in attendance at the event (it found 19 people with pending arrest warrants.

In the 2000 presidential election, the Mexican government employed facial recognition software to prevent voter fraud. Some individuals had been registering to vote under several different names, in an attempt to place multiple votes. By comparing new facial images to those already in the voter database, authorities were able to reduce duplicate registrations Similar technologies are being used in the United States to prevent people from obtaining fake identification cards and driver's licenses.

There are also a number of potential uses for facial recognition that are currently being developed. For example, the technology could be used as a security measure at ATM's;

instead of using a bank card or personal identification number, the ATM would capture an image of your face, and compare it to your photo in the bank database to confirm your identity. This same concept could also be applied to computers; by using a webcam to capture a digital image of yourself, your face could replace your password as a means to log-in.

As part of the investigation of the disappearance of Madeleine McCann the British police are calling on visitors to the Ocean Club Resort, Praia da Luz in Portugal or the surrounding areas in the two weeks leading up to the child's disappearance on Thursday 3 May 2007 to provide copies of any photographs of people taken during their stay, in an attempt to identify the abductor using a biometric facial recognition application.

Comparative Study

Among the different biometric techniques facial recognition may not be the most reliable and efficient but its great advantage is that it does not require aid from the test subject. Properly designed systems installed in airports, multiplexes, and other public places can detect presence of criminals among the crowd. Other biometrics like fingerprints, iris, and speech recognition cannot perform this kind of mass scanning. However, questions have been raised on the effectiveness of facial recognition software in cases of railway and airport security.

Criticisms

Weaknesses

Face recognition is not perfect and struggles to perform under certain conditions. Ralph Gross, a researcher at the Carnegie Mellon Robotics Institute, describes one obstacle related to the viewing angle of the face: "Face recognition has been getting pretty good at full frontal faces and 20 degrees off, but as soon as you go towards profile, there've been problems."

Other conditions where face recognition does not work well include poor lighting, sunglasses, long hair, or other objects partially covering the subject's face, and low resolution images.

Effectiveness

Critics of the technology complain that the London Borough of Newham scheme has, as of 2004, never recognized a single criminal, despite several criminals in the system's database living in the Borough and the system having been running for several years. "Not once, as far as the police know, has Newham's automatic facial recognition system spotted a live target." This information seems to conflict with claims that the system was credited with a 34% reduction in crime - which better explains why the system was then rolled out to Birmingham also.

An experiment by the local police department in Tampa, Florida, had similarly disappointing results.

"Camera technology designed to spot potential terrorists by their facial characteristics at airports failed its first major test at Boston's Logan Airport".

Privacy Concerns

Despite the potential benefits of this technology, many citizens are concerned that their privacy will be invaded. Some fear that it could lead to a "total surveillance society," with the government and other authorities having the ability to know where you are, and what you are doing, at all times. This is not to be an underestimated concept as history has shown that states have typically abused such access before.

Recent Improvements

In 2006, the performance of the latest face recognition algorithms were evaluated in the Face Recognition Grand Challenge. High-resolution face images, 3-D face scans, and iris images were used in the tests. The results indicated that the new algorithms are 10 times more accurate than the face recognition algorithms of 2002 and 100 times more accurate than those of 1995. Some of the algorithms were able to outperform human participants in recognizing faces and could uniquely identify identical twins.

Early Development

Pioneers of Automated Facial Recognition include: Woody Bledsoe, Helen Chan Wolf, and Charles Bisson.

During 1964 and 1965, Bledsoe, along with Helen Chan and Charles Bisson, worked on using the computer to recognize human faces (Bledsoe 1966a, 1966b; Bledsoe and Chan 1965). He was proud of this work, but because the funding was provided by an unnamed intelligence agency that did not allow much publicity, little of the work was published. Given a large database of images (in effect, a book of mug shots) and a photograph, the problem was to select from the database a small set of records such that one of the image records matched the photograph. The success of the method could be measured in terms of the ratio of the answer list to the number of records in the database. Bledsoe (1966a) described the following difficulties:

> "This recognition problem is made difficult by the great variability in head rotation and tilt, lighting intensity and angle, facial expression, aging, etc. Some other attempts at facial recognition by machine have allowed for little or no variability in these quantities. Yet the method of correlation (or pattern matching) of unprocessed optical data, which is often used by some researchers, is certain to fail in cases where the variability is great. In particular, the correlation is very low between two pictures of the same person with two different head rotations."

This project was labeled man-machine because the human extracted the coordinates of a set of features from the photographs, which were then used by the computer for recognition. Using a graphics tablet (GRAFACON or RAND

TABLET), the operator would extract the coordinates of features such as the center of pupils, the inside corner of eyes, the outside corner of eyes, point of widows peak, and so on. From these coordinates, a list of 20 distances, such as width of mouth and width of eyes, pupil to pupil, were computed. These operators could process about 40 pictures an hour. When building the database, the name of the person in the photograph was associated with the list of computed distances and stored in the computer. In the recognition phase, the set of distances was compared with the corresponding distance for each photograph, yielding a distance between the photograph and the database record. The closest records are returned.

This brief description is an oversimplification that fails in general because it is unlikely that any two pictures would match in head rotation, lean, tilt, and scale (distance from the camera). Thus, each set of distances is normalized to represent the face in a frontal orientation. To accomplish this normalization, the program first tries to determine the tilt, the lean, and the rotation. Then, using these angles, the computer undoes the effect of these transformations on the computed distances. To compute these angles, the computer must know the three-dimensional geometry of the head. Because the actual heads were unavailable, Bledsoe (1964) used a standard head derived from measurements on seven heads.

After Bledsoe left PRI in 1966, this work was continued at the Stanford Research Institute, primarily by Peter Hart. In experiments performed on a database of over 2000 photographs, the computer consistently outperformed humans when presented with the same recognition tasks (Bledsoe 1968). Peter Hart (1996) enthusiastically recalled the project with the exclamation, "It really worked!"

By about 1997, the system developed by Christoph von der Malsburg and graduate students of the University of Bochum in Germany and the University of Southern

California in the United States outperformed most systems with those of Massachusetts Institute of Technology and the University of Maryland rated next. The Bochum system was developed through funding by the United States Army Research Laboratory. The software was sold as ZN-Face and used by customers such as Deutsche Bank and operators of airports and other busy locations. The software was "robust enough to make identifications from less-than-perfect face views. It can also often see through such impediments to identification as mustaches, beards, changed hair styles and glasses—even sunglasses".

In about January 2007, image searches were "based on the text surrounding a photo," for example, if text nearby mentions the image content. Polar Rose technology can guess from a photograph, in about 1.5 seconds, what any individual may look like in three dimensions, and thought they "will ask users to input the names of people they recognize in photos online" to help build a database.

FUTURE DEVELOPMENTS - RETAILING

A possible future application for facial recognition systems lies in retailing. A retail store (for example, a grocery store) may have cash registers equipped with cameras, the cameras would be aimed at the faces of customers, so pictures of customers could be obtained. The camera would be the primary means of identifying the customer, and if visual identification failed, the customer could complete the purchase by using a PIN (personal identification number). After the cash register had calculated the total sale, the face recognition system would verify the identify of the customer and the total amount of the sale would be deducted from the customer's bank account. Hence, face-based retailing would provide convenience for retail customers, since they could go shopping simply by showing their faces, and there would be no need to bring debit cards, or other financial media. Wide-reaching applications of face-based retailing are possible, including retail stores, restaurants, movie theaters, car rental companies, hotels, etc.

AUTOMATIC NUMBER PLATE RECOGNITION

Automatic number plate recognition (ANPR) is a mass surveillance method that uses optical character recognition on images to read the licence plates on vehicles. As of 2006, systems can scan number plates at around one per second on cars travelling up to 100 mph (160 km/h) They can use existing closed-circuit television or road-rule enforcement cameras, or ones specifically designed for the task. They are used by various police forces and as a method of electronic toll collection on pay-per-use roads, and monitoring traffic activity such as red light adherence in an intersection.

ANPR can be used to store the images captured by the cameras as well as the text from the licence plate, with some configurable to store a photograph of the driver. Systems commonly use infrared lighting to allow the camera to take the picture at any time of day. A powerful flash is included in at least one version of the intersection-monitoring cameras, serving to both illuminate the picture and make the offender aware of his or her mistake. ANPR technology tends to be region specific, owing to plate variation from place to place.

Concerns about these systems have centered on privacy fears of government tracking citizens' movements and media reports of misidentification and high error rates. However, as they have developed, the systems have become much more accurate and reliable.

Other Names

ANPR is sometimes known by various other terms:

- Automatic licence plate recognition (ALPR)
- Automatic vehicle identification (AVI)
- Car plate recognition (CPR)
- Licence plate recognition (LPR)
- Lecture Automatique de Plaques d'Immatriculation (LAPI)

Development History

The ANPR was invented in 1976 at the Police Scientific Development Branch in the UK. Prototype systems were working by 1979 and contracts were let to produce industrial systems, first at EMI Electronics then at Computer Recognition Systems (CRS) in Wokingham, UK. Early trial systems were deployed on the A1 road and at the Dartford Tunnel. The first arrest due to a detected stolen car was made in 1981.

Components

The software aspect of the system runs on standard PC hardware and can be linked to other applications or databases. It first uses a series of image manipulation techniques to detect, normalise and enhance the image of the number plate, and finally optical character recognition (OCR) to extract the alphanumerics of the licence plate. ANPR/ALPR systems are generally deployed in one of two basic approaches; one allows for the entire process to be performed at the lane location in real-time, the other transmits all the images from many lanes to a remote computer location and performs the OCR process there at some later point in time. When done at the lane site, the information captured of the plate alphanumeric, date-time, lane identification, and any other information that is required is completed in somewhere around 250 milliseconds. This information, now small data packets, can easily be transmitted to some remote computer for further processing if necessary, or stored at the lane for later retrieval. In the other arrangement there are typically large numbers of PCs used in a server farm to handle high workloads, such as those found in the London congestion charge project. Often in such systems there is a requirement to forward images to the remote server and this can require larger bandwidth transmission media.

Technology

ANPR uses optical character recognition (OCR) on images taken by cameras. When Dutch vehicle registration plates switched to a different style in 2002 one of the changes made was to the font, introducing small gaps in some letters (such as P and R) to make them more distinct and therefore more legible to such systems. Some licence plate arrangements use variations in font sizes and positioning – ANPR systems must be able to cope with such differences in order to be truly effective. More complicated systems can cope with international variants, though many programs are individually tailored to each country.

The cameras used can include existing road-rule enforcement or closed-circuit television cameras as well as mobile units which are usually attached to vehicles. Some systems use infrared cameras to take a clearer image of the plates.

ANPR in Mobile Systems

Advances in technology have taken Automatic Number Plate Reader (ANPR) systems from fixed applications to mobile ones. Scaled-down components at more cost-effective price points have led to a record number of deployments by law enforcement agencies around the world. Smaller cameras with the ability to read license plates at high speeds, along with smaller, more durable processors that fit in the trunks of police vehicles, allow law enforcement officers to patrol daily with the benefit of license plate reading in real time, when they can interdict immediately.

Despite their effectiveness, there are noteworthy challenges related with mobile ANPRs. One of the biggest is that the processor and the cameras must work fast enough to accommodate relative speeds of more than 100 mph (160 km/h), a likely scenario in the case of oncoming traffic. This equipment must also be very efficient since the power source is the vehicle battery and equipment must be small to minimize the space it requires.

Relative speed is only one issue that affects the camera's ability to actually read a license plate. Algorithms must be able to compensate for all the variables that can affect the ANPR's ability to produce an accurate read, such as time of day, weather and angles between the cameras and the license plates. A system's illumination wavelengths can also have a direct impact on the resolution and accuracy of a read in these conditions.

Installing ANPR cameras on law enforcement vehicles requires careful consideration of the juxtaposition of the cameras to the license plates they are to read. Using the right number of cameras and positioning them accurately for optimal results can prove challenging given the various missions and environments at hand. Highway patrol requires forward-looking cameras that span multiple lanes and are able to read license plates at very high speeds. City patrol needs shorter range, lower focal length cameras for capturing plates on parked cars. And parking lots with perpendicularly parked cars often require a specialized camera with a very short focal length. Most technically advanced systems are flexible and can be configured with a number of cameras ranging from one to four which can easily be repositioned as needed. States with rear-only license plates have an additional challenge since a forward-looking camera is ineffective with incoming traffic. In this case one camera may be turned backwards.

Difficulties

Early ANPR systems were unable to read white or silver lettering on black background, as permitted on UK vehicles built prior to 1973.

There are a number of possible difficulties that the software must be able to cope with. These include:

- Poor image resolution, usually because the plate is too far away but sometimes resulting from the use of a low-quality camera.

- Blurry images, particularly motion blur.
- Poor lighting and low contrast due to overexposure, reflection or shadows.
- An object obscuring (part of) the plate, quite often a tow bar, or dirt on the plate.
- A different font, popular for vanity plates (some countries do not allow such plates, eliminating the problem)
- Circumvention techniques.
- Lack of coordination between countries or states. Two cars from different countries or states can have the same number but different design of the plate.

  Must be able to recognise foreign licence plates as such.

While some of these problems can be corrected within the software it is primarily left to the hardware side of the system to work out solutions to these difficulties. Increasing the height of the camera may avoid problems with objects (such as other vehicles) obscuring the plate, but introduces and increases other problems such as the adjusting for the increased skew of the plate.

On some cars, towbars may obscure one or two characters of the licence plate. Bikes on bike racks can also obscure the number plate, though in some countries and jurisdictions, such as Victoria, Australia, "bike plates" are supposed to be fitted.

Some small-scale systems allow for some errors in the licence plate. When used for giving specific vehicles access to a barriered area the decision may be made to have an acceptable error rate of one character. This is because the likelihood of an unauthorised car having such a similar licence plate is seen as quite small. However, this level of inaccuracy would not be acceptable in most applications of an ANPR system.

Imaging Hardware

At the front end of any ANPR system is the imaging hardware which captures the image of the license plates. The initial image capture n accordance to the Garbage In, Garbage Out principle of computing, will often determine the overall performance.

Licese plate capture is typically performed by specialized cameras designed specifically for the task. Factors which pose difficulty for license plate imaging cameras include speed of the vehicles being recorded, varying ambient lighting conditions, headligh glare and harsh environmental conditions. Most dedicated license plate capture cameras will incorporate infrared illumination in order to solve the problems of lighting and plate reflectivity.

Many countries now use licence plates that are retroreflective This returns the light back to the source and thus improves the contrast of the image. In some countries, the characters on the plate are not reflective, giving a high level of contrast with the reflective background in any lighting conditions. A camera that makes use of active infrared imaging (with a normal colour filter over the lens and an infrared illuminator next to it) benefits greatly from this as the infrared waves are reflected back from the plate. This is only possible on dedicated ANPR cameras, however, and so cameras used for other purposes must rely more heavily on the software capabilities. Further, when a full-colour image is required as well as use of the ANPR-retrieved details it is necessary to have one infrared-enabled camera and one normal (colour) camera working together.

Blurry images make OCR difficult or impossible. ANPR systems should have fast shutter speeds to avoid motion blur.

To avoid blurring it is ideal to have the shutter speed of a dedicated camera set to 1/1000th of a second. Because the car is moving, slower shutter speeds could result in an image which is too blurred to read using the OCR software, especially if the camera is much higher up than the vehicle. In slow-moving traffic, or when the camera is at a lower level and the vehicle is at an angle approaching the camera, the shutter speed does not need to be so fast. Shutter speeds of 1/500th of a second can cope with traffic moving up to 40 mph (64 km/h) and 1/250th of a second up to 5 mph (8 km/h). License plate capture cameras can now produce usable images from vehicles traveling at 120 mph (190 km/h).

To maximize the chances of effective license plate capture, installers should carefully consider the positioning of the camera relative to the target capture area. Exceeding threshold angles of incidence between camera lens and license plate will greatly reduce the probability of obtaining usable images due to distortion. Manufacturers have developed tools to help eliminate errors from the physical installation of license plate capture cameras.

Circumvention Techniques

Vehicle owners have used a variety of techniques in an attempt to evade ANPR systems and road-rule enforcement cameras in general. One method increases the reflective properties of the lettering and makes it more likely that the system will be unable to locate the plate or produce a high enough level of contrast to be able to read it. This is typically done by using a plate cover or a spray, though claims regarding the effectiveness of the latter are disputed. In most jurisdictions, the covers are illegal and covered under existing laws, while in most countries there is no law to disallow the use of the sprays. Other users have attempted to smear their license plate with dirt or utilize covers to mask the plate.

Novelty frames around Texas license plates were made illegal in Texas on 1 September 2003 by Texas Senate Bill 439 because they caused problems with ANPR devices. That law made it a Class C misdemeanor (punishable by a fine of up to US $200), or Class B (punishable by a fine of up to US $2,000 and 180 days in jail) if it can be proven that the owner did it to deliberately obscure their plates.

If an ANPR system cannot read the plate it can flag the image for attention, with the human operators looking to see if they are able to identify the alphanumerics.

In order to avoid surveillance or penalty charges, there has been an upsurge in car cloning. This is usually achieved by copying registration plates from another car of a similar model and age. This can be difficult to detect, especially as cloners may change the registration plates and travel behavior to hinder investigations.

In principle, it may be possible to foil infrared detection simply by heating the license plate to a sufficient temperature so that the infrared brightness of the license plate exceeds that of the reflected signal that would otherwise be detected in the camera.

Other Uses

ANPR systems may also be used for/by:

- Section control, to measure average vehicle speed over longer distances.
- Border crossings.
- Filling stations to log when a motorist drives away without paying for their fuel.
- A marketing tool to log patterns of use.
- Traffic management systems, which determine traffic flow using the time it takes vehicles to pass two ANPR sites.
- How ANPR can be used.
- Where ANPR can be used.
- Drive Through Customer Recognition, to automatically recognize customers based on their license plate and offer them their last selection, improving service to the customer.

Measuring ANPR System Performance

It is not uncommon to read claims of Automatic Number Plate Recognition read rates in excess of 98%. The experience of system operators is that overall read rates for licence plates are 90% to 94% in ideal conditions with excellent modern systems. In some older systems overall performance rates are rumoured to be between 60% and 80%. ANPR is a developing technology which is coming of age and functional applications are expanding on a steady basis. Although there has been a significant improvement in recent years in the performance of ANPR systems, how operators can assess and monitor ANPR/LPR systems has not advanced as much.

12

Face Perception

Face perception is the process by which the brain and mind understand and interpret the face, particularly the human face.

The face is an important site for the identification of others and conveys significant social information. Probably because of the importance of its role in social interaction, psychological processes involved in face perception are known to be present from birth, to be complex, and to involve large and widely distributed areas in the brain. These parts of the brain can be damaged to cause a specific impairment in understanding faces known as prosopagnosia.

Development

While there is no question that the majority of face perception skills developed by adults are not present in babies, there is evidence of an innate tendency to pay attention to faces from birth. It is known that early perceptual experience is crucial to the development of visual perception and this orienting response undoubtedly encourages the rapid development of face specific skills such as the ability to identify friendly others and relatively complex pre-verbal communication. By two months of age face perception has developed so specific areas of the brain are known to be activated by viewing faces.

Adult Face Perception

Theories about the processes involved in adult face perception have largely come from two sources: research on normal adult face perception and the study of impairments in face perception that are caused by brain injury or neurological illness.

One of the most widely accepted theories of face perception argues that understanding faces involves several stages: from basic perceptual manipulations on the sensory information to derive details about the person (such as age, gender or attractiveness), to being able to recall meaningful details such as their name and any relevant past experiences of the individual.

This model (developed by psychologists Vicki Bruce and Andrew Young) argues that face perception might involve several independent sub-processes working in unison.

> A 'view centred description' is derived from the perceptual input. Simple physical aspects of the face are used to work out age, gender or simple facial expressions. Most analysis at this stage is on feature-by-feature basis.
>
> This initial information is used to create a structural model of the face, which allows it to be compared to other faces in memory, and across views. This explains why the same person seen from a novel angle can still be recognised. This structural encoding can be seen to be specific for upright faces as demonstrated by the Thatcher effect.
>
> The structurally encoded representation is transferred to notional 'face recognition units' which in conjunction with 'person identity nodes' allow the person to be

identified by information from semantic memory. Interestingly, the ability to produce someone's name when presented with their face has been shown to be selectively damaged in some cases of brain injury, suggesting that naming may be a separate process from being able to produce other information about a person.

The study of *prosopagnosia* (an impairment in recognising faces which is usually caused by brain injury) has been particularly helpful in understanding how normal face perception might work. Individuals with prosopagnosia may differ in their abilities to understand faces, and it has been the investigation of these differences which has suggested that several stage theories might be correct.

Face perception is an ability which involves a great deal of the brain, however some areas have been shown to be particularly important. Brain imaging studies typically show a great deal of activity in an area of the temporal lobe known as the fusiform gyrus, an area also known to cause prosopagnosia when damaged (particularly when damage occurs on both sides). This evidence has led to a particular interest in this area and it is sometimes referred to as the fusiform face area for that reason.

Neuroanatomy of Facial Processing

Facial perception has well identified, neuroanatomical correlates in the brain. Most scientists agree that during the perception of faces, major activations occur in the extrastriate areas bilaterally, particularly in the fusiform gyri and in the inferior temporal gyri. Others have shown that the fusiform gyri are preferentially responsive to faces, whereas the para-hippocampal/lingual gyri are responsive to buildings. Ishai and colleagues have proposed the object form topology hypothesis, which posits that there is a topological organisation of neural substrates for object and facial processing. However, Gauthier disagrees and suggests that the category-specific and process-map models could accommodate most other proposed models for the neural underpinnings of facial processing. Most neuroanatomical substrates for facial processing are perfused by the middle cerebral artery (MCA). Therefore, facial processing has been studied using measurements of mean cerebral blood flow velocity in the middle cerebral arteries bilaterally. During facial recognition tasks, greater changes in the right middle cerebral artery (RMCA) than the left (LMCA) have been observed. It has been demonstrated that men were right lateralised and women left lateralised during facial processing tasks.

Gender-related Asymmetry in Facial Processing

The mechanisms underlying gender-related differences in facial processing have not been studied extensively. Studies using electrophysiological techniques have demonstrated gender-related differences during a face recognition memory (FRM) task and a facial affect identification task (FAIT). The male subjects used a right, while the female subjects used a left, hemisphere neural activation system in the processing of faces and facial affect. Moreover, in facial perception there was no association to estimated intelligence, suggesting that face recognition performance in women is unrelated to several basic cognitive processes. Gender-related differences may suggest a role for sex hormones. In females there may be variability for psychological functions related to differences in hormonal levels during different phases of the menstrual cycle. Data obtained in norm and in pathology support asymmetric face processing. Gorno-Tempini and others in 2001, suggested that the left inferior frontal cortex and the bilateral occipitotemporal junction respond equally to all face conditions. Some neuroscientists contend that both the left inferior frontal cortex (Brodmann area 47) and the occipitotemporal junction are implicated in facial memory. The right inferior temporal/fusiform gyrus responds selectively to faces but not to non-faces. The right temporal pole is activated during the discrimination of familiar faces and scenes from unfamiliar ones. Right asymmetry in the mid temporal lobe for faces has also been shown using 133-Xenon measured cerebral blood flow (CBF). Other investigators have observed right lateralisation for facial recognition in previous electro-physiological and imaging studies.

The implication of the observation of asymmetry for facial perception would be that different hemispheric strategies would be implemented. The right hemisphere would be expected to employ a holistic strategy, and the left an analytic strategy. In 2007, Philip Njemanze using a novel functional transcranial Doppler (fTCD)] technique called functional transcranial Doppler spectroscopy (fTCDS) demonstrated that men were right lateralised for object and facial perception, while women were left lateralised for facial tasks but showed a right tendency or no lateralisation for object perception Njemanze demonstrated using fTCDS, summation of responses related to facial stimulus complexity, which could be presumed as evidence for topological organisation of these cortical areas in men. It may suggest that the latter extends from the area implicated in object perception to a much greater area involved in facial perception. This agrees with the object form topology hypothesis proposed by Ishai and colleagues in 1999. However, the relatedness of object and facial perception was process based, and appears to be associated with their common holistic processing strategy in the right hemisphere. Moreover, when the same men were presented with facial paradigm requiring analytic processing, the left hemisphere was activated. This agrees with the suggestion made by Gauthier in 2000, that the extrastriate cortex contains areas that are best suited for different computations, and described as the process-map model. Therefore, the proposed models are not mutually exclusive, and this underscores the fact that facial processing does not impose any new constraints on the brain other than those used for other stimuli. It may be suggested that each stimulus was mapped by category into face or non-face, and by process into holistic or analytic.

Therefore, a unified category-specific process-mapping system was implemented for either right or left cognitive styles. Njemanze in 2007, concluded that, for facial perception, men used a category-specific process-mapping system for right cognitive style, but women used same for the left.

Controversies

While a great deal of resources seem to be used by the mind and brain to understand the face, opinion is divided as to whether we genuinely develop specific skills for understanding faces, or whether face perception is just part of a general skill for making within-category discriminations, such as recognising and differentiating between similar animals or plants. Recognising a face involves a process of analogy.

Proponents of this view argue that the differences seen between faces and non-face objects in experimental studies are due to faces being particularly difficult to distinguish and observers having acquired expertise at making these discriminations. Although we often assume that faces are relatively unique, statistically they are quite similar, so a great deal of cognitive effort is needed to differentiate them. According to this view, faces are nothing more than a particularly difficult class of perceptual object which we have learned to distinguish at the expert level, much as we would learn to distinguish between other similar objects if much of our communication and survival depended on it.

Cognitive Neuroscientists Isabel Gauthier and Michael Tarr are two of the major proponents of the view that face recognition involves expert discrimination of similar objects. Other scientists, in particular Nancy Kanwisher and her colleagues, argue that face recognition involves processes that are face-specific and that are not recruited by expert discriminations in other object classes.

Studies by Gauthier have shown that an area of the brain known as the fusiform gyrus (sometimes called the 'fusiform face area' because it is active during face recognition) is also active when study participants are asked to discriminate between different types of birds and cars, and even when participants become expert at distinguishing computer generated nonsense shapes known as greebles This suggests that the fusiform gyrus may have a general role in the recognition of similar visual objects. Yaoda Xu, then a post doctoral fellow with Nancy Kanwisher, replicated the car and bird expertise study using an improved fMRI design that was less susceptible to attentional accounts.

The activity found by Gauthier when participants viewed non-face objects was not as strong as when participants were viewing faces, however this could be because we have much more expertise for faces than for most other objects. Furthermore, not all of findings of this research have been successfully replicated, for example, other research groups using different study designs have found that the fusiform gyrus is specific to faces and other nearby regions deal with non-face objects.

However, these failures to replicate are difficult to interpret, because studies vary on too many aspects of the method. It has been argued that some studies test experts with objects that are slightly outside of their domain of expertise. More to the point, failures to replicate are null effects and can occur for many different reasons. In contrast, each replication adds a great deal of weight to a particular argument. With regard to "face specific" effects in neuroimaging, there are now multiple replications with Greebles, with birds and cars nd two unpublished studies with chess experts.

Although it is sometimes found that expertise recruits the FFA (e.g. as hypothesized by a proponent of this view in the preceding paragraph), a more common and less controversial finding is that expertise leads to focal category-selectivity in the fusiform gyrus - a pattern similar in terms of antecedent factors and neural specificity to that seen for faces. As such, it remains an open question as to whether face recognition and expert-level object recognition recruit similar neural mechanisms across different subregions of the fusiform or whether the two domains literally share the same neural substrates. Moreover, at least one study argues that the issue as to whether expertise-predicated category-selective areas overlap with the FFA is nonsensical in that multiple measurements of the FFA within an individual person often overlap no more with each other than do measurements of FFA and expertise-predicated regions At the same time, such expertise effects have been characterized as extremely small , and numerous well done studies have failed to replicate them altogether. For example, four published fMRI studies have asked whether expertise has any specific connection to the FFA in particular, by testing for expertise effects in both the FFA and a nearby but not face-selective region called LOC. In all four studies, expertise effects are significantly stronger in the LOC than in the FFA, and indeed expertise effects were only borderline significant in the FFA in two of the studies, while the effects were robust and significant in the LOC in all four studies. Thus, there is no evidence that increased fMRI activations due to perceptual expertise affect the FFA in particular, as opposed to nearby cortex.

Therefore, it is still not clear in exactly which situations the fusiform gyrus becomes active, although it is certain that face recognition relies heavily on this area and damage to it can lead to severe face recognition impairment.

Differences in own- versus other-race face recognition and perceptual discrimination have been shown across a series of studies This phenomenon is often referred to as the own-race effect, cross-race face effect, other-race effect, own race bias or interracial-face-recognition-deficit.

A meta-analysis, Mullen found evidence that the other-race effect is larger among White subjects than among African American subjects, whereas Brigham and Williamson (1979, cited in Shepherd, 1981) obtained the opposite pattern. Shepherd also reviewed studies that found a main effect for race efface like that of the present study, with better performance on White faces, other studies in which no difference was found and yet other studies in which performance was better on African American faces. Overall, Sheperd reports a reliable positive correlation between the size of the effect of target race (indexed by the difference in proportion correct on same- and other-race faces) and self-ratings of amount of interaction with members of the other race, $r(30) = .57$, $p < .01$. This correlation is at least partly an artifact of the fact that African American subjects, who performed equally well on faces of both races, almost always responded with the highest possible self-rating of amount of interaction with White people ($M = 4.75$), whereas their White counterparts both demonstrated an other-race effect and reported less other-race interaction ($M = 2.13$); the difference in ratings was reliable, £(30) = 7.86, $p < .01$.

Further research points to the importance of other-race experience in own-versus other-race face processing (O'Toole et al., 1991; Slone et al., 2000; Walker & Tanaka, 2003). In a series of studies, Walker and colleagues showed the relationship between amount and type of other-race contact and the ability to perceptually differentiate other-race faces. Participants with greater other-race experience were consistently more accurate at discriminating between other-race faces than were participants with less other-race exprience.

In addition to other-race contact, there is suggestion that the own-race effect is linked to increased ability to extract information about the spatial relationships between different features. Richard Ferraro writes that facial recognition is an example of a neuropsychological measure that can be used to assess cognitive abilities that are salient within African-

American culture. The deficit occurs because people emphasize visual information specifying race at the expense of individuating information when recognizing faces of other races Further research using perceptual tasks could shed light on the specific cognitive processes involved in the other-race effect. They had observed that people from New Guinea and Ethopia who had had contact to white people before had a significantly better emotional recognition rate. The German university spin-off company Global Emotion uses this knowledge to overcome the Caucasian-Asian other-race effect with an online-training.

Studies on adults have also shown sex differences in face recognition. Men tend to recognise fewer faces of women than women do, whereas there are no sex differences with regard to male faces.

Artificial Face Perception

A great deal of effort has been put into developing software that can recognise human faces; see facial recognition system. Much of the work has been done by a branch of artificial intelligence known as computer vision which uses findings from the psychology of face perception to inform software design. Recent breakthroughs using noninvasive functional transcranial Doppler spectroscopy as demonstrated by Njemanze, 2007, to locate specific responses to facial stimuli have led to improved systems for facial recognition. The new system uses input responses called cortical long-term potentiation (CLTP) derived from Fourier analysis of mean blood flow velocity to trigger target face search from a computerized face database system Such a system provides for brain-machine interface for facial recognition, and the method has been referred to as cognitive biometrics.

PROSOPAGNOSIA

Prosopagnosia (sometimes known as face blindness) is a disorder of face perception where the ability to recognize faces is impaired, while the ability to recognize other objects may be relatively intact. The term originally referred to a condition following acute brain damage, but recently a congenital form of the disorder has been identified, which is inherited by about 2.5% of the population The specific brain area usually associated with prosopagnosia is the fusiform gyrus.

Few successful therapies have so far been developed for affected people, although individuals often learn to use 'piecemeal' or 'feature by feature' recognition strategies. This may involve secondary clues such as clothing, hair color, body shape, and voice. Because the face seems to function as an important identifying feature in memory, it can also be difficult for people with this condition to keep track of information about people, and socialize normally with others.

Some also use the term prosophenosia, which refers to the inability to recognize faces following extensive damage of both occipital and temporal lobes.

Overview

Selective inabilities to recognize faces were reported throughout the 19th century, and included case studies by Hughlings Jackson and Charcot. However, it was not named until the term *prosopagnosia* was first used in 1947 by Joachim Bodamer, a German neurologist. He described three cases, including a 24-year old man who suffered a bullet wound to the head and lost his ability to recognise his friends, family, and even his own face. However, he was able to recognize and identify them through other sensory modalities such as auditory, tactile, and even other visual stimuli patterns (such as gait and other physical mannerisms). Bodamer gave his paper the title *Die Prosop-Agnosie*, derived from classical Greek (*prosopon*) meaning "face" and (*agnosia*) meaning "non-knowledge".

The study of prosopagnosia has been crucial in the development of theories of face perception. Because prosopagnosia is not a unitary disorder (i.e., different people may show different types and levels of impairment) it has been argued that face perception involves a number of stages, each of which can be separately damaged This is reflected not just in the amount of impairment displayed but also in the qualitative differences in impairment that a person with prosopagnosia may present with.

This sort of evidence has been crucial in supporting the theory that there may be a specific face perception system in the brain. This is counter-intuitive to many people as we do not experience faces as 'special' or perceived in a different way from the rest of the world.

There is some debate about the specificity of both face perception and prosopagnosia and some people have argued that it is just a subtype of visual agnosia. While prosopagnosia is often accompanied by problems with recognising visual objects, cases have been reported where perception for faces seems to be selectively impaired.

A report of a case described a closely related condition called prosopamnesia, in which the subject, from birth, could perceive faces normally but had a severely impaired ability to remember them.

It has also been argued that prosopagnosia may be a general impairment in understanding how individual perceptual components make up the structure or gestalt of an object. Psychologist Martha Farah has been particularly associated with this view.

Until early in the 21st century, prosopagnosia was thought to be quite rare and solely associated with brain injury or neurological illness affecting specific areas of the brain. However, recently a form of congenital prosopagnosia has been identified, in which people are born with a selective impairment in recognising and perceiving faces. The cases that have been reported suggest that this form of the disorder may be highly variable and some newer research suggests that it may be heritable and much more common than previously thought (about 2.5% of the population may be affected) It has been suggested that very mild cases of face blindness are much more common, perhaps affecting 10% of the population, although there have not been any studies confirming this. The inability to keep track of the identity of characters in movies is a common complaint.

A classic case of a prosopagnosia is presented by "Dr P" in Oliver Sacks' 1985 book The Man Who Mistook His Wife for a Hat. Although Dr. P could not recognize his wife from her face, he was able to recognize her by her voice. His recognition of pictures of his family and friends appeared to be based on highly specific features, such as his brother's chipped tooth.

Subtypes

Apperceptive Prosopagnosia

Apperceptive prosopagnosia is thought to be a disorder of some of the earliest processes in the face perception system. People with this disorder cannot make any sense of faces and are unable to make same-different judgements when they are presented with pictures of different faces. They may also be unable to work out attributes such as age or gender from a face. However, they may be able to recognise people based on non-face clues such as their clothing, hairstyle or voice.

Associative Prosopagnosia

Associative prosopagnosia (AP) is thought to be an impairment to the links between early face perception processes and the semantic information we hold about people in our memories. People with this form of the disorder may be able to say whether photos of people's faces are the same or different and derive the age and gender from a face (suggesting they can make sense of some face information) but may not be able to subsequently identify the person or provide any information about them such as their name, occupation or when they were last encountered. They may be able to recognise and produce such information based on non-face information such as voice, hair, or even particularly distinctive facial features (such as a distinctive moustache) that does not require the structure of the face to be understood. Typically such people do not report that 'faces make no sense' but simply that they do not look distinctive in any way.

Developmental Prosopagnosia

Developmental prosopagnosia (DP) is thought to be a form of 'congenital prosopagnosia', and that some people are born with a selective impairment in recognizing and perceiving faces. The cases that have been reported suggest that this form of the disorder may be highly variable and there is some suggestion that it may be hereditary.

It is known that there are many developmental disorders that incorporate within themselves an increased likelihood that the person will have differences in face perception, of which the person may or may not be aware. That is to say, the person may or may not have insight in the clinical sense of the word. However, the mechanism by which these effects take place is largely unknown. A partial list of some disorders that often have prosopagnosiac components would include nonverbal learning disorder, Williams syndrome, and autism spectrum disorders in general. However these types of disorders are very complicated, so arbitrary assumptions should be avoided.

Unconscious Face Recognition

One particularly interesting feature of prosopagnosia is that it suggests both a conscious and unconscious aspect to face recognition. Experiments have shown that when presented with a mixture of familiar and unfamiliar faces, people with prosopagnosia may be unable to successfully identify the people in the pictures, or even make a simple familiarity judgement ("this person seems familiar/ unfamiliar"). However, when a measure of emotional response is taken (typically a measure of skin conductance) there tends to be an emotional response to familiar people even though no conscious recognition takes place.

This suggests emotion plays a significant role in face recognition, perhaps unsurprising when basic survival (particularly security) relies on identifying the people around you.

It is thought that Capgras delusion may be the reverse of prosopagnosia. In this condition people report conscious recognition of people from faces, but show no emotional response, perhaps leading to the delusional belief that their relative or spouse has been replaced by an impostor.

13

Microspectrophotometer

The UV-visible-NIR microspectrophotometer is an instrument used to measure spectra of microscopic samples or microscopic areas on samples. They have many functions and are known by many names:

- microspectrometer or microspectrophotometer
- microscope spectrometer or microscope spectrophotometer
- microscope photometer or microphotometer
- cytospectrophotometer or cytospectrometer
- microfluorimeter or microfluorometer
- Raman microspectrometer

While some have a specific function, such as the microfluorometer or the Raman microspectrometer, most are designed to measure spectra of microscopic areas or microscopic samples. The UV-visible-NIR microspectrophotometer can be configured to measure the transmittance, absorbance, reflectance, polarization, fluorescence and luminescence microspectra of sample areas smaller than a micron. They are also capable of non-destructive and non-contact colorimetry and thin film thickness measurement. Because UV-visible-NIR micro-spectrometers are so flexible, they are used in many fields of research and industry.

Some of these instruments are designed to be added to standard microscopes or probe stations, such as the QDI 302™ microscope spectrophotometer, while others are fully integrated, purpose built instruments such as the QDI 2010™ microspectrophotometer. As such, microspectrophotometers have greater spectral ranges, better results and a number of features that are not possible with add-on units.

Why Use a Microspectrophotometer?

The microspectrophotometer allows the scientist or engineer to acquire spectra of extremely small sample areas non-destructively. Measurements can be made while light is transmitted through the sample, reflected from it or even when the sample is made to emit light such as from an OLED pixel. The UV-visible-NIR range is especially important as more substances . . . even colorless ones . . . absorb in the UV than in the visible and infrared regions. Therefore, a UV microscope spectrometer is very useful for analysis of most samples for any application.

Microspectrophotometers are widely used in many different fields and are found in both scientific laboratories and production facilities. In the production environment, for example, they are used for quality control of everything from color masks in flat panel displays to the thickness of films on semiconductor integrated circuits. Microspectrometers are used by analytical laboratories to identify and quantify microscopic samples ranging from the kinetics of cells by a biologist, diagnosis of cancer by a doctor, matching fibers or paints by a forensic chemist, the qualification of gems or coal by a geologist, the determination of the colour of ink or paint by a process chemist or even the analysis of great works of art by conservators. As such, the microspectrometer is a highly flexible instrument with many different applications.

Science of Microspectroscopy

The UV-visible-NIR microspectrophotometer is designed to measure spectra of microscopic areas or microscopic samples. It can be configured to measure the transmittance, absorbance, reflectance, polarization and fluorescence of sample areas as small as one micron.

Absorbance

Microspectroscopy is the study of the quantized energy transfer between radiation and matter. The energy of light is directly related to its wavelength by the Einstein-Planck relationship:

$$E = hv = \frac{hc}{\lambda}$$

The electromagnetic energy of a photon is inversely proportional to its wavelength. In other words, short wavelength or blue light is higher energy than red light. Due to the differences, the light causes different effects when it interacts with molecules. In the ultraviolet-visible region, electronic transitions are mainly observed. Namely, when a photon of the proper energy is absorbed by a molecule, an electron is excited to higher energy level or shell. This is most commonly described in what is called a Jablonski diagram (as shown to the left).

For a photon to be absorbed, the energy of the photon must correspond to the difference in energy between the ground state and the excited state to which the electron transfers. As can be seen in the diagram, the electron jumps to the first excited state (S1) when an electron of the corresponding energy is absorbed. If a photon of a higher energy, one that corresponds to the difference between the ground and say the second excited state (S2), were absorbed, the electron would jump the S2 state.

The energy levels of the molecules are due to the types of atoms and how they are bound to one another. Additionally, the shape of the molecule as well as its environment can also play a part in structuring the energy levels. In fact, a dye chemist can "tune" a dye molecule by adding or removing functional groups or atoms of a molecule, thereby changing its color.

Fluorescence

After the electron has jumped to the excited state, it then decays by internal conversion to the lowest excited state, S1. From there it can decay back to the ground state by a number of paths. The most common is a radiation-less transition whereby the electron drops from the S1 excited state to the ground state losing energy without the emission of a photon. However, when the electron drops from the S1 state to the ground state *with* the emission of a photon, the process is called fluorescence. It is a rapid process and fluorescence lifetimes usually follow first order kinetic rules. It should be noted that the fluorescence intensity is governed by many factors, some of which include excitation wavelength, quantum yield, quenching materials and even molecular structure.

Reflectance

Reflectance microspectroscopy simply measures the spectra of electromagnetic energy reflected from the sample. The portion that is not reflected may have been absorbed or transmitted through the sample (if transparent to that wavelength of light) or even scattered. Reflected light may be divided into two types: specular and diffuse. Simply put, specular reflectance is like the reflectance from a mirror. The light is reflected at the same angle as it impinges upon the mirror surface. Diffuse reflectance is similar to what occurs with white paper. Light is effectively reflected at all angles.

Chemistry and Colour

Substances absorb, reflect or emit light in ways that are dependant upon their chemical structure and their environment. Examples include the pigments found in automotive paints that reflect specific wavelengths of light which we perceive as a colour . . . or quantum dots, commonly used for biological analysis, that emit light of specific wavelengths when excited and then decay back to the ground state with the emission of photons. The optical properties of these colorants depend upon the molecular structure of their chromophores (the molecules that interact with the light) as well as their environment. Measuring the optical properties of these molecules on the microscale is called microspectroscopy.

Microspectrophotometer Design

The UV-visible-NIR microspectrophotometer is designed to measure the spectrum of microscopic areas or microscopic samples. It can be configured to measure the transmittance, absorbance, reflectance, polarization and fluorescence of sample areas as smaller than a micron.

Microspectrophotometer Components

The microspectrophotometer is sometimes called a microscope spectrophotometer as it combines an optical microscope and a highly sensitive spectrophotometer. In actuality, the microspectrophotometer is a fully integrated, purpose built instrument while the microscope spectrophotometer is an add-on component for a standard microscope. As such, add-on components have certain performance limitations due to the microscope itself. An integrated instrument avoids those limitations as it is designed specifically for microspectroscopy.

Individually, the microscope is an optical instrument that uses lenses and mirrors to produce magnified images of microscopic objects or microscopic areas of larger objects. The sample is illuminated in one several ways:

- Transmission illumination where light is focused onto the sample by the condenser. The portion collected by the microscope objective has been transmitted through the sample.

- Incident or reflectance illumination where light is again focused onto the sample but through the objective. The reflected light from the sample is collected by the same objective. Reflectance can be further subdivided into specular and diffuse incident illumination.
- Emission: where the sample emits light after the sample has been stimulated in some manner. One example is fluorescence where a fluorophore is excited with one wavelength of light and emits light of a different wavelength. The emitted light is collected by the microscope objective.

The objective of the microscope is used to collect the light from the sample and focus it on the spectrophotometer aperture. The digital imaging system images both the aperture and the sample simultaneously so that it can present an image that shows what the spectrophotometer aperture is measuring.

The spectrophotometer portion of the microspectrophotometer is an optical instrument for measuring the intensity of light relative to its wavelength. The electromagnetic energy, collected from the sample, enters the device through the aperture and is separated into its component wavelengths by a diffraction grating. The separated light is then focused onto a CCD array detector where the intensity of each wavelength is then measured by a pixel of the array. The CCD is then read-ff to a computer and the result is a spectrum which displays the intensity of each wavelength of light. By making measurements of reference materials, corrected microspectra.

In a microspectrophotometer, such as those made by CRAIC Technologies, the spectrophotometer is integrated with a specially designed microscope. The microscope optics and light sources are of the highest quality and able to operate in the ultraviolet, visible and near infrared regions (normal microscopes only operate in the visible range). The spectrophotometer is built into the microscope, along with a digital imaging system, so that the maximum amount of light can be collected from the smallest samples. As such, microspectrophotometers are very flexible instruments able to measure absorbance, transmittance, reflectance, and emission (such as fluorescence) spectra of even sub-micron sized samples.

14

Forensic Psychology

Forensic psychology is the intersection between psychology and the criminal justice system. It involves understanding criminal law in the relevant jurisdictions in order to be able to interact appropriately with judges, attorneys and other legal professionals. An important aspect of forensic psychology is the ability to testify in court, reformulating psychological findings into the legal language of the courtroom, providing information to legal personnel in a way that can be understood Further, in order to be a credible witness, for example in the United States, the forensic psychologist must understand the philosophy, rules and standards of the American judicial system. Primary is an understanding of the adversarial model under which the system functions. There are also rules about hearsay evidence and importantly the exclusionary rule. Lack of a firm grasp of these procedures will result in the forensic psychologist losing credibility in the courtroom. A forensic psychologist can be trained in clinical, social, organizational or any other branch of psychology In the United States, the salient issue is the designation by the court as an expert witness by training, experience or both by the judge. Generally, a forensic psychologist is designated as an expert in a particular jurisdiction. The number of jurisdictions in which a forensic psychologist qualifies as an expert increases with experience and reputation.

Questions asked by the court of a forensic psychologist are generally not questions regarding psychology but are legal questions and the response must be in language the court understands. For example, a forensic psychologist is frequently appointed by the court to assess a defendant's competency to stand trial. The court also frequently appoints a forensic psychologist to assess the state of mind of the defendant at the time of the offense. This is referred to as an evaluation of the defendant's sanity or insanity (which relates to criminal responsibility) at the time of the offense These are not primarily psychological questions but rather legal ones. Thus, a forensic psychologist must be able to translate psychological information into a legal framework.

Forensic psychologists also provide sentencing recommendations, treatment recommendations, and any other information the judge requests, such as information regarding mitigating factors, assessment of future risk, and evaluation of witness credibility. Forensic psychology also involves training and evaluating police or other law enforcement personnel, providing law enforcement with criminal profiles and in other ways working with police departments. Forensic psychologists work both with the Public Defender, the States Attorney, and private attorneys. Forensic psychologists may also help with jury selection.

Distinction between Forensic and Therapeutic Evaluation

A forensic psychologist's interactions with and ethical responsibilities to the client differ widely from those of a psychologist dealing with a client in a clinical setting.

- **Scope**. Rather than the broad set of issues a psychologist addresses in a clinical setting, a forensic psychologist addresses a narrowly defined set of events or interactions of a nonclinical nature.

- **Importance of client's perspective**. A clinician places primary importance on understanding the client's unique point of view, while the forensic psychologist is interested in accuracy, and the client's viewpoint is secondary.
- **Voluntariness**. Usually in a clinical setting a psychologist is dealing with a voluntary client. A forensic psychologist evaluates clients by order of a judge or at the behest of an attorney.
- **Autonomy**. Voluntary clients have more latitude and autonomy regarding the assessment's objectives. Any assessment usually takes their concerns into account. The objectives of a forensic examination are confined by the applicable statutes or common law elements that pertain to the legal issue in question.
- **Threats to validity**. While the client and therapist are working toward a common goal, although unconscious distortion may occur, in the forensic context there is a substantially greater likelihood of intentional and conscious distortion.
- **Relationship and dynamics**. Therapeutic interactions work toward developing a trusting, empathic therapeutic alliance, a forensic psychologist may not ethically nurture the client or act in a "helping" role, as the forensic evaluator had divided loyalties and there are substantial limits on confidentiality he can guarantee the client. A forensic evaluator must always be aware of manipulation in the adversary context of a legal setting. These concerns mandate an emotional distance that is unlike a therapeutic interaction.
- **Pace and setting**. Unlike therapeutic interactions which may be guided by many factors, the forensic setting with its court schedules, limited resources, and other external factors, place great time constrains on the evaluation without opportunities for reevaluation. The forensic examiner focuses on the importance of accuracy and the finality of legal dispositions.

Forensic Psychology Practice

The forensic psychologist views the client or defendant from a different point of view than does a traditional clinical psychologist. Seeing the situation from the client's point of view or "empathizing" is not the forensic psychologist's task. Traditional psychological tests and interview procedure are not sufficient when applied to the forensic situation. In forensic evaluations, it is important to assess the consistency of factual information across multiple sources. Forensic evaluators must be able to provide the source on which any information is based. Unlike more traditional applications of clinical psychology, informed consent is not required when the assessment is ordered by the court. Instead, the defendant simply needs to be notified regarding the purpose of the evaluation and the fact that he or she will have no control over how the information obtained is used While psychologists infrequently have to be concerned about malingering or feigning illness in a non-criminal clinical setting, a forensic psychologist must be able to recognize exaggerated or faked symptoms. Malingering exists on a continuum so the forensic psychologist must be skilled in recognizing varying degrees of feigned symptoms.

Forensic psychologists perform a wide range of tasks within the criminal justice system. By far the largest is that of preparing for and providing testimony in the court room. This task has become increasingly difficult as attorneys have become sophisticated at undermining psychological testimony. Evaluating the client, preparing for testimony, and the testimony itself require the forensic psychologist to have a firm grasp of the law and the legal situation at issue in the courtroom, using the Crime Classification Manual and other sources. This knowledge must be integrated with the psychological information obtained from testing, psychological and mental status exams, and appropriate assessment of background materials, such as police reports, prior psychiatric or psychological evaluations, medical records and other available pertinent information.

Malingering

An overriding issue in any type of forensic assessment is the issue of malingering and deception. A defendant may be intentionally faking a mental illness or may be exaggerating the degree of symptomatology. The forensic psychologist must always keep this possibility in mind. It is important if malingering is suspected to observe the defendant in other settings as it is difficult to maintain false symptoms consistently over time In some cases, the court views malingering or feigning illness as obstruction of justice and sentences the defendant accordingly. In United States v. Binion, malingering or feigning illness during a competency evaluation was held to be obstruction of justice and led to an enhanced sentence As such, fabricating mental illness in a competency-to-stand-trial assessment now can be raised to enhance the sentencing level following a guilty plea.

Competency Evaluations

If there is a question of the accused's competency to stand trial, a forensic psychologist is appointed by the court to examine and assess the individual. The individual may be in custody or may have been released on bail. Based on the forensic assessment, a recommendation is made to the court whether or not the defendant is competent to proceed to trial. If the defendant is considered incompetent to proceed, the report or testimony will include recommendations for the interim period during which an attempt at restoring the individual's competency to understand the court and legal proceedings, as well as participate appropriately in their defense will be made. Often, this is an issue of the defendant complying with prescribed psychiatric medication for a period long enough for the medication to take effect. If the individual does not gain competence after a suitable period of time, that person may be involuntarily committed, on the advice of a forensic psychologist, to a psychiatric treatment facility until such time as the individual is deemed competent.

As a result of Ford v. Wainwright, a case by a Florida inmate on death row that was brought before the Supreme Court of the United States, forensic psychologists are appointed to assess the competency of an inmate to be executed in death penalty cases.

Sanity Evaluations

The forensic psychologist may also be appointed by the court to evaluate the defendant's state of mind at the time of the offense. These are defendants who the judge, prosecutor or public defender believe, through personal interaction with the defendant or through reading the police report, may have been significantly impaired at the time of the offense. In other situations, the defense attorney may decide to have the defendant plead not guilty by reason of insanity. In this case, usually the court appoints forensic evaluators and the defense may hire their own forensic expert. In actual practice, this is rarely a plea in a trial. Usually any judgments about the defendant's state of mind at the time of the offense are made by the court before the trial process begins.

Sentence Mitigation

Even in situations where the defendant's mental disorder does not meet the criteria for a not guilty by reason of insanity defense, the defendant's state of mind at the time, as well as relevant past history of mental disorder and psychological abuse can be used to attempt a mitigation of sentence. The forensic psychologist's evaluation and report is an important element in presenting evidence for sentence mitigation. In *Hamblin v. Mitchell*, 335 F.3d 482 (6th Cir. 2003), the Sixth Circuit Court of Appeals reversed the decision of a lower court because counsel did not thoroughly investigate the defendant's mental history in preparation for the sentencing phase of the trial. Specifically, the court stated that such investigation should include members of the defendant's immediate and extended family, medical history, and family and social history (including physical and mental abuse,domestic violence, exposure to traumatic events and criminal violence) his issue was further addressed in Wiggins v. Smith and Bigby v. Dretke.

Other Evaluations

Forensic psychologists are frequently asked to make an assessment of an individual's dangerousness or risk of re-offending. They may provide information and recommendations necessary for sentencing purposes, grants of probation, and the formulation of conditions of parole, which often involves an assessment of the offender's ability to be rehabilitated. They are also asked questions of witness credibility and malingering. Occasionally, they may also provide criminal profiles to law enforcement.

Due to the Supreme Court decision upholding involuntary commitment laws for predatory sex offenders in Kansas v. Hendricks, it is likely that forensic psychologists will become involved in making recommendations in individual cases of end-of-sentence civil commitment decisions.

Ethical Implications

A forensic psychologist generally practices within the confines of the courtroom, incarceration facilities, and other legal setting. It is important to remember that the forensic psychologist is equally likely to be testifying for the prosecution as for the defense attorney. A forensic psychologist does not take a side, as do the psychologists described below he ethical standards for a forensic psychologist differ from those of a clinical psychologist or other practicing psychologist because the forensic psychologist is not an advocate for the client and nothing the client says is guaranteed to be kept confidential. This makes evaluation of the client difficult, as the forensic psychologist needs and wants to obtain certain information while it is often not in the client's best interest to provide it. The client has no control over how that information is used Despite the signing of a waiver of confidentiality, most clients do not realize the nature of the evaluative situation. Furthermore, the interview techniques differ from those typical of a clinical psychologist and require an understanding of the criminal mind and criminal and violent behavior For example, even indicating to a defendant being interviewed that an effort will be made to get the defendant professional help may be grounds for excluding the expert's testimony.

In addition, the forensic psychologist deals with a range of clients unlike those of the average practicing psychologist. Because the client base is by and large criminal, the forensic psychologist is immersed in an abnormal world As such, the population evaluated by the forensic psychologist is heavily weighted with specific personality disorders.

The typical grounds for malpractice suits also apply to the forensic psychologist, such as wrongful commitment, inadequate informed consent, duty and breach of duty, and standards of care issues. Some situations are more clear cut for the forensic psychologist. The duty to warn, which is mandated by many states, is generally not a problem because the client or defendant has already signed a release of information, unless the victim is not clearly identified and the issue of the identifiability of the victim arises. However, in general the forensic psychologist is less likely to encounter malpractice suits than a clinical psychologist. The forensic psychologist does have some additional professional liability issues. As mentioned above, confidentiality in a forensic setting is more complicated that in a clinical setting as the client or defendant is apt to misinterpret the limits of confidentiality despite being warned and signing a release.

FORENSIC PSYCHIATRY

Forensic psychiatry is a sub-specialty of psychiatry. It encompasses the interface between law and psychiatry. Some practitioners of forensic psychiatry have taken extra training in that specific area. In the United States, one year fellowships are offered in this field to psychiatrists who have completed their general psychiatry training. Such psychiatrists may then be eligible to sit for a board certification examination in forensic psychiatry. In Britain one is required to complete a three-year subspeciality training in forensic psychiatry, after completing one's general psychiatry training, before receiving a Certificate of Completion of Training as a forensic psychiatrist. In some countries general psychiatrists can practice forensic psychiatry as well. However, some countries, such as Japan, require a specific certification from the government to do this type of work.

Court Work

Forensic psychiatrists work with courts in evaluating an individual's competency to stand trial, defenses based on mental diseases or defects (e.g., the "insanity" defense), and sentencing recommendations. There are two major areas of criminal evaluations in forensic psychiatry. These are Competency to Stand trial (CST) and Mental State at the Time of the Offence (MSO).

Competency to Stand Trial (CST)

This is the competency evaluation to determination that a defendant has the mental capacity to understand the charges and assist his attorney. This is seated in the Fifth Amendment to the US Constitution, which ensures the right to be present at your trial, to face your accusers, and to have help from an attorney.

In English and Welsh law a similar concept is that of "fitness to plead".

As an Expert Witness

Forensic psychiatrists are often called to be expert witnesses in both criminal and civil proceedings. Expert witnesses give their opinion about a specific issue. Often the psychiatrist will have prepared a detailed report before testifying. The primary duty of the expert witness is to provide an independent opinion to the court.

Mental State Opinion

This gives the Court an opinion, and only an opinion, as to whether a defendant was able to understand what he was doing at the time of the crime. This is worded differently in many states, and has been rejected altogether in some, but in every setting, the intent to do a criminal act and the understanding that it was a criminal act bear on the final disposition of the case. Much of forensic psychiatry is guided by significant Court rulings or laws that bear on this area which include the following three standards:

- **M'Naghten rules:** Excuses a defendant who, by virtue of a defect of reason or disease of the mind, does not know the nature and quality of the act, or, if he does, does not know that the act is wrong.
- **Durham rule:** Excuses a defendant whose conduct is the product of mental disease or defect.
- **ALI test:** Excuses a defendant who, because of a mental disease or defect, lacks substantial capacity to appreciate the criminality (wrongfulness) of his conduct or to conform his conduct to the requirements of law.

"Not guilty by reason of insanity" (NGRI) is one potential outcome in this type of trial. It is important to note that insanity is a legal and not a medical term. Often there will be a psychiatrist(s) testifying for both the defense and the prosecution.

Forensic psychiatrists are also involved in the care of prisoners, both those in jails and those in prisons, and in the care of the mentally ill and dangerous (such as those who have been found not guilty by reason of insanity).

Risk Management

Many past offenders against other people, and suspected or potential future offenders with mental health problems or an intellectual or developmental disability, are supervised in the community by forensic teams containing a variety of professionals, including psychiatrists, psychologists, nurses and care workers. These teams have dual responsibilities, to promote both the welfare of their clients and the safety of the public. The aim is not so much to predict as to prevent violence, by means of risk management.

Risk assessment and management is a growth area in the forensic field, with much academic work being done in Ontario and British Columbia. This began with the attempt to predict the likelihood of a particular kind of offence being repeated, by combining "static" indicators from personal history and offence details in actuarial instruments such as the RRASOR and Static-99, which were shown to be more accurate than unaided professional judgement. More recently, use is being made also of "dynamic" risk factors, such as attitudes, impulsivity, mental state, family and social circumstances, substance use, availability and acceptance of support, to make a "structured professional judgement." The aim of this is to move away from prediction to prevention, by identifying and then managing risk factors. This may entail monitoring, treatment, rehabilitation, supervision and victim safety planning and depends on the availability of funding and legal powers. These schemes may be based on published assessments such as the HCR-20 (which incorporates 10 Historical, 5 Clinical and 5 Risk Management factors) and the RSVP (Risk of Sexual Violence Protocol) from Simon Fraser University, BC.

Britain

In Britain most forensic psychiatrists work for the National Health Service, in specialist secure units caring for mentally ill offenders (as well as people whose behaviour has made them impossible to manage in other hospitals). These can be either medium secure units (of which there are many throughout the country) or maximum security hospitals (also known as Special Hospitals), of which there are three in England and one in Scotland (The State Hospital, Carstairs), the best known of which being Broadmoor Hospital. The other 'specials' are Ashworth hospital in Maghull, Liverpool and Rampton hospital in Nottinghamshire. There are also a number of private sector medium secure units, which sell their beds exclusively to the NHS, as there are not enough secure beds available in the NHS system. (There are no 'private' paying patients in Forensic Psychiatry!)

Forensic psychiatrists often also do prison inreach work, in which they go into prisons and assess and treat people suspected of having mental disorders; much of the day to day work of these psychiatrists comprises care of very seriously mentally ill patients, especially those suffering from schizophrenia. Some units also treat people with severe personality disorder, learning disabilities (by which is meant, in Britain, intellectual impairment), autistic spectrum disorders or other illnesses.

The areas of assessment for courts are also somewhat different in Britain, because of differing mental health law. Fitness to plead, and mental state at the time of the offence are indeed issues given consideration, but the mental state at the time of trial is also a major issue, and it is this assessment which most commonly leads to the use of mental health legislation to detain people in hospital, as opposed to their getting a prison sentence.

Learning disabled offenders who are a continuing risk to others may be detained in learning disability hospitals (or specialised community-based units with a similar regime, as the hospitals have mostly been closed) as suffering from "Mental Impairment" in England and Wales, and without use of that term in Scotland. This includes those who commit serious crimes of violence, including sexual violence, and fire-setting. They would be cared for by learning disability psychiatrists and registered learning disability nurses (RNLD). Some psychiatrists doing this work have dual training in learning disability and forensic psychiatry or learning disability and adolescent psychiatry. Some nurses would have training in mental health also (RMN and RNLD).

Many past offenders against other people, and suspected or potential future offenders with mental health problems or a learning disability, are supervised in the community by forensic teams containing a variety of professionals, including psychiatrists, psychologists, nurses and care workers. These teams have dual responsibilities, to promote both the welfare of their clients and the safety of the public. The aim is not so much to predict as to prevent violence, by means of risk management.

Court work (medico-legal work) is generally but not exclusively undertaken by psychiatrists (most often 'forensic' psychiatrists who are also consultants (senior doctors) in the National Health Service (NHS).

FORENSIC TOXICOLOGY

Forensic toxicology is the use of toxicology and other disciplines such as analytical chemistry, pharmacology and clinical chemistry to aid medicolegal investigation of death, poisoning, and drug use. The primary concern for forensic toxicology is not the legal outcome of the toxicological investigation, but rather the technology and techniques for obtaining and interpreting the results. A toxicological analysis can be done to various kinds of samples.

A forensic toxicologist must consider the context of an investigation, in particular any physical symptoms recorded, and any evidence collected at a crime scene that may narrow the search, such as pill bottles, powders, trace residue, and any available chemicals. Provided with this information and samples with which to work, the forensic toxicologist must determine which toxic substances are present, in what concentrations, and the probable effect of those chemicals on the person.

Determining the substance ingested is often complicated by the body's natural processes (see ADME), as it is rare for a chemical to remain in its original form once in the body. For example: heroin is almost immediately metabolised into another substance and further to morphine, making detailed investigation into factors such as injection marks and chemical purity necessary to confirm diagnosis. The substance may also have been diluted by its dispersal through the body; while a pill or other regulated dose of a drug may have grams or milligrams of the active constituent, an individual sample under investigation may only contain micrograms or nanograms.

Samples

Urine

A urine sample is quick and easy for a live subject, and is common among drug testing for employees and athletes. Urine samples do not necessarily reflect the toxic substance(s) the subject was influenced by at the time of the sample collection. An example of this is THC from cannabinoid (for example, marijuana) use, which in heavy users can be detected in urine for up to 14 days following use. Note also that it can take as long as 8 hours until a given substance can be detected. Specific to workplace drug testing, urine collection must be directly observed due to the prevalence of substance abusers "beating the test" via sample substitution or adulteration.

Blood

A blood sample of approximately 10 cm^3 is usually sufficient to screen and confirm most common toxic substances. A blood sample provides the toxicologist with a profile of the substance that the subject was influenced by at the time of collection; for this reason, it is the sample of choice for measuring blood alcohol content in drunk driving cases.

Hair Sample

Hair is capable of recording medium to long-term or high dosage substance abuse. Chemicals in the bloodstream may be transferred to the growing hair and stored in the follicle, providing a rough timeline of drug intake events. Head hair grows at rate of approximately 1 to 1.5 cm a month, and so cross sections from different sections of the follicle can give estimates as to when a substance was ingested. Testing for drugs in hair is not standard throughout the population. The darker and coarser the hair the more drug that will be found in the hair. If two people consumed the same amount of drugs, the person with the darker and coarser hair will have more drug in their hair than the lighter haired person when tested. This raises issues of possible racial bias in substance tests with hair samples.

Oral Fluid

Oral fluid is the proper term, however saliva is used commonly. Saliva is a component of oral fluid. Oral fluid is composed of many components and concentrations of drugs typically parallel to those found in blood. Sometimes referred to as ultra filtrate of blood, it is thought that drugs pass into oral fluid predominantly through a process known as passive diffusion. Drugs and pharmaceuticals that are highly protein bound in blood will have a lower concentration in oral fluid. The use of oral fluid is gaining importance in forensic toxicology for showing recent drug use, e.g. in clinical settings or investigation of driving under influence of substances.

Other

Other bodily fluids and organs may provide samples, particularly samples collected during an autopsy. A common autopsy sample is the gastric contents of the deceased, which can be useful for detecting undigested pills or liquids that were ingested prior to death. In highly decomposed bodies, traditional samples may no longer be available. The vitreous humour from the eye may be used, as the fibrous layer of the eyeball and the eye socket of the skull protects the sample from trauma and adulteration. Other common organs used for toxicology are the brain, liver, spleen and stomach contents.

The inspection of the contents of the stomach must be part of every postmortem examination if possible because it may provide qualitative information concerning the nature of the last meal and the presence of abnormal constituents. Using it as a guide to the time of death, however, is theoretically unsound and presents many practical difficulties, although it may have limited applicability in some exceptional instances. Generally, using stomach contents as a guide to time of death involves an unacceptable degree of imprecision and is thus liable to mislead the investigator and the court. Characteristic cell types from food plants can be used to identify a victim's last meal; knowledge about which can be useful in determining the victim's whereabouts or actions prior to death. Some of these cell types include:

- sclereids (pears)
- starch grains (potatoes and other tubers)
- raphide crystals (pineapple)
- druse crystals (citrus, beets, spinach)
- silica bodies (cereal grasses and bamboos)

In a case where a young woman had been stabbed to death, witnesses reported that she had eaten her last meal at a particular fast food restaurant. However, her stomach contents did not match the limited menu of the restaurant, leading investigators to conclude that she had eaten at some point after being seen in the restaurant. The investigation led to the apprehension of a man whom the victim knew, and with whom she had shared her actual final meal. Time since death can be approximated by the state of digestion of the stomach contents. It normally takes at least a couple of hours for food to pass from the stomach to the small intestine; a meal still largely in the stomach implies death shortly after eating, while an empty or nearly-empty stomach suggests a longer time period between eating and death. However, there are numerous mitigating factors to take into account: the extent to which the food had been chewed, the amount of fat and protein present, physical activity undertaken by the victim prior to death, mood of the victim, physiological variation from person to person. All these factors affect the rate at which food passes through the digestive tract. Pathologists are generally hesitant to base a precise time of death on the evidence of stomach contents alone.

Other Organisms

Bacteria, maggots and other organisms that may have ingested some of the subject matter may have also ingested any toxic substance within it.

Detection and Classification

Detection of drugs and pharmaceuticals in biological samples is usually done by an initial screening and then a confirmation of the compound(s), which may include a quantitation of the compound(s). The screening and confirmation are usually, but not necessarily, done with different analytical methods. Every analytical method used in forensic toxicology should be carefully tested by performing a validation of the method to ensure correct and indisputable results at all times. A testing laboratory involved in forensic toxicology should adhere to a quality programme to ensure the best possible results and safety of any individual.

The choice of method for testing is highly dependent on what kind of substance one expects to find and the material on which the testing is performed. Biological samples are more complex to analyze because of factors such as the matrix effect and the metabolism and conjugation of the target compounds.

Gas Chromatography

Gas-liquid chromatography is of particular use in examining volatile organic compounds.

Detection of Metals

The compounds suspected of containing a metal are traditionally analyzed by the destruction of the organic matrix by chemical or thermal oxidation. This leaves the metal to be identified and quantified in the inorganic residue, and it can be detected using such methods as the Reinsch test, emission spectroscopy or X-ray diffraction. Unfortunately, while this identifies the metals present it removes the original compound, and so hinders efforts to determine what may have been ingested. The toxic effects of various metallic compounds can vary considerably.

Nonvolatile Organic Substances

Drugs, both prescribed and illicit, pesticides, natural products, pollutants and industrial compounds are some of the most common nonvolatile compounds encountered. Screening methods include thin-layer chromatography, gas-liquid chromatography and immunoassay. For complete legal identification, a second confirmatory test is usually also required. The trend today is to use liquid chromatography tandem mass spectrometry, predeced with sample workup as liquid-liquid extraction or solid phase extraction. Older methods include: spot test (see Pill testing), typically the Marquis Reagent, Mecke Reagent, and Froehde's Reagent for opiates, Marquis Reagent and Simon's reagent for amphetamine, methamphetamine and other analogs, like MDMA, the Scott's test for cocaine, and the modified Duquenois reagent for marijuana and other cannabinoids. For compounds that don't have a common spot test, like benzodiazepines, another test may be used, typically mass spectroscopy, or spectrophotometry.

15

Forensic Dentistry

Forensic dentistry or forensic odontology is the proper handling, examination and evaluation of dental evidence, which will be then presented in the interest of justice. The evidence that may be derived from teeth, is the age (in children) and identification of the person to whom the teeth belong. This is done using dental records or *ante-mortem* (prior to death) photographs. Forensic odontology is derived from Latin, meaning forum or where legal matters are discussed. The first forensic dentist in the United States was Paul Revere who was known for the identification of fallen revolutionary soldiers.

The other type of evidence is that of bite marks, left on either the victim (by the attacker), the perpetrator (from the victim of an attack), or on an object found at the crime scene. Bite marks are often found on children who are abused.

Forensic dentists are responsible for six main areas of practice:

- Identification of found human remains
- Identification in mass fatalities
- Assessment of bite mark injuries
- Assessment of cases of abuse (child, spousal, elder)
- Civil cases involving malpractice
- Age estimation

Background

Forensic odontology is the study of dental applications in legal proceedings. The subject covers a wide variety of topics including individual identification, mass identification, and bite mark analysis. The study of odontology in a legal case can be a piece of incriminating evidence or an aspect of wide controversy. There have been many cases throughout history which have made use of bite marks as evidence. Bite marks are usually seen in cases involving sexual assault, murder, and child abuse and can be a major factor in leading to a conviction. Biting is often a sign of the perpetrator seeking to degrade the victim while also achieving complete domination . Bite marks can be found anywhere on a body, particularly on soft, fleshy tissue such as the stomach or buttocks. In addition, bite marks can be found on objects present at the scene of a crime. Bite marks are commonly found on a suspect when a victim attempts to defend him/ herself. Even though using bite mark evidence began around 1870, the first published account involving a conviction based on bite marks as evidence was in the case of *Doyle v. State*, which occurred in Texas in 1954 The bite mark in this case was on a piece of cheese found at the crime scene of a burglary. The defendant was later asked to bite another piece of cheese for comparison. A firearms examiner and a dentist evaluated the bite marks independently and both concluded that the marks were made by the same set of teeth. The conviction in this case set the stage for bite marks found on objects and skin to be used as evidence in future cases

Another landmark case was *People v. Marx,* which occurred in California in 1975 woman was murdered by strangulation after being sexually assaulted. She was bitten several times on her nose. Walter Marx was identified as a suspect and dental impressions were made of his teeth. Impressions and photographs were also taken of the woman's injured nose. These samples along with other models and casts were evaluated using a variety of techniques, including two-dimensional and three-dimensional comparisons, and acetate overlays. Three experts testified that the bite marks on the woman's nose were indeed made by Marx and he was convicted of voluntary manslaughter.

High-profile Criminal Cases

Forensic odontology has played a key role in famous criminal cases:

- Wayne Boden - The first case of Forensic Dentistry
- State of Florida v. Ted Bundy
- State of New Jersey v. Jesse Timmendequas (Megan's Law case)
- People of California v. Marx, the 1975 case which established evidentiary standards for forensic odontology
- People of Arizona v. Ray Krone, bite mark evidence led to a wrongful conviction.

Organizations

Three organizations are dedicated to the field of forensic odontology. These organizations include: the Bureau of Legal Dentistry (BOLD), the American Board of Forensic Odontology (ABFO), and the International Organization for Forensic Odonto-Stomatology (IOFOS). In 1996, BOLD was created at the University of British Columbia to develop new technology and techniques in forensic odontology. The University of British Columbia program is the only one in North America that provides graduate training in forensic odontology The Bureau of

Legal Dentistry encourages the use of multiple dental impressions to create a "dental lineup", similar to a suspect lineup used to identify alleged perpetrators of crime. Currently, dental impressions collected as evidence are compared only to those collected from a given suspect, which may bias the resulting outcome. Using multiple dental impressions in a lineup may enable forensic odontologists to significantly decrease the current bias in matching bite marks to the teeth of a suspect The organization BOLD also supports the creation of a database of dental records, which could help in verifying dental uniqueness This database could be created using criminal records or possibly all dental patients. In 1984, the ABFO began making an attempt to diminish the discrepancies and increase the validity of bite mark analysis by creating bite mark methodology guidelines. The guidelines attempt to establish standard terminology in describing bite marks and that reduces the risk of biased results. The ABFO also provides advice on how to effectively collect and preserve evidence. For example, they recommend that the collection of DNA evidence and detailed photographs of bites be taken together at the crime scene. The guidelines also outline how and what a forensic odontologist should record, such as the location, contours, shape, and size of a bite mark. They also provide a system of scoring to assess the degree to which a suspect's dental profile and bite mark match. According to the ABFO, the guidelines are not a mandate of methods to be used, but a list of generally accepted methods The guidelines are intended to prevent potentially useful evidence from being thrown out simply because the forensic odontologist's collection methods were not standardized. Kouble and Craig used a simplified version of the ABFO scoring guidelines in order to retain accuracy with a larger sample of comparisons. A numerical score was assigned to represent the degree of similarity between the bite mark and model/overlay. The higher the score, the greater the similarity. In order to simplify the model, some features that were individually scored in the ABFO guidelines such as arch size and shape were assessed together while certain distinctive features such as spacing between teeth were treated as a separate variable. The authors believe that a simplified version would increase the strength of the comparison process. In an attempt to improve guidelines used to collect dental evidence, IOFOS developed one of the most recognized systems for the collection of forensic dental evidence.

Bite Mark Analysis

Upon collection of dental evidence, the forensic odontologist analyzes and compares the bite marks. Studies have been performed in an attempt to find the simplest, most efficient, and most reliable way of analyzing bite marks. Factors that may affect the accuracy of bite mark identification include time-dependent changes of the bite mark on living bodies, effects of where the bite mark was found, damage on soft tissue, and similarities in dentition among individuals. Other factors include poor photography, impressions, or measurement of dentition characteristics. Most bite mark analysis studies use porcine skin (pigskin) since it is comparable to the skin of a human because it is considered unethical to bite a human for study in the United States. Limitations to the bite mark studies include differences in properties of pigskin compared to human skin and the technique of using simulated pressures to create bite marks. Although similar histologically, pigskin and human skin behave in dynamically different ways due to differences in elasticity. Furthermore, postmortem bites on nonhuman skin, such as those used in the experiments of Martin-de-las Heras et al., display different patterns to those seen in antemortem bite injuries In recognition of the limitations of their study, Kouble and Craig suggest using a G-clamp on an articulator in future studies to standardize the amount of pressure used to produce experimental bite marks instead of applying manual pressure to models on pigskin. Future research and technological developments may help reduce the occurrence of such limitations. Kouble and Craig compared direct methods and indirect methods of bite mark analysis. In the past, the direct method compared a model of the suspect's teeth to a life-size photograph of the actual bite mark. In these experiments, direct comparisons were made between dental models and either photographs or "fingerprint powder lift-models." The "fingerprint powder lift" technique involves dusting the bitten skin with black fingerprint powder and using fingerprint tape to transfer the bite marks onto a sheet of acetate. Indirect methods involve the use of transparent overlays to record a suspect's biting edges. Transparent overlays are made by free-hand tracing the occlusal surfaces of a dental model onto an acetate sheet. When comparing the "fingerprint powder lift" technique against the photographs, the use of photographs resulted in higher scores determined by a modified version of the ABFO scoring guidelines The use of transparent overlays is considered subjective and irreproducible because the tracing can be easily manipulated. On the other hand, photocopier-generated overlays where no tracing is used is considered to be the best method in matching the correct bite mark to the correct set of models without the use of computer imaging While the photocopier-generated technique is sensitive, reliable, and inexpensive, new methods involving digital overlays have proven to be more accurate. Two recent technological developments include the 2D polyline method and the painting method. Both methods use Adobe Photoshop. Use of the 2D polyline method entails drawing straight lines between two fixed points in the arch and between incisal edges to indicate the tooth width. Use of the painting method entails coating the incisal edges of a dental model with red glossy paint and then photographing the model. Adobe Photoshop is then used to make measurements on the image. A total of 13 variables were used in analysis. Identification for both methods were based on canine-to-canine distance (1 variable), incisor width (4 variables), and rotational angles of the incisors (8 variables). The 2D polyline method relies heavily on accurate measurements, while the painting method depends on precise overlaying of the images. Although both methods were reliable, the 2D polyline method gave efficient and more objective results The latest indirect analysis method uses Dental Print which generates biting edges to compare overlays from 3-dimensional images of a dental cast to those generated from Adobe Photoshop. Martin-de las Heras et al suggests using this method to identify negative dentitions. The purpose of this study was to make a comparison between Dental Print and Adobe Photoshop and to determine the impact of an examiner's experience in influencing the accuracy of results. Use of the DentalPrint method involves three stages. First, the teeth involved in the bite mark are identified. Next, a contact plane is created from the three highest points detected in the 3-dimensional image of the dental cast. Lastly, Dental Print software is used to extend the contact plane deep into the teeth to acquire all biting edges of the cast. In a blind trial, an expert and a non-expert were asked to make comparisons (n=128). Martin-de las Heras et al ound that experienced examiners performed significantly better than non-experts when using either Dental Print software or Adobe Photoshop software in correctly identifying the biter.

Criticism

The scientific foundation of forensic odontology, and especially bite mark comparison, has been called into question. A 1999 study, frequently referenced in news stories but difficult to actually locate, by a member of the American Board of Forensic Odontology found a 63 percent rate of false identifications. However, the study was based on an informal workshop during an ABFO meeting which many members did not consider a valid scientific setting.

An investigative series by the *Chicago Tribune* entitled "Forensics under the Microscope" examined many forensic science disciplines to see if they truly deserve the air of infallibility that has come to surround them. The investigators concluded that bite mark comparison is always subjective and no standards for comparison have been accepted across the field. The journalists discovered that no rigorous experimentation has been conducted to determine error rates for bite mark comparison, a key part of the scientific method.

Critics of bite mark comparison cite the case of Ray Krone, an Arizona man convicted of murder on bite mark evidence left on a woman's breast. DNA evidence later implicated another man and Krone was released from prison. Similarly, Roy Brown was convicted of murder due in part to bite-mark evidence, and freed after DNA testing of the saliva left in the bite wounds matched someone else.

Although bite mark analysis has been used in legal proceedings since 1870, it remains a controversial topic due to a variety of factors. DeVore and Barbenel and Evans have shown that the accuracy of a bite mark on skin is limited at best. Skin is not a good medium for dental impressions; it is liable to have a number of irregularities present before the imprint that could cause distortion. Also, bite marks can be altered through stretching, movement or a changing environment during and after the actual bite. Furthermore, the level of distortion tends to increase after the bite mark was made. Both studies suggest that for the bite mark to be accurately analyzed, the body must be examined in exactly the same position it was in when the bite occurred which can be a difficult if not an impossible task to accomplis Bite mark distortion can rarely be quantified. Therefore, bite marks found at the scene are often analyzed under the assumption that they have undergone minimal distortion Only limited research has been done in trying to quantify the level of distortion of a bite mark on human skin since the 1970s. The lack of research may largely be due to the fact that such studies are difficult to organize and are very expensive.

Bite mark analysis is also controversial because dental profiles are subject to change. The loss of teeth or the alteration of arch configuration through a variety of procedures is common in human populations. The onset of oral diseases such as dental caries has been shown to alter the arch and tooth configuration and must be taken into account when comparing a dental profile to the bite mark after a significant amount of time has passed since the mark was made.

While the methods behind collecting bite mark evidence at the scene are leading toward greater standardization, the methodology behind analyzing bite marks is extremely variable because it depends upon the preference of the specific odontologist. As discussed earlier, there are several methods used to compare bite marks ranging from life sized photographs to computer enhanced 3-dimensional imaging. These methods vary in precision and accuracy, and there is no set standard by which to compare or analyze them The lack of analytical standards leads to a wide array of interpretation with any bite mark evidence. Some odontologists even disagree on whether or not a mark on the body is the result of a bite Therefore, the interpretation of evidence lies largely on the expertise of the forensic odontologist handling the case.

One possible issue facing bite mark analysis is a lack of bite mark uniqueness in any given population. Bite mark analysis is based on the assumptions that the dental characteristics of anterior teeth involved in biting are unique amongst individuals, and this asserted uniqueness is transferred and recorded in the injury. However, there is very little reliable research to support these assumptions. However, this study suffered from a small sample size (n=5), with the intent to extrapolate the data to the general population. They also used plaster of paris as the substrate to simulate skin, yet the two materials have very different properties In a review conducted by Strom, he references a study conducted by Berg and Schaidt which suggested that at least four to five teeth need to be present in the mark to ensure its uniqueness and make a positive identification. However, this study was done long before many of the current evaluation methods, and this sheds doubt on how applicable these conclusions are today.

One of the most well known papers attempting to provide empirical data on bite mark uniqueness was done by Rawson et al. In this study, researchers determined that if five teeth marks can be matched to five teeth, it can be said with confidence that only one person could have caused the bite, and if eight teeth were matched to marks this would be a certainty. However, in this study the probabilities used to make this claim are based on the assumption that the position of each tooth was independent of all the others. This is probably unrealistic because there are a number of ways that the dental profile can be changed. For example, braces apply force to specific teeth, in order to shift the placement of multiple teeth.

One particular case that highlighted the lack of uniqueness in bite marks involved two suspects accused of attacking a man that had sustained a bite mark injury. Two separate forensic dentists, one representing the prosecution and one the defense, were brought in to analyze the mark. They reported conflicting results. One found the mark to come from suspect A and the other said it was from suspect B. This disagreement resulted from the fact that even though the two suspects had dental features making them unique, the bite mark itself was not detailed enough to reflect them. Therefore, the mark could have reasonably come from either of the men. The equivocal outcome demonstrated in the case emphasizes the difficulty in proving uniqueness.

Most of the controversies facing bite mark analysis are due to the lack of empirical supporting evidence. When searching the entire MedLine database from 1960–1999, only 50 papers in English were found that related to bite mark analysis. Of these 50 papers, most of which were published in the 1980's, only 8% came from well designed experimentation providing empirical data The lack of research has led to the continued use of a few outdated and limited studies to support the validity of bite mark analysis. This brings into question whether or not there is enough scientific support for bite mark analysis to be employed in court.

There have been several instances when forensic dentists have made claims, accusations, and guarantees supported by bite mark evaluation that have been proven incorrect through other forensic sciences DNA analysis has shed some light on the limitations of bite mark analysis because often the DNA from saliva surrounding the area of the bite mark proves to be a more reliable form of identification. In the case of *Mississippi vs. Bourne*, the DNA of a suspect excluded them from the crime after a dentist claimed the bite marks on the victim matched the defendant's teeth In the case of *State vs. Krone*, the defendant was sentenced to death, which was overturned. Then Krone was later reconvicted and given life in prison. Both convictions were based largely on bite mark evidence, but ten years later DNA evidence surfaced that identified the real killer and Krone was set free.

TRACE EVIDENCE

Trace evidence is normally caused by objects or substances contacting one another, and leaving a minute sample on the contact surfaces. Material is often transferred by heat induced by contact friction.

The importance of trace evidence in criminal investigations was shown by Dr. Edmond Locard in the early 20th Century. Throughout the past century, forensic scientists have used trace evidence to reconstruct crimes, as well as to describe the people, places and things involved in them. Case studies of real life homicides have been published in the forensic science literature showing how trace evidence has been used to solve these crimes, free the innocent, and bring the guilty to justice.

Examples

Examples of typical trace evidence in criminal cases include fingerprints, hairs, cosmetics, plant fibers, mineral fibers, synthetic fibers, glass, paint chips, soils, botanical materials, gunshot residue, explosives residue, and volatile hydrocarbons (arson evidence). For such evidence to be useful, it must be compared to similar items from suspects, but particular care is necessary to ensure a thorough analysis.

Ladder feet often leave a trace pattern on the ground, so showing how the ladder moved and caused an accident to the user. Skid marks from tires are often critical in determining the sequence of events before and during a car crash. Vehicular accident reconstruction relies on such marks to estimate vehicle speed before and during an accident, as well as braking and impact forces. Fabric prints of clothing worn by pedestrians in the paint and/or road grime of the striking vehicle can match a specific vehicle involved in a Hit and Run collision. Such traces are also known as "witness marks", especially in engineering and may be critical in understanding how a product failed. A typical witness mark could be an impact depression which broke a product, especially if that mark can be matched to the product which made the impact such as a hammer or nail. Such marks are also commonly encountered in criminal cases, and include bite marks, puncture marks, bullet holes etc.

Protection

The best form of preservation is first to photograph it *in situ* or where you first found the object, and then take the object which shows key traces, protect it and analyse later under controlled laboratory conditions.

Many different techniques are used in the protection of trace evidence from criminal investigations, although all must be photographed when fresh and still in place. Samples may be collected by shaking, brushing, taping, vacuuming, swabbing and hand picking, although great care may be needed to prevent contamination with other substances (such as natural oil and sweat on the hand of the collector). In some cases, such as with oil or grease, a solvent extraction can be used to collect the evidence for analysis. The method used for collection is generally dependent on both the type of evidence and from where or what sort of object it is being collected from.

Analysis

Analysis of trace materials most often begins with a visual examination of the evidence usually involving macro-photography. This is then usually followed by microscopic analysis, of which a number of different types are available depending on the type of material to be analysed, such as a stereomicroscope, scanning electron microscope (SEM) or comparison microscope. SEM is especially useful because X-ray analysis can be conducted on selected areas of the sample, so is a form of microanalysis. It is useful where chemical residues can show unusual elements present which may indicate chemical attack of the product. A car accident caused by a diesel fuel leak, for example, showed traces of sulfur on the cracked tube indicative of attack by sulfuric acid from the battery.

Gunshot residue may be identified by elemental analysis using atomic absorption or with a scanning electron microscope equipped with an energy dispersive spectroscope. Small amounts of explosives, volatile hydrocarbons, and other chemicals are identified with the use of analytical instruments, such as gas chromatography, mass spectrometry, and infrared spectroscopy, all of which separate out the components of the chemicals.

Similar comments apply to damaged items from an accident scene, but care is needed in ensuring that the sample is not damaged by the testing, or sampling for testing. Such nondestructive testing must always be used first before considering destructive methods which involve taking small samples from the item for more detailed tests, such as spectroscopic analysis. Use of all such methods must be done in consultation with other experts and the relevant authorities, such as lawyers on both sides of a case.

Problems

False positives and contamination by subsequent handling, for example, are problems owing to the presence of many common substances and the necessity of human involvement in the collection of trace evidence. Samples from accidents or crimes should therefore be protected as musch as possible by enclosure in a sealable container as soon as possible after the incident being investigated.

FORENSIC PHOTOGRAPHY

Forensic photography (sometimes referred to as forensic imaging or crime scene photography) is the art of producing an accurate reproduction of a crime scene or an accident scene for the benefit of a court or to aid in the investigation. It is part of the process of evidence collecting. It provides investigators with photos of bodies, places and items involved in the crime. Pictures of accidents show broken machinery, or a car crash, and so on. Photography of this kind involves choosing correct lighting, accurate angling of lenses, and a collection of different viewpoints. Scales are often used in the picture so that dimensions of items are recorded on the image.

Methods

Crime or accident scene photographers capture images commonly in color, but also in black and white. The photograph of the skid mark was made during reconstruction at the accident scene to show how and why the ladder had slipped and caused a serious injury to the user. Color pictures are generally preferred because color may be an important aspect of the trace evidence, for example. Thus traces of paint or dye on a piece of evidence may be crucial to linking the evidence with a crime or accident.

Various forces and different countries have different policies in regards to 35 mm film or digital photography. There are advantages and disadvantages to both. Conventional photography (even using disposable cameras) have a high resolution, enabling great enlargement should details in a picture need closer examination. Pictures from surveillance cameras are a growing source of evidence for courts, as are pictures taken by bystanders on mobile phones. The former are being used increasingly at accident blackspots, and bystanders may take pictures of events when no policeman or investigator is present, but yet may be critical to a case. Digital photographs usually have an automatic date and time marker on each image, so that authenticity can be verified. Conventional photographs without such marks must be authenticated by the photographer, usually in a witness statement. Pictures of the relative position of objects (as in a Palimpsest) can establish a sequence of events at a crime or accident scene. Due to continued advances in digital technology and software, digital single-lens reflex (DSLR) cameras are increasingly being used by most Police forces.

Fit for Court

The images must be clear and usually have scales. They serve to not only remind CSIs and investigators of the scene but also to provide a tangible image for the court to better enable them to understand what happened. The use of several views taken from different angles helps to minimise the problem of parallax.

Overall images do not have scales and serve to show the general layout (e.g. the house where the murder is thought to have occurred). Context images show evidence in context (e.g. how the knife was next to the sofa). Close up images show fine detail of an artifact (e.g. a bloody fingerprint on the knife).

Road Traffic Incident (RTI) photographs show the overall layout at the scene taken from many different angles, with close-ups of significant damage, or trace evidence such as tire marks at a car crash scene. As with crime scene photography, it is essential that the site is pristine and untouched as far as is possible. Some essential intervention (rescuing a trapped victim, for example) must be recorded in the notes made at the time by the photographer, so that the authenticity of the photographs can be verified.

Untampered

Like all evidence a chain of custody must be maintained for crime scene photographs. Sometimes a CSI (Forensic Photographer) will process his/her own film or there is a specific lab for it. Regardless of how it is done any person who handles the evidence must be recorded. Accident scene pictures should also be identified and sourced, police photographs taken at the scene often being used in civil cases.

Index

C

❑❑❑